THE GREAT CONVERGENCE

THE GREAT CONVERGENCE

Asia, the West, and
the Logic of One World

KISHORE MAHBUBANI

PUBLICAFFAIRS

New York

Published in the United States by PublicAffairs™, a Member of the Perseus Books Group

Library of Congress Cataloging-in-Publication Data
Mahbubani, Kishore, author.
    The great convergence : Asia, the West, and the logic of one world / Kishore Mahbubani.
    pages   cm
    Includes bibliographical references and index.
    ISBN 978-1-61039-033-0 (hardcover) — ISBN 978-1-61039-034-7 (e-book)
1. Asia—Foreign relations. 2. Asia—Foreign economic relations. 3. International relations. 4. International economic relations. 5. Globalization. 6. Global Financial Crisis, 2008-2009. 7. East and West. I. Title.
    JZ1670.M33 2013
    327.50182'1—dc23
                                                              2012046077

First Edition
10 9 8 7 6 5 4 3 2 1

To my parents' grandchildren—
Deepika, Jhamat, Kishore, Lal, Poonam, Sapna, Shelagh, and Veena—
who will inherit the great convergence

CONTENTS

Introduction

Deep in our guts we all know that our world has changed significantly. Indeed, the world has experienced greater change in the past thirty years than it did in the previous three hundred. What we are all struggling to find is the one big idea that explains what we feel. I believe that the concept of "the great convergence" explains the massive change we are experiencing. Since human history began, we have lived in different communities and tribes and in different cultures and civilizations. Today, the massive forces unleashed by globalization are creating a new global civilization. Until recently, terms like "North and South" and "developed and developing" were used to describe the global condition. Today, the terms appear irrelevant. In a *Financial Times* column titled "In the Grip of a Great Convergence," Martin Wolf said, "Convergent incomes and divergent growth—that is the economic story of our times. We are witnessing the reversal of the 19th and early 20th century era of divergent incomes. In that epoch, the peoples of western Europe and their most successful former colonies achieved a huge economic advantage over the rest of humanity. Now it is being reversed more quickly than it emerged. This is inevitable and desirable."[1]

The great convergence also explains the rapidly rising living standards of the vast majority of the world's population. Never before in human history have so many people been lifted out of absolute poverty. Nor have there been so many entrants into the global middle class. Simple things like a flush toilet, electricity at home, a cell phone, a TV set, and a refrigerator have represented the aspirations of billions. For a long time, they seemed out of reach. Now many, if not most, people believe that these aspirations are achievable. One statistic exemplifies the scale of the change. Today, 500 million Asians enjoy middle-class living standards. By 2020, this number will explode to 1.75 billion, an increase of three and a half times in eight years. The *McKinsey Quarterly Report* of August 2012 provided equally dramatic statistics that the world is converging: "For centuries, less than 1 percent of the world's population enjoyed sufficient income to spend it on anything beyond basic needs. As recently as 1990, the number of people earning more than $10 a day,[2] the level at which households can contemplate discretionary purchases of products such as refrigerators or televisions, was around one billion, out of a total world population of roughly five billion. The vast majority of those consumers were based in developing countries in North America, Western Europe, or Japan." After noting that by 2010 the number had reached 2.4 billion, the report continued, "By 2025, MGI research suggests, that number will nearly double again, to 4.2 billion consumers out of a global population of 7.9 billion people. For the first time in world history, the number of people in the consuming class will exceed that number still struggling to meet their most basic needs."[3] The world will have never seen anything like it.

The human condition is not just improving in the material sphere. For millennia, peace was an elusive condition. Now a long peace has arrived. The number of people dying in wars is presently the lowest it has ever been since statistics began to be kept. Until recently, it appeared that only North America and the European Union (EU) had abolished war from their soil. Now the rest of the world is also converging toward peace. Major interstate wars have become a sunset industry.

I can speak with great passion and conviction about this massive change in the human condition as I have experienced it personally. As a child in Singapore in the 1950s and 1960s, I lived in a typical Third World city. Our per capita income was the same as Ghana's. We had no flush toilets, some malnutrition, ethnic riots, and, most importantly of all, no sense of hope for the future. Singapore was then a British colony. No one believed that Singapore could become as prosperous as London. Yet the unthinkable happened. Now this "impossible" feat is being replicated in all corners of the world. We are building a new and better civilization.

And we are also creating one world. Never before in history has humanity been so interconnected and interdependent. When Greece totters,

Europeans are not the only ones who worry. Barack Obama knew in his guts that Greece could derail his reelection. And stock markets from Latin America to Asia, Africa to Australia also fell. Greece was a tiny domino. But it could bring down larger dominoes because we have become fundamentally intertwined. Yet despite this, we still do not have the right conceptual structures to capture this new global condition.

The nation-state was invented in 1648 with the Treaty of Westphalia. And it has served humanity reasonably well as an organizing concept, overcoming the old divisions of tribes and sects, clans and classes. But it is hard to believe that a human construct invented more than three hundred fifty years ago can serve humanity when everything has changed so totally. A simple analogy will explain this fundamental change.

Before the era of modern globalization, when humanity lived discretely in more than one hundred separate countries, humankind was like a flotilla of more than one hundred separate boats. What the world then needed was a set of rules designed to ensure that these many boats did not collide and to facilitate their cooperation on the high seas if they chose to do so. This is what the 1945 rules-based order strived to do, and despite some obvious failures, it succeeded in producing a relatively stable global order for more than fifty years.

Today, global circumstances have changed dramatically. The 7 billion people who inhabit planet earth no longer live in more than one hundred separate boats. Instead, they all live in 193 separate cabins on the same boat. But this boat has a problem. It has 193 captains and crews, each claiming exclusive responsibility for one cabin. However, it has no captain or crew to take care of the boat as a whole. None of us would sail into an ocean of rapidly changing currents and looming storms without a capable captain and crew at the helm of our boat. Yet the global policy community proposes to do exactly that: sail into the uncertain waters of the twenty-first century without a captain.

Many of the major global challenges we face demonstrate well the degree to which all 7 billion of us sail on the same boat. The global financial crisis of 2008–2009 began with the collapse of Lehman Brothers in September 2008. Yet within months, the entire global economy came crashing down. No country could detach itself from this crisis because we were all in the same boat. The world came close to a total global economic meltdown in January 2009. Yet, amazingly, few people are aware that total meltdown was averted only because a captain and crew emerged in time to take care of the boat as a whole.

It happened at a G-20 leaders meeting in London. Traditionally, all G-20 leaders are programmed to put the interests of their cabins ahead of the interests of the boat as a whole. This is natural behavior. They are elected by their cabins, not by the boat as a whole. Yet when they came to London on April 2, 2009, they clearly sensed that the boat was sinking. To save their own cabins, they had to save the boat. Hence, they mounted a major coordinated global exercise to bring the world economy back from the brink. They pooled all their resources and decided to stimulate the global economy with US $1.1 trillion. For all practical purposes, even though the G-20 leaders will deny this emphatically, the G-20 meeting functioned like a global government—and it performed well.

Common sense would dictate that if all 7 billion people now live on the same boat, we should elect or select a captain and crew to take care of the boat as a whole. We have to create a global government of some sort, but not even the boldest political leaders want to mention the words "global government." It is out of reach as a practical idea; the world's electorates are not ready for it. Still, there are times when we will need it. For the next century or more, the world will have to live with a slew of imperfect solutions for solving major and growing global challenges. Imperfect solutions can solve some global problems. In the late 1970s and 1980s, the realization that there was an ever-expanding ozone hole, created by man-made chemicals called chlorofluorocarbons (CFCs), spurred concerted action. Good sense prevailed, and in 1987 forty-three nations came together to sign and ratify the Montreal Protocol, which aimed to phase out the production and use of CFCs. A decade or two later, the problem disappeared. The Montreal Protocol worked.

In academic literature, the multilateral institutions (like the UN) and processes (like the Montreal Protocol) we have created to solve global problems are described as components of "global governance." As long as a "global government" with mandatory powers is considered unacceptable, it is essential to strengthen cooperative institutions of global governance. But even as we do so, we should understand why global governance solutions are imperfect. This process is akin to sailing out to sea and selecting a different committee to manage the boat each time a new storm emerges. Moreover, the committee will inevitably be chosen after the storm emerges, not before. George W. Bush, probably the most unilateralist American president of modern times, resorted to the G-20 only when it became clear that the economic storm was too big for the US or the G-8 to handle alone. We were lucky that the G-20 could be assembled just in time, before the world economy crashed. We may not be so lucky next time.

Why? To strengthen institutions and processes of global governance, we clearly have to see a willingness on the part of different nations to make the necessary sacrifices to achieve global compromise and consensus. Even under normal circumstances, this can be difficult. However, we do not live under "normal" circumstances. We are living in an extraordinary period with massive changes taking place on several fronts. And all these changes complicate the efforts to strengthen global governance.

Many of these geopolitical challenges are also a result of old thinking. They will not disappear soon. However, this does not mean that we cannot improve the "systems" for managing these rivalries. Here a useful glimpse into the future can be provided by looking at Europe as a microcosm. The single biggest achievement of the European Union is not the story of its economic integration. It is simply the fact that the continent, which unleashed the two most disastrous wars of human history, has managed to achieve *zero prospect* of war. This is absolutely amazing. The existential question for all of us as we march into the twenty-first century is whether the modern world outside Europe can also match this European achievement of zero prospect of war.

Ironically, Europe's imperfect record provides reason for hope. Geopolitical rivalries in Europe did not cease after the EU was born, nor have they vanished today. In the 1990s, several decades after the EU was born, Yugoslavia fell apart. Despite their superficial cooperation in the overt peace efforts, the separate EU states covertly supported their old World War II allies. In the initial phase of Yugoslavia's breakup, Germany supported Slovenia and Croatia while the UK and France sympathized with Serbia. Adam LeBor describes well these European divisions:

> Not everyone in the UN wanted to cosy up with [the Serbians]. Yet those
> officials who pushed for a tougher line to be taken were sidelined by

peacekeeping officers, often British and French, many of whom simply felt more comfortable with the Bosnian Serbs. . . . For years, London and Paris insisted on seeing the Serbs as the inheritors of Tito's multi-national Yugoslavia, even as Gen. Mladic and his soldiers systematically destroyed it. It is Europe's shame that in the end it was an American, Bill Clinton, who finally took the decision to bomb.[4]

Indeed, they even sent arms covertly to their respective proxies. Yet despite all these tense geopolitical rivalries, Germany, France, and the UK never even came close to declaring war on each other.

The big question is, why not? Here again the answer is complex, but part of it is due to the fact that the EU states have accepted a rules-based order to guide their relations with each other. This order is made up of legal instruments and a complex political ecosystem that reflects the values of the European populations. Despite enormous geopolitical and other rivalries, there are major constraints on the behavior of EU states. Significantly, while there are some legal sanctions on violations of some rules and norms, the adherence to rules reflects values rather than fear of sanctions.

There is no fundamental reason why this European ecosystem of perpetual peace cannot be shared with the rest of humanity. This is not utopianism. I have lived most of my life in Asia, indeed in the Balkans of Asia—Southeast Asia. When the Cold War ended, most of the experts expected the Balkans of Europe to remain in peace and the Balkans of Asia to explode into conflict. Instead, the exact opposite happened. The march to modernity in Asia has already begun to reap dividends of peace. The Association of Southeast Asian Nations (ASEAN), a minireplica of the EU, played a critical role in delivering peace, just as the EU did for its member states.

Optimism about the future is emphatically not equivalent to utopianism. We are far from achieving utopia. Major geopolitical and economic challenges continue to plague our world. Humanity has never progressed forward in a straight line. For every two steps forward that we take, we may take one or two steps backward from time to time. History will, as usual, zigzag. For this reason, this book will focus on many of the major geopolitical challenges we have to overcome. Continuing on autopilot is not an option. We have to work even harder to navigate geopolitical fault lines and use all the political skills and cunning (yes, cunning) we can muster to overcome these challenges.

Ideally, we should try to reinvent the global institutional order to deal with this new human condition. But this won't happen. To put it bluntly, humanity lacks both the imagination and the courage to deliver bold new solutions. It does not help that political leaders continue to use old language and old concepts to explain the new world to their populations. One of the key goals of this book is to spark a new kind of discourse about the global condition. The great convergence requires nothing less.

Fortunately, we do not have to wait until we have reinvented the world order to solve major geopolitical challenges. We can build on existing postwar models of cooperation to deal with them. And we can also work together to strengthen the 1945 rules-based order (including the UN and the Bretton Woods institutions) that has been a major gift from the West, especially America, to the rest of the world. Overall, there is no doubt that America and Europe have been good custodians of the imperfect but mostly positive 1945 rules-based order. However, there is change afoot on that front: the populations of America and Europe have shifted their attitudes. They used to support global institutions and global liberalization processes because they assumed that they would be the biggest beneficiaries of them. Now most fear that all the benefits will go to China and India. Hence, why should they continue to be custodians of this benevolent world order? The situation poses a sharp message to the new emerging powers: they have to step up to the plate and take on greater global responsibilities. They should stop pretending that they are still "developing countries."

If they do step up and agree to take on more responsibility, the West should welcome it. The headships of the International Monetary Fund (IMF) and World Bank may no longer remain European and American. But there will be more "responsible stakeholders" whose views on global order have begun to converge with the Western worldview. But will America begin to share power and work with the rest of the world in strengthening global multilateral institutions? America has long had an ambivalent attitude toward multilateral institutions. It has done as much to undermine them as it has to strengthen them. As long as the United States remained the strongest power in the world, such ambivalence did not lead to real costs for the country. However, with America facing the prospect of becoming the second-largest economy in the world sometime soon, it may be wiser for America to change course and work to strengthen, rather than undermine, the 1945 rules-based order.

Former president Bill Clinton put across this point well when he spoke at Yale University in 2003:

> If you believe that maintaining power and control and absolute freedom of movement and sovereignty is important to your country's future, there's nothing inconsistent in that [the US continuing to behaving unilaterally]. [The US is] the biggest, most powerful country in the world now. We've got the juice and we're going to use it. . . . But if you believe that we should be trying to create a world with rules and partnerships and habits of behavior that we would like to live in when we're no longer the military political economic superpower in the world, then you wouldn't do that. It just depends on what you believe.[5]

Clinton had wanted to say as much to America when he was president. However, as Strobe Talbott, then deputy secretary of state, documents in his book *The Great Experiment*, political realities prevented the president from speaking out:

> Clinton's view was diametrically opposed to Charles Krauthammer's concept of the "unipolar moment," which held that the United States had a several-decade window of opportunity to get its way unilaterally—unencumbered by the need for consensus-building and compromise—before the world became multipolar. Clinton believed just the opposite: what we had in the wake of the cold war was a *multilateral* moment—an opportunity to shape the world through our active leadership of the institutions Clinton admired and Krauthammer disdained. But Clinton kept that belief largely to himself while he was in office. In public, and even in meetings with administration insiders and political supporters, Clinton's political instincts told him it would be inviting trouble to suggest that the sun would someday set on American preeminence. Ronald Reagan's optimism about "morning in America" had helped him defeat Jimmy Carter, who had, in the eyes of many, inadvertently associated his

presidency—and, therefore, for some time to come, his party—with the word *malaise*.[6]

Talbott goes on to remind us that Clinton could *not* mention that something like a self-governing world community would have to eventually emerge:

> For most of his time in office, Clinton was equally careful not to broadcast his belief in a version of Darwinism in its most optimistic form—the notion that globalization was conducive to the emergence—or evolution—of an increasingly cooperative international system. In off-the-cuff public remarks, in prepared speeches, and in private conversation, I heard him field-test the idea that the spread of democracy, open society, market economy, and individual empowerment was the wave of the future. An example came during a joint press conference in Beijing with President Jiang Zemin of China on June 27, 1998, when Clinton ad-libbed, "It is important that whatever our disagreements over past action, China and the United States must go forward on the right side of history for the future sake of the world. The forces of history have brought us to a new age of human possibility but our dreams can only be recognized by nations whose citizens are both responsible and free." He stopped well short of endorsing the idea that something like a self-governing world community was a desirable outcome, not to mention a pre-determined one.[7]

We now live in a different world. The unipolar moment, if it ever existed, has passed. Slowly, even the most unilateral minds in Washington are beginning to acknowledge that some global rules may actually benefit and enhance American interests. Again, as usual, it was an immediate geopolitical challenge that triggered this new thinking. Speaking at the Shangri-La dialogue in 2011, Robert Gates, then secretary of defense, pressed China to abide by the Law of the Sea Treaty in its behavior in the South China Sea. This was a reasonable call. However, Gates was quite naturally embarrassed when someone asked him, "When is the USA going to ratify the Law of the Sea Treaty?"

There is a lot of wisdom in the adage that people who live in glass houses should not throw stones. If America is going to succeed in persuading

China to abide by global rules and conventions, it has to lead by example. This is exactly what happened. In May 2012, the Obama administration made a genuine effort to persuade the US Senate to ratify the Law of the Sea Treaty. Secretary of State Hillary Rodham Clinton led the charge by saying that the treaty was "critical to the leadership and security of the United States." "U.S. interests are deeply tied to the oceans," she added. "No country is in a position to gain more from the Law of the Sea Convention than the United States."[8] She concluded by saying, "The United States is long past due in joining this Convention. Our global leadership on maritime issues is at stake. I therefore urge the Committee to give its swift approval for U.S. accession to the Law of the Sea Convention and ratification of the 1994 Agreement, and urge the Senate to give its advice and consent before the end of this year."[9] Even major Republican voices like George W. Bush and George P. Shultz, secretary of state to President Ronald Reagan, supported US accession to the treaty, which is still unratified.[10]

Why did Washington's brahmins change their minds? Simple. The set of rules that America thought would only constrain it would now constrain a power that could become more powerful than America. This could happen sooner than most Americans expect. Indeed, almost no American knows that according to IMF data and in purchasing power parity (PPP) terms, the American economy could become number two in the world as early as 2016.[11] And who will tell the people that this has happened?

The world will not end when America becomes number two. Nor will it end when two centuries of Western domination of the world order come to a natural end. I have to emphasize this because the Western world is filled with new books that exude pessimism over the general global situation. Gideon Rachman succinctly captures the spirit of the Western mind with his appropriately titled *Zero-Sum World*. As he says in his Foreword, "My prognosis for the future of international politics is undoubtedly bleak."[12] Similarly, Ian Bremmer's book *Every Nation for Itself*, suggests that the world is careening toward disorder. Charles Kupchan has a similar theme with his appropriately titled *No One's World*. Even *The Economist* has concurred that

> the West's growing pessimism is reshaping political life. Two years after Barack Obama's hope-filled inauguration the mood in Washington is as glum as it has been since Jimmy Carter argued that America was suffer-

ing from "malaise." The Democrats' dream that the country was on the verge of a 1960s-style liberal renaissance foundered in the mid-terms. But the Republicans are hardly hopeful: their creed leans towards anger and resentment rather than Reaganite optimism. Europe, meanwhile, has seen mass protests, some of them violent, on the streets of Athens, Dublin, London, Madrid, Paris and Rome. If the countries on the European Union's periphery are down in the dumps it is hardly surprising, but there is pessimism at its more successful core too.[13]

By way of contrast, *The Economist* added that "according to the Pew Research Centre, some 87% of Chinese, 50% of Brazilians and 45% of Indians think their country is going in the right direction, whereas 31% of Britons, 30% of Americans and 26% of the French do. Companies, meanwhile, are investing in "emerging markets" and sidelining the developed world. 'Go east, young man' looks set to become the rallying cry of the 21st century."[14]

Ironically, for a book that retains an optimistic outlook, it may well appear in print in the middle of a perfect economic storm in the West in 2013. In July 2012, former Treasury Secretary Robert Rubin warned that America was headed straight toward a "fiscal cliff" with a potential contraction of $600 billion a year—or about 4 percent of GDP—if Congress took no action to stop the automatic budget cuts by January 2, 2013. All this could trigger a double-dip recession in the US. Rubin warned that the "uncertainty" surrounding this "could begin to affect decisions in the real economy."[15] At the same time, another squabble in Congress over raising the debt ceiling could further damage market confidence. Such major uncertainty in America coupled with major uncertainty over the future of the Euro could well deliver a perfect economic storm in 2013.

I have lived through one perfect economic storm in the Asian financial crisis of 1997–1998. The prices of everything collapsed in Southeast Asia. It seemed as though the world was coming to an end. As we now know, it did not. Nor will the world come to an end for the West if it has to struggle massively to get out of a perfect economic storm. At the end of the day, the strong inner resilience of Western societies will come through, in one way or another.

So there is no reason for the West to be pessimistic. The West will not lose power. It will have to share power. And the 88 percent of the world's population who live outside the West want to cooperate with the 12 percent who live in the West. The massive new middle-classes emerging all around the world have begun to accept many of the values and aspirations of the Western middle classes. In retrospect, this should not surprise us. Millions of the best minds from Asia, Africa, and Latin America have studied either in Western universities or, equally importantly, in Western-style universities in their own countries. Consequently, their perception of what constitutes "good societies" has also changed.

In the past few decades, the world has produced the greatest flock of university-educated brains ever seen in human history. Never before have we nurtured talent at the scale occurring today. The rising tide of new talent is one of the key driving forces producing the great convergence. The hundreds of thousands of Asians, for example, who have been educated in American universities and who have returned home want to re-create the "American dream" of a stable and prosperous middle-class society. In previous centuries when leaders met, they had to overcome their deep cultural differences. Some cultural differences remain. But it helps enormously when leaders of different countries have been trained at Harvard or Yale, Columbia or Stanford. And it is quite astonishing how often this happens now. We can and must take advantage of this new convergence to solve some of our world's new pressing problems. And it can be done.

A New Global Civilization

HUMANITY IS ONE. THAT HAS ALWAYS BEEN A NOBLE ASPIRATION espoused by leading global thinkers, from Albert Einstein to Mahatma Gandhi. Einstein famously said:

> When we survey our lives and endeavors, we soon observe that almost the whole of our actions and desires is bound up with the existence of other human beings. We notice that our whole nature resembles that of the social animals. We eat food that others have produced, wear clothes that others have made, live in houses that others have built. The greater part of our knowledge and beliefs has been communicated to us by other people through the medium of a language which others have created. Without language our mental capacities would be poor indeed, comparable to those of the higher animals; we have, therefore, to admit that we owe our principal advantage over the beasts to the fact of living in human society. The individual, if left alone from birth, would remain primitive and beastlike in his thoughts and feelings to a degree that we can hardly conceive.[1]

Einstein, in his usual brilliant fashion, was reminding us that we belong to a larger whole. Gandhi echoed a similar spirit with the remark "All humanity is one undivided and indivisible family." Yet even as we listen to their exhortations calling on us to confer equal moral worth to each human being regardless of race, religion, language, or culture, few of us believed that we could improve the condition of humanity as a whole. Renowned Swedish economist Gunnar Myrdal explained well the general pessimism that the human lot could be fundamentally improved: "In recent years there have been sudden, major changes in the world economy. They have radically affected the economic situation of all underdeveloped countries, though in different directions and degrees, and thereby the entire setting of the equality problem I am discussing in this lecture. For by far the larger part of the peoples in underdeveloped countries, these changes have been worsening their development prospects and in many countries are now threatening the survival of large numbers of their poor masses."[2]

Today, we can replace that Zeitgeist of pessimism with a new Zeitgeist of optimism. Without any grand strategy or a comprehensive plan of action, humanity has succeeded in creating a new global civilization. The goal of this chapter is to document in detail how the human condition has improved dramatically for the vast majority of the earth's inhabitants. And this chapter will demonstrate how the world is becoming a more "civilized" place. We are killing each other less and less. We are understanding each other better and cooperating more and more. There is a lot of goodness about our world that has gone unnoticed. If present trends continue, as they are likely to, the human condition will become the best we have experienced since human history began.

Fewer Wars and Combat Deaths

Not only is the danger of war between any two major powers the lowest it has been in human history, there is now also abundant data to confirm that the number of people dying on battlefields is the lowest it has ever been since records have been kept. "The number of people killed in battle—calculated per 100,000 population—has dropped by 1,000-fold over the centuries as civilizations evolved. Before there were organized countries, battles killed on average more than 500 out of every 100,000 people. In 19th century France, it was 70. In the 20th century with two world wars and a few genocides, it was 60. Now battlefield deaths are down to three-tenths of a person per 100,000."[3] The "2010 Human Security Report" argues that long-term trends are reducing the risks of both international and civil wars. Andrew Mack, director of the Human Security Report Project and a former adviser to United Nations (UN) Secretary-General Kofi Annan, comments:

> The most reassuring finding is that high-intensity wars, those that kill at least 1,000 people a year, have declined by 78% since 1988. . . . In the 1950s there was an average of six international conflicts (including anti-colonial wars) being fought around the world each year; in the new millennium the average was less than one. Recent international wars have also been far less deadly than those of the Cold War era, and the major powers have not fought each other for more than six decades—the longest period of major power peace in centuries. . . . France, the UK, USA, Russia/USSR, and India (in that order) were the world's most war-prone countries between 1946 and 2008 in that they have been involved in the most state-based armed conflicts. . . . The demise of colonialism, the end of the Cold War, a dramatic increase in the number of democratic states, and a shift in elite attitudes towards warfare are among the key political changes that have reduced the incidence of international warfare since the end of World War II. . . . Since the 1930s, public and elite attitudes towards war have changed substantially. Wars of colonial conquest would be unthinkable today. Whereas in earlier eras war was seen as acceptable, even desirable, now it is proscribed except in self-defense, or with the authority of the UN Security Council [UNSC]. . . .

Equally important, argues Mack, has been the dramatic long-term increase in levels of global economic interdependence. "Interdependence," he says, "has increased the costs of war while reducing its benefits. . . . Greatly increased levels of international trade and foreign direct investment have raised the costs of conquest and shrunk its benefits. One recent study found that, on average, a 10 percent increase in foreign direct investment reduced the risk of net conflict numbers by 3 percent. In today's open global trading system, it is almost always cheaper to acquire goods and raw materials by trade, than to invade a country in order to steal them."[4]

Mack also points out that

identifying the determinants of peace with any degree of precision is difficult—not because there are too few plausible explanations, but rather
there are too many. This complicates the task of analysis, but the range
of causes suggests that—other things being equal—the decline in interstate warfare is likely to prove enduring. Equally importantly, the UN,
liberated from four decades of political stasis in the Cold War, led the
huge increase in international initiatives directed at stopping wars and
preventing those that had stopped from re-starting. The UN was joined
by other international agencies, donor governments, governments of the
war-affected countries. Countless international and national NGOs were
also actively involved. The strongest finding to emerge from statistical
studies of the causes of civil war is that as levels of economic development rise, the risk of war falls. It is no accident that civil wars have been
concentrated in the poorest countries in the world.[5]

Mack is not the only scholar to document this remarkable secular decline in wars and war-related deaths. Another study, entitled "Global
Trends in Armed Conflict," by Halvard Buhaug, Scott Gates, Håvard Hegre,
and Håvard Strand, of the Centre for the Study of Civil War, Peace Research Institute Oslo (PRIO), has also confirmed that "the number of ongoing conflicts has declined since shortly after the end of the Cold War and
the severity of armed conflict has generally declined since World War II.
We are now in the longest period since World War II without interstate
war (those fought between two or more countries)."[6]

One statistic from Steven Pinker's *The Better Angels of Our Nature* con-
firms how dramatically the world has changed in the area of interstate conflict: annual war deaths have fallen between 1950 and 2010 by more than
an order of magnitude, from about 500,000 to 30,000 per year by one estimate (see Figure 1.1).

Many in the West live in fear of terrorist attacks. But even in the case of
terrorist attacks, the probabilities are illuminating. According to Ronald
Bailey, science correspondent of *Reason* magazine, an American was more
likely to be killed by lightning (1 in 5,500,000) or by a car accident (1 in
19,000) than by a terrorist attack (1 in 20 million) in the last five years

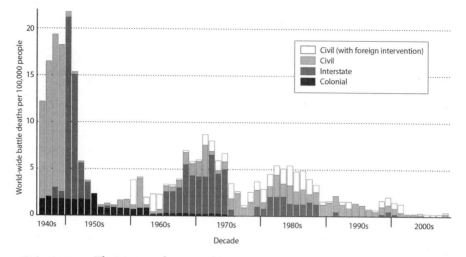

FIGURE 1.1 The Waning of War: Worldwide Battles Deaths per 100,000 People. *Source*: Adapted from Human Security Report Project, the Uppsala Conflict Data Program, and the Peace Research Institute Oslo, http://flatrock.org.nz/static/frontpage/06_the_waning _of_war.jpg.

(2005–2010).[7] President George W. Bush used to say frequently, "We live in a dangerous world."[8] He was dead wrong.

Pinker provides a trove of data and argument to confirm that the world has really turned a corner in the field of war and conflict. As he says, since 1945 we have seen a new phenomenon he describes as a "long peace" (a concept coined in 1989 by the brilliant Cold War historian John Lewis Gaddis, who wrote a book of that name).[9] Pinker describes how, since the end of the Cold War, a broader "new peace" appears to have taken hold. As I will describe later in this chapter, even corners of the world that have traditionally been perceived as dangerous, such as Southeast Asia (the Balkans of Asia),[10] are experiencing a "new peace" that is both profound and durable. It is an undeniable fact that for most of human history, human beings treated each other terribly. Conflicts were frequent. With each conflict, more and more human beings were killed. The decline of senseless killing and the dawn of a new peace clearly mean that the world is becoming a more civilized place. With each passing decade, we worry less and less about being killed by a fellow human being. Surely, there can be no clearer standard of treating fellow human beings in a more "civilized" manner.

Steady Decline in Absolute Poverty and Its Effects

A second positive trend we are seeing globally is the steady disappearance of absolute poverty. At the turn of the new millennium, the UN set many new Millennium Development Goals (MDGs) to be achieved by the year 2015. Not all the MDGs will be accomplished. But one key MDG will be reached ahead of time: the halving of global poverty. A lot of this will be due to the rapid economic growth experienced by China and India in recent decades. But Africa is also contributing significantly to the reduction of poverty. "The Millennium Development Goals Report 2011," published by the UN, notes that poverty continues to decline in many countries and regions: "Despite significant setbacks after the 2008–2009 economic downturn, exacerbated by the food and energy crisis, the world is still on track to reach the poverty-reduction target. By 2015, it is now expected that the global poverty rate will fall below 15 per cent, well under the 23 per cent target."[11] The US National Intelligence Council is even more optimistic, projecting that global poverty will be virtually eliminated by 2030.[12]

A *Time* magazine article, quoting a report issued by the UN and the Overseas Development Institute, noted that

> in 2010, about 1.4 billion of the world's 6.7 billion people lived in extreme poverty, which seems daunting until you consider that before the Millennium Development Program was launched, the figure was 1.8 billion. The 22% improvement rate is all the more impressive considering that it's been achieved in the face of a growing global population. Nearly 45% of signatory countries were on track to meet their goal of halving childhood hunger rates by 2015, and 75% have succeeded in bringing the number down in the critical under-5-year-old group. A whopping 95% of all countries have improved their under-5 mortality rate, with the worldwide figure falling from 101 deaths per 1,000 live births to 69.[13]

In addition to reducing poverty, many developing countries have made great strides in education. Sub-Saharan Africa as a region made an 18 percentage point gain between 1999 and 2009, the best record of improvement worldwide. Benin, Bhutan, Burkina Faso, Ethiopia, Guinea, Mali, Mozambique, and Niger have increased net enrollment ratios by 25 percentage points in the same time period.

Targeted interventions have also been met with much success. Today, 12,000 fewer children are dying each day than in 1990. Between 2000 and 2008, improved first- and second-dose immunization coverage led to a 78 percent drop in measles deaths, which represents one-quarter of the decline in mortality among children under five.[14] The human condition is improving significantly in this arena too.

With all these dramatic improvements in the developing world, the world is becoming a less unequal place. The Center for Global Development (CGD), a think tank based in Washington, DC, has produced a major report, edited by Charles Kenny, that describes "the great convergence in quality of life" between the rich and the poor states: "The next bit of good news regarding development is that looking at almost any measure of the quality of life except for income suggests rapid and ubiquitous global improvement. Since 1960, global average infant mortality has more than halved, for example. Nine million children born in 2005 were alive to celebrate their first birthday in 2006 who would have died if global mortality rates had remained unchanged since 1960. And the vast majority of those children lived in developing countries."

The same CGD report makes another fascinating comparison, which strongly supports the great convergence thesis. Many in the West continue to believe that Africa made little progress in the twentieth century and is not likely to make any meaningful progress in the future. Few expected that infant mortality rates would decline, life expectancy would go up, hunger would diminish, and literacy would increase. And yet Africa is progressing well on all these counts. They will be shocked to learn, then, that even the poorest parts of the world are performing faster than they ever have in human history. For instance, between 1275 and 1775 the British population and wage rates stayed the same. In contrast, in the much shorter period between 1913 and 2000, Ghana's per capita income increased by 63 percent.[15] We can see clearly here that even the poorest parts of our world are progressing faster than ever before in human history.

The Ghanaian recent track record in development is even more impressive. Economist Jeffrey Sachs notes, "Ghana is on track to achieve most, if not all, of the Millennium Development Goals. . . . It is one of the strongest performers in Africa on the MDGs because it has been investing for a long time in health and education, gender and equality, and it has made a lot of progress."[16] The *Christian Science Monitor* also reports, in a January 2012 article, that "Ghana was one of world's fastest growing economies in 2011 with an annual growth rate of 14 percent and it achieved middle-income status according the World Bank. Inflation has been on the decline in the past year and the Ghana Investment and Promotion Council said that Foreign Direct Investment (FDI) totaled $4.13 billion in the first three quarters of the 2011, a massive increase from the level of investment in the same quarter in 2010 that was at $216.71 million."[17]

Charles Kenny eloquently states:

> Countries in every region of the world, from the poorest to the richest, with stagnant or vibrant economies, have all seen improvements in average levels of health and education over the past half century. Most countries, regardless of economic performance, have taken strides towards gender equality, civil and political rights. Progress in quality of life has been particularly rapid in countries previously the furthest behind. There are concerns—the picture regarding global violence is mixed, the quality of education in particular remains extremely low in many developing countries, and recent progress on health has slowed, not least because of the crisis of AIDS. Nonetheless, the overall picture from the last 50 years is of a planet with a growing number of people living a better life.[18]

One truly little known feature of our contemporary world is that poor developing countries, including poor developing countries that have experienced traumatic internal conflicts, have begun to outperform some developed countries in the delivery of public services. Many years ago, the British government privatized its water authorities to improve their services. They did improve. Yet a water authority in a country that had just emerged from a painful genocidal experience outperformed all these British water authorities. That country was Cambodia.

All this happened because of a remarkable man, Ek Sonn Chan. During the brutal rule of Pol Pot from 1975 and 1979, Ek lost his entire family and barely managed to survive. In 1979, when the Khmer Rouge was evicted, he worked in a municipal abattoir. He took over the Phnom Penh Water Supply Authority (PPWSA) in 1993 and transformed it dramatically, leading the PPWSA to outperform its British counterparts. As a result, he was awarded the Ramon Magsaysay Award in 2006, and the PPWSA won the Stockholm Industry Water Award in 2010. The Magsaysay Award citation describes well Ek Sonn Chan's tremendous achievements:

> Ek combed his bloated workforce for the best and brightest and set them to work—locating and repairing the system's myriad leaks, installing thousands of water meters, and closing hundreds of illegal connections. He installed a computerized billing program, financed by France, and persuaded other international lenders that his agency was a good risk. In 1997, the Phnom Penh Water Supply Authority (PPWSA) became an autonomous public enterprise. With major loans from the World Bank, the Asian Development Bank, and the government of Japan, General Director Ek Sonn Chan embarked upon a major overhaul.
>
> He laid 1,500 kilometers of new pipelines and expanded the Authority's water output by 600 percent. He confronted VIP nonpayers and cut off their water when persuasion failed, achieving a collection rate of 99 percent by 2003. He raised prices, resulting in strong revenues and an enviable reputation for paying the Authority's debts ahead of schedule. With pricing policies favoring light users as well as subsidized connection fees and installment payment plans, he made cheap water available to the city's poorest neighborhoods. New and refurbished water-treatment plants ensured that this water met WHO water-safety standards. At the same time, Ek professionalized the Authority's workforce, building its technical capacity and instilling in its employees a work ethic of discipline, competence, and teamwork.[19]

I lived in Phnom Penh for one year, not long before the Khmer Rouge took over in 1975. The city was shelled almost every day when I was there, as it was under siege then. Hence, I experienced firsthand the painful civil war Phnom Penh experienced from 1970 to 1975, before the Khmer Rouge took over. When the civil war finally ended in 1990, I expected Cambodia to emerge as a broken nation, with the country in danger of falling apart. On this unpromising soil, Ek Sonn Chan managed to deliver a public service comparable to the best in the world. Stories like his illustrate well the great convergence that the world is enjoying.

A More Educated World Population

These positive trends are leading to a more educated world. The whole world is moving toward virtually universal primary school enrollment. As Joel Cohen, David Bloom, Helen Anne Curry, and Martin Malin describe:

> Over the past century, formal schooling spread remarkably, as measured by the primary gross enrolment ratio (GRE)—the ratio of total primary enrolment, regardless of age, to the population of the age group that officially belongs in primary education. In 1900, estimated primary GREs were below 40 percent in all regions, except . . . in northwestern Europe, North America, and Anglophone regions of the Pacific. . . . Within the past few years, [the equivalent figure] reached 86 percent. . . . Over the twentieth century, literacy tripled in developing countries, from 25 percent to 75 percent.[20]

The spread of primary education is also leading to more informed citizens. To quote the CGD report again:

> People around the world are also more "informed consumers" than they used to be. They not only demand soap to wash their hands, they want schools to educate their girls, and they want governments that respect their rights. The increasing demand for education in particular is an important part of the story behind climbing primary enrolments. Less than half of primary-age kids worldwide were enrolled in school in 1950, but by the end of the century the figure was closer to 9 out of 10. Valuing ABCs and getting DPTs—these are the forces behind global improvements in quality of life.[21]

In addition, the report explains, "the proportion of the world's infants vaccinated against diphtheria, pertussis, and tetanus—the DPT shot—climbed from one-fifth to nearly four-fifths between 1970 and 2006. And ideas that save lives—wash your hands, don't defecate in the fields you eat from—are increasingly accepted."[22]

Education helps to improve the human condition. Steven Pinker suggests that as well as becoming better educated, we are also becoming more intelligent. Pinker describes this as the "Flynn effect," which is "the remarkable finding by the philosopher James Flynn that ever since I.Q. tests were first administered, the scores achieved by those taking the test have been rising. The average I.Q. is, by definition, 100; but to achieve that result, raw test scores have to be standardized. If the average teenager today could go back in time and take an I.Q. test from 1910, he or she would have an I.Q. of 130, which would be better than 98 percent of those taking the test then."[23]

More People Joining the Middle Class

These rising levels of intelligence, education, and prosperity are in turn associated with a rising number of people joining the middle class. Homi Kharas, a senior fellow at the Brookings Institution in the United States and an expert on the burgeoning middle class in developing countries, has defined members of a global middle class as follows: "Those households with daily expenditures between $10 and $100 per person in PPP terms. This excludes those who are considered poor in the poorest advanced countries and rich in the richest advanced countries." The greatest improvements in history have occurred in the past thirty years, coinciding with the decision of China and India to open up and reform their economies in 1979 and 1991, respectively. As a result of this opening up of the world's two most populous countries, a staggering number of people are seeing their living standards improve, especially in Asia. Kharas describes these changes well: "Asia accounts for less than one-quarter of today's middle class. But by 2020, that share could double. More than half the world's middle class could be in Asia and Asian consumers could account for over 40 per cent of global middle class consumption. This is because a large mass of Asian households have incomes today that position them just below the global middle class threshold and so increasingly large numbers of Asians are expected to become middle class in the next ten years."[24]

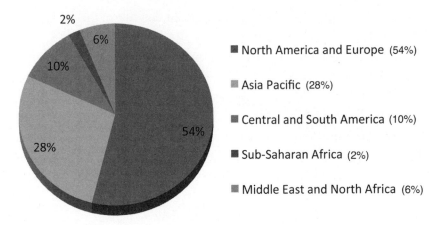

FIGURE 1.2 Regional Share of the Global Middle Class, 2009. *Source:* Based on Homi Kharas, "The Emerging Middle Class in Developing Countries," Working Paper No. 285 (Paris: OECD Development Center, 2010), http://www.oecd.org/dataoecd/12/52/4445 7738.pdf.

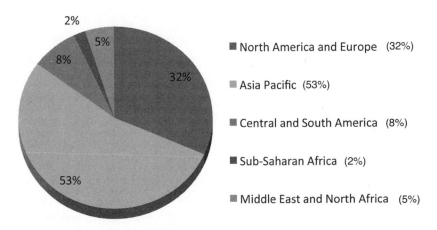

FIGURE 1.3 Regional Share of the Global Middle Class, 2020. *Source:* Based on Homi Kharas, "The Emerging Middle Class in Developing Countries," Working Paper No. 285 (Paris: OECD Development Centre, 2010), http://www.oecd.org/dataoecd/12/52/4445 7738.pdf.

Indeed, Figures 1.2 and 1.3 highlight rather dramatically the extent to which Asia will soon become home to the world's largest middle class. In 2009, the North American and European middle classes were by far the largest on the planet. But in the space of just one decade, Asia will easily take their place.[25]

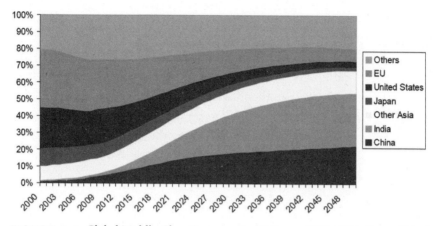

FIGURE 1.4 Global Middle-Class Consumption Patterns, 2000–2050. *Source:* Based on Homi Kharas, "The Emerging Middle Class in Developing Countries," Working Paper No. 285 (Paris: OECD Development Center, 2010), http://www.oecd.org/dataoecd/12/52/44457738.pdf.

Figure 1.4 should put to rest any doubts that the first five decades of the twenty-first century will experience a great transformation.[26]

We must keep in mind at this point that all the trends described so far—the decline of war, the rise of education, and burgeoning middle-class aspirations—tend to reinforce each other. As the European Union states have taught us, the development of middle class societies and the decline of conflict are correlated. Human nature has not changed. Europeans have always been Europeans, at war or in peace. What has changed is the social order. As a result of modernization, people can improve their living standards and those of their children without having to resort to war. Indeed, wars leave societies worse off, not better off. This may well be the biggest contribution of George W. Bush in creating a more civilized human order: when the colossal military power of the US could not easily crush a small state like Iraq and when the US had to pay massive material and human costs in trying to conquer and pacify it, this provided a living and daily demonstration of the futility of war. The Iraq war is estimated to have cost American taxpayers anywhere between $1 and $3 trillion (the estimate of Nobel economist Joseph Stiglitz).[27] Living standards of Americans have been damaged by the wars in Iraq and Afghanistan. Indeed, wars have become unfashionable. Australian historian Geoffrey Blainey once observed,

"For every thousand pages published on the causes of wars there is less than one page directly on the causes of peace."[28]

Blainey is absolutely right. We have not absorbed the new reality that the human condition is the most peaceful that it has ever been. Nor have we really understood why this has happened. I suggest simply that the world is becoming a more peaceful and prosperous place because a consensual cluster of norms has been sweeping the globe and has been accepted by policymaking elites all around the world. Policymakers in all corners have essentially developed the same set of perspectives on how to improve and develop their societies.

Greater University-Educated Populations

Even though there is increasingly broad agreement in the world on how to improve societies, it will still not be easy to unpack with precision what is included in these norms. But there are clues to where we might find the origins of such a global consensus. Let's begin by investigating leading North American universities, such as Harvard or Yale, Stanford or Carnegie Mellon. Although these elite campuses might once have been remote "ivory towers" that offered students and professors a cloistered and paralyzed life, isolated from the rest of the world, they are now places admitting hundreds of thousands of foreign students, especially from Asia. The resulting norms of these North American campuses have spread like a healthy virus across the globe. The numbers are staggering: the International Institute of Education (IIE) in New York has documented that in the year 2011, 723,277 foreign students studied in North American universities.[29] This number included 157,558 from China, 103,895 from India, and 73,351 from South Korea.[30] Figure 1.5 illustrates well the growing number of foreigners studying in American universities.

While more international students studied in the US in 2011, less than 2 percent of US college and university students studied abroad during the same period, according to the IIE report. This may explain why Secretary of State Hillary Clinton urged US students to apply for passports and "not just think globally but get out there and study globally as well."[31] The world has learned a lot from America. Is America ready to learn from the world?

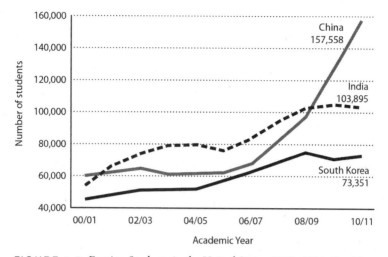

FIGURE 1.5 Foreign Students in the United States, 2000–2011: Top Three Countries of Origin. *Source:* Based on Institute of International Education, 2011, http://www.iie.org/Research-and-Publications/~/media/Files/Corporate/Open-Doors/Open-Doors-2011-Briefing-Presentation.ashx.

The millions of foreign graduates from American universities (and, to be fair, European, Canadian, Australian, and New Zealand universities) have returned home to replicate the Western university experience. As a consequence, our world now has the highest percentage of university-educated populations ever. China provides the most dramatic example. As recently as 1990, only around 3 percent of each secondary school cohort went on to university or another higher education institute. However, by 2010, less than twenty years later, China was able to increase the number of each cohort going to higher education to 29 percent. *The Economist* has reported that the number of students in China enrolled in degree courses rose from 1 million in 1997 to 5 million in 2011. The number of higher education institutions in China more than doubled from 2001 to 2011, from 1,022 to 2,263.[32] By 2020, forecasts predict that China will account for 29 percent of the world's graduates aged between twenty-five and thirty-four.[33]

A paper produced by the East Asian Institute of the National University of Singapore (NUS) provides more data on this absolutely remarkable transformation. It notes:

Enrolment in China's higher education has expanded rapidly since 1999. In 1995, only 5% in the age group 18–22 had access to higher education, putting China in the same rank as Bangladesh, Botswana and Cameroon; in 2007, the ratio increased to 23%. The pace of expansion was unprecedented. Yearly tertiary student enrolment did not reach one million until 1997; a decade later it exceeded 5.5 million. There was an increase of about half a million every year from 1999 to 2006. Thanks to the unprecedented expansion, China is now in the stage of mass higher education. With more than 20 million students, China has overtaken the U.S. in having the world's largest higher education sector since 2005.[34]

Similarly, according to the National Science Foundation's Science and Engineering Report of 2012, India and China were the countries of origin for nearly two-thirds of the foreign science and engineering graduates in the United States in November 2010. In 2008, about 5 million first university degrees were awarded in science and engineering worldwide. Students in China earned about 23 percent, those in the European Union earned about 19 percent, and those in the United States earned about 10 percent of these degrees. In the United States, about 4 percent of all bachelor's degrees awarded in 2008 were in engineering, compared with about 19 percent throughout Asia and 31 percent in China specifically. In 2008, China overtook the United States as the world leader in the number of doctoral degrees awarded in the natural sciences and engineering. Students from China earned the largest number of US science and engineering doctorates awarded to foreign students during the 1989–2009 period (57,700), followed by those from India (24,800), South Korea (21,800), and Taiwan (17,800). Ten percent of foreign recipients of science and engineering doctorates in the United States between 1989 and 2009 were Indian, and 25 percent of them were Chinese. As a consequence of all this, China is going to overtake the US in citations of scientific literature, as illustrated in Figure 1.6.

China awarded more than 500,000 doctorates in 2009, up from 1,900 in 1993. The nation also graduated 500,000 engineers in 2010, including 10,000 PhDs. The US graduated only 8,000 PhD engineers in 2010, an estimated two-thirds of whom were not US citizens. Since 2008, substantially more PhD engineers and scientists have graduated in China than in the United States. In 2001, only 5 percent of American twenty-four-year-olds with a bachelor's degree were engineers, compared to 39 percent in

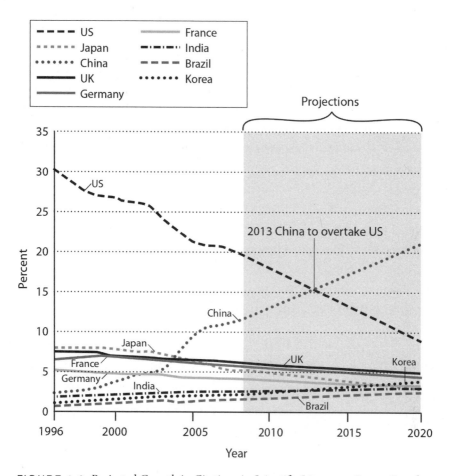

FIGURE 1.6 Projected Growth in Citations in Scientific Literature. *Source:* Based on http://www.bbc.co.uk/news/science-environment-12885271 and data from Britain's Royal Society.

China and 19 percent or more in South Korea, Taiwan, and Japan. R. E. Smalley, a Nobel Prize–winning scientist from Rice University, reckoned that in 2010, 90 percent of all PhD physical scientists and engineers in the world were Asians living in Asia. And among Asian PhD engineers and scientists, most will be produced by China.[35]

Even though these Chinese and Indians graduate from their own universities, not North American universities, they often graduate with the same cultural and intellectual approaches I referred to earlier. Just look, for example, at the remarkable contributions of Indian Institute(s) of Technology (IIT) graduates, many of whom have helped to fuel the Silicon

Valley revolutions and have gone on to become CEOs of major American corporations or the deans of leading American business schools. In the last six decades the IIT system has produced more than 170,000 graduates. It is generally estimated that about one-third or more of these alumni have found opportunities in other countries, where they are universally acknowledged to be leaders in their fields of endeavor.[36]

Many IIT alumni have become entrepreneurs. They include N. R. Narayana Murthy (cofounder and former chairman of Infosys), Rajendra S. Pawar (cofounder and chairman of NIIT), Vinod Khosla (cofounder of Sun Microsystems), Anurag Dikshit (cofounder of PartyGaming), and Suhas S. Patil (founder and chairman emeritus of Cirrus Logic). Other alumni have achieved leading corporate positions, such as Rajat Gupta (former managing director of McKinsey), Arun Sarin (former CEO of Vodafone), Vijay K. Thadani (cofounder and CEO of NIIT), Victor Menezes (senior vice chairman of Citigroup), and Kanwal Rekhi (CTO of Novell).

Khosla, a graduate of the Indian Institute of Technology in Delhi, helped turn a computer science project into Sun Microsystems, a multibillion-dollar phenomenon. He is now a venture capitalist. His firm, Khosla Ventures, focuses on venture investments in various technology sectors, in particular clean energy technology. He said, "Most people who do well might go spend $100 million buying a yacht. And I've known plenty of people who have done that. My yacht is 100 little $1 million startups. . . . That sounded a lot more fun, backing 100 young entrepreneurs than buying a yacht and sailing it once a week. . . . These startups are my yacht."[37]

This is how *The Economist* reports his goals:

"We need 1,000% change if billions of people in China and India are to enjoy a Western, energy-rich lifestyle." Forget today's green technologies like electric cars, wind turbines, solar cells and smart grids, in other words. None meets what Mr Khosla calls the "Chindia price"—the price at which people in China and India will buy them without a subsidy. "Everything's a toy until it reaches that point," he says. Mr Khosla has a different plan to save the planet. He is investing over $1 billion of his clients' money in "black swans"—ideas with the potential for sudden jumps in technology that promise huge environmental benefits, easy scalability and rapid payback. The catch? Mr Khosla expects nine out of ten of his investments to fail. "I am only interested in technologies that have a 90% chance of failure but, if they do succeed, would change the infrastructure of society in some radical way," he says. Khosla Ventures' portfolio reads like an eco-utopian wish-list: non-polluting nuclear reactors; diesel from microbes; carbon-negative cement; quantum batteries; and a system for extracting methane from coal while it is still underground. "Any one of these things is improbable but, if you have enough shots on goal, then it's very likely that something improbable will win," he says. "Ten years ago, no analyst in the world would have predicted 650m cellphone subscribers in India but only 300m people with access to latrines and toilets. Even five years ago, no one would have predicted the way that Twitter took off. These are the black swan outliers."[38]

Murthy founded Infosys Technologies in 1981 with an initial investment of $250 borrowed from his wife. At Infosys, Murthy articulated, designed, and implemented the Global Delivery Model that became the foundation for the huge success in IT services outsourcing from India. In 2011, thirty years later, Infosys has become one of the largest wealth creators in India. It is valued at more than $7.5 billion. This growth translates into a thirty-year annual return of 78 percent, thereby surpassing Warren Buffett's thirty-six-year Berkshire Hathaway annual return of 22 percent, Peter Lynch's thirteen-year Magellan Fund annual return of 29 percent, and George Soros's thirty-two-year Quantum Fund annual return of 30 percent. Now retired, Murthy hopes to replicate what Infosys did for middle-class India for the poor in India with Catamaran, the $129 million venture fund he set up in 2009 after selling his and his wife Sudha's part holdings in Infosys. Believing that the only way to deal with the challenge of poverty is to create jobs and generate wealth through private entrepreneurship, he will encourage small entrepreneurs in a wide spectrum of fields. The fund has already made eight investments, the biggest of them in SKS Microfinance, Manipal Global Learning, and energy drink maker Tzinga. Every business has to make money, grow, and make a difference by investing more in technology, creating new products, and creating more jobs, says Murthy.[39]

The contributions of IIT graduates have only just begun. Many more of them will continue to transform our world. In December 2009, I was invited to go to Chennai to address the PanIIT Conference. The organizers assigned a young student, Midhun Salim, to act as my host. He was chosen because he was coming to the NUS, where I am the dean of the Lee Kuan Yew School of Public Policy, on an exchange program the following year. He was among twenty students from Asia-Pacific chosen for the Leadership Enrichment and Regional Networking scholarship instituted by Temasek Foundation.

I then met him in Singapore. He did well there. He traveled throughout Southeast Asia and forged lasting friendships. His first international experience opened his mind to the challenges facing the wider world and the innumerable opportunities it offered. He was particularly fascinated by the debate around the high cost of health care. From Singapore, he went to Canada. There he worked as a research assistant at the Sauder School of Business. His project was focused on delivering cost-efficient treatment for patients suffering from end stage renal disease. The project was a success, and the lessons from the project are currently being implemented at British Columbia hospitals.

After returning from Canada, he became involved in another of his passions—energy. His team won the 2009 Edison Challenge (sponsored by General Electric in association with the Department of Science and Technology, India) for its thesis on a rural energy model based on AC-coupled microgrids and decentralized power generation. Initial parts of the proposed model are being currently tested at the village of Natham in Tamil Nadu state in India. Capitalizing on the experience he had gained during the course of the project, he founded a startup (Greenext Technology Solutions) that provided sophisticated algorithms for battery management systems and electricity markets. This business plan won the New York City Economic Development Corporation's Next Idea 2009 competition. His team was offered office space for two years and legal and administrative support for starting the business. His team is currently working on acquiring intellectual property rights on the algorithms.

Midhun has currently taken up an offer from Deutsche Bank to work in its Global Markets Division. He is hoping to acquire corporate experience before he continues with his long-term interests in entrepreneurship. I often tell this story about Midhun to my friends to illustrate how a young Muslim boy of India who had never stepped out of India in 2008 went on to win places and competitions in Canada and New York City within a few years. A hundred years ago, or perhaps even fifty years ago, Midhun Salim would not have ventured far away from the village of his birth. Nor would he have gone to university or traveled to developed cities. The new global environment has changed all this. As a consequence, young men, like Midhun Salim, and young women have been swept into the global mainstream, improving it as they join it.

The New Norms

The increasingly common patterns of behavior among policymaking elites around the world provide another clue to what is the new normal. With the possible exception of North Korea, the last remaining hermit kingdom in the world, these new norms have seeped into every society. Let me look at five of them here: acceptance of the frameworks of modern science, reliance on logical reasoning, embrace of free-market economics, transformation of the social contract between ruler and ruled, and increasing focus on multilateralism.

Modern Science

The first key element is the acceptance of modern science and the scientific method. This acceptance means that when a society anywhere on the planet encounters a major problem (like floods or droughts, earthquakes or violent storms), it scours the world to find the best scientific solution. For many in the West, this is a natural response; indeed, any other choice is inconceivable. But that wasn't my personal experience: I had the good fortune of growing up in a poor developing country with parents who never went to high school, let alone university. Indeed, I was probably the first descendant of all my ancestors to ever study in a university. Hence, I could see clearly the threshold a person had to cross in going from the pre-scientific world into the scientific era.

As a result of going to school, I learned that electricity was a relatively recent scientific discovery, one that had significantly improved the human

condition. Without modern science, humanity would never have har-
nessed electricity. I tried to convince my mother of this simple fact. She
would always smile kindly at me and say that she had no doubt that electricity had divine origins. The light came from heaven. Nor was she too
impressed with modern aviation. She mentioned that several Hindu epics
had documented how our ancestors used to fly before modern aviation
came along. Recalling these conversations and encounters fifty years later,
I can see that I was fortunate to have glimpsed the premodern scientific
universe. But this universe is disappearing. Modern science is now accepted universally and is clearly one of the key driving forces creating the
new global civilization we live in.

Many in the West assume that the Islamic world remains resistant to
modern science. Certainly, the levels of education in science are lower in
the Islamic world, especially the Arab world, than anywhere else in Asia.
The Arab world continues to underinvest in research. According to Mouïn
Hamzé, the secretary-general of the National Council for Scientific Research in Lebanon, "Funding for research and development in the Arab
world remains far below that of most other regions. In 2007–2008, for example, countries throughout the region spent just 0.3% of their gross domestic product (GDP) on R&D. China, in contrast, now spends 1.5% of
its GDP on R&D and India more than 1.0%."[40]

Yet there is no doubt over the direction the Islamic world is heading in
the field of science. Roger Highfield, editor of *New Scientist* magazine,
notes, "From the empire of Islam came the astrolabe, algebra and the collective wisdom of the likes of Ptolemy and Aristotle, ideas that would pave
the way to the Renaissance and shape the modern world. This golden age
of Arabic science faltered centuries ago but what is notable is the magnitude of the current efforts to rekindle the flame of this influential scientific tradition."[41] According to a UNESCO report on higher education in
the Arab world, "Three regional initiatives exemplify recent top-down initiatives in higher education: Qatar's Education City, the Masdar Institute
in Abu Dhabi, and the King Abdullah University of Sciences and Technology in Saudi Arabia."[42]

Although Saudi Arabia remains one of the most conservative societies
in the world—it still does not allow its women to drive cars—it has also invested the largest amount of money to build the world's newest and largest

scientific university, the King Abdullah University of Science and Technology (KAUST). KAUST is an international, graduate-level research university supported by a multi-billion dollar endowment and accepts students (men and women) from all over the world. KAUST's research agenda focuses on four strategic areas: energy and the environment, biosciences and bioengineering, material sciences and engineering, and applied mathematics and computational science.[43]

If the Saudi Arabian policymaking elite did not believe in modern science, it would not have made such a major investment. The other rich Gulf Cooperation Council members, such as the United Arab Emirates and Qatar, are following suit. According to the UNESCO report just mentioned:

> The Qatar Foundation founded Education City in 2001 as a hub for capacity-building and character development. At the heart of Education City are branches of six international universities: Carnegie Mellon University, Georgetown University's School of Foreign Service, Virginia Commonwealth University, Weill Medical College of Cornell University and the Texas Agricultural and Mechanical University (Texas A&M). A significant percentage of the Qatari students enrolled in these branch campuses are girls seeking to pursue higher education close to home. For instance, 75 of the 120 Qatari students at the Carnegie Mellon satellite campus are female. On Georgetown's satellite campus, 68 of the 107 students are female. Education City includes an Academic Bridge Programme which prepares students for study in world-class universities.[44]

"Qatar now aims to spend 2.8 per cent of its GDP on research in a region where figures typically range from 0.02 to 0.07 per cent."[45]

Moreover, according to the UNESCO report,

> Abu Dhabi in the United Arab Emirates launched the Masdar Initiative in 2006 as a global co-operative scientific platform to address pressing issues, such as energy security, climate change and the development of human expertise in sustainability science. Masdar aims to position Abu Dhabi as a world-class R&D hub for new energy technologies and to drive the commercialization and adoption of these and other technologies in

sustainable energy, carbon management and water conservation. Developed in co-operation with the Massachusetts Institute of Technology (MIT), the Masdar Institute of Science and Technology emulates MIT's high standards and offers Master's and PhD programmes focused on the science and engineering of advanced energy and sustainable technologies. MIT is working with Masdar to establish a sustainable, home-grown academic and scientific research institute. The Masdar Institute aspires to become a centre of high-calibre renewable energy and sustainability research capable of attracting leading scientists from around the world.[46]

Abu Dhabi is attempting to establish the world's first fully sustainable city and innovation hub, with 50,000 people and 1,500 businesses.

When it comes to Iran, the most demonized Islamic society in the West, many Westerners could be forgiven for believing that Iran is run by some mad mullahs who are opposed to modern scientific education and certainly opposed to sharing this scientific education with women, who are, in this view, totally oppressed in Iran. But the facts speak otherwise.

According to a 2008 study of women in Iran's higher education conducted by Iran's Parliament (Majlis) Research Center, Iranian women constituted 65 percent of the student population in Iran's higher education, a twofold increase compared to 32 percent in 1983, the base year in the study. In 2008, Iranian female high school graduates constituted 65 percent of participants in the nationwide university entrance exam, compared to 42 percent in 1983.[47] According to UN data, girls outnumbered boys in primary school enrollment in 2005, making up 54 percent of primary students. Women outnumbered men in tertiary education as well, making up 51 percent of tertiary-level students. In tertiary-level science programs, 67 percent of students were women, and 58 percent of those studying social sciences, business, and law at the tertiary level were also women.[48] Author Robert D. Kaplan has also commented on the more liberal nature of Iranian women relative to women from other Muslim countries. He observed during his travels: "Women in Teheran stare you in the face. Their eyes meet you dead-on. Cairo has little of this, and Istanbul much less than Teheran. . . . In Iran, a male traveler communicated with both sexes, not just with his own."[49]

The willingness of the hugely conservative Iranian leadership to endorse female education in massive numbers in modern science and technology demonstrates how the new consensus has seeped into some of the most conservative societies on our planet.

Logic

Scientific reasoning, especially logic, is a second vital shared norm. We are now using effectively a common conceptual framework in much of our decisionmaking. This is another major contribution that Western universities have made: they have unleashed the virus of logical reasoning in all corners of the world.

The emergence of American-style MBAs and American-style business schools in all corners of the world has had an enormous positive effect. Business school graduates may be less idealistic and more focused on making money than most other graduates. Yet they may have done far more good for the world than any other graduates because, while they are taught to be competitive, they are also taught to look for optimal win-win solutions in making deals.

This search for win-win solutions has now become even more pervasive worldwide and explains why traditionally adversarial countries, like Germany and France, Greece and Turkey, Brazil and Argentina, or even the US and China, can begin to speak to each other with a common language. Pinker describes this dynamic as "an accelerating escalator of reason [that] carried us away from impulses that lead to violence."[50]

I have seen this escalator of reason at work firsthand in my own backyard, Southeast Asia. In 1954, President Dwight Eisenhower described well the grim prospects facing Southeast Asia:

> Finally, you have broader considerations that might follow what you would call the "falling domino" principle. You have a row of dominoes set up, you knock over the first one, and what will happen to the last one is the certainty that it will go over very quickly. So you could have a beginning of a disintegration that would have the most profound influences. . . . With respect to more people passing under this domination, Asia, after all, has already lost some 450 million of its peoples to the

Communist dictatorship, and we simply can't afford greater losses. But when we come to the possible sequence of events, the loss of Indochina, of Burma, of Thailand, of the Peninsula, and Indonesia following, now you begin to talk about areas that not only multiply the disadvantages that you would suffer through loss of materials, sources of materials, but now you are talking really about millions and millions and millions of people.[51]

In 1975, American political scientist Donald E. Nuechterlein wrote that in the decade following Eisenhower's speech the situation in Southeast Asia had not improved:

> In sum, none of the nations which currently make up the region of Southeast Asia was strong enough internally to withstand pressures from outside the region. Since these nations had for varying periods of their history lived under different colonial systems, the communications among them had to start from nearly a zero baseline. The foundations for both nationhood and for regional cooperation were just beginning.... It is little wonder, therefore, that the former colonial powers should have been deeply involved in the process of providing their former colonies a defense shield behind which they might hopefully buy time to develop their political institutions and internal security. The decade from 1954 to 1964 proved this was a vain hope; fundamentally, the nations of Southeast Asia were little better prepared in 1964 than they were in 1954 to assume full responsibility for working out their own destinies.[52]

In this unpromising and inauspicious environment, the Southeast Asian states created a regional organization, the Association of Southeast Asian Nations, in August 1967. Few expected ASEAN to survive, as both of its immediate predecessors, ASA and Maphilindo, had died quick deaths. The conventional wisdom was that ASEAN would perish soon enough as well. It is therefore truly astonishing that it has survived for forty-five years and is now widely recognized globally as the second most successful regional organization after the European Union. How did this happen?

The simple answer is that ASEAN has traveled up the escalator of reason. I first started attending ASEAN meetings in 1971. We had five members then: Indonesia, Malaysia, the Philippines, Singapore, and Thailand. Each of the five members traditionally had experienced problems with at least one of the other ASEAN members. I remember vividly the suspicion and distrust in the room when ASEAN meetings were held in the 1970s. There were not many glimpses of win-win solutions. Instead, each member tried to gain advantages at the expense of the others.

Two decades later when I began attending ASEAN meetings again, I was astonished at the reduced levels of distrust and increased levels of goodwill, even though the membership had doubled to ten members. Even more remarkably, one of the newest members was Vietnam, against whom the original five founding members had engaged in a major struggle during the Cold War, right up to 1990. But by the mid-1990s, we were all working together. The culture of the Southeast Asian people did not change between the 1970s and 1990s. Ancient cultures do not change overnight. However, their attitudes toward regional cooperation did, as they rationally worked out the costs and benefits. The rational process of analysis overcame decades of distrust, demonstrating that Pinker's "escalator of reason" was working well in Southeast Asia.

The story of Southeast Asia is a particularly inspiring one for our global community because no other region is as diverse—in religious, ethnic, cultural, and political terms—as Southeast Asia. The region has almost 600 million people. This population comprises 300 million Muslims, 80 million Christians, 150 million Hinayana Buddhists, 80 million Mahayana Buddhists, and 5 million Hindus. Some Vietnamese Buddhists also practice Taoism and Confucianism, in addition to being Communists. On the ethnic front there is even greater diversity, and on the political front ASEAN has the full spectrum of political systems. By contrast, the European Union is a simple club of Christian majority states with only one kind of political system. Hence, if the most diverse region of our world can use the forces of logical reasoning to achieve real and meaningful cooperation, it demonstrates well how we all are moving toward creating a more civilized global community. ASEAN shows that a clash of civilizations is not inevitable. This may be why Kofi Annan, a former UN secretary-general, says, "ASEAN is one of the most successful organisations which I look up to and admire."[53]

Free-Market Economics

The third key element in this consensual cluster is the acceptance of free-market economics as the only viable instrument for promoting prosperity. There was a time when there were competing systems of economic development. History has dealt a deathblow to the Communist centrally planned economic management systems, with North Korea once again remaining the only holdout. Even Cuba is gradually opening its economy, following cautiously in the footsteps of China and Vietnam, two of the most dynamic economies of the world.

Of course, there are varieties of economic subsystems within the free-market universe. The French economy is not a replica of the American economy. Nor is the Indonesian economy a replica of the Indian economy. However, despite these variations, they agree fundamentally with Adam Smith's major insight: that the "invisible hand" guides the individual to pursue his own self-interest but in doing so, he "frequently promotes [the interest] of the society more effectually than when he really intends to promote it."[54]

The Social Contract

The fourth key element is a fundamental change in the traditional social contract between the rulers and the ruled. One reason that the West leaped ahead of the rest of the world is that it was the first to destroy the feudal assumption that the people were accountable to their lords and masters, but not the other way around. The West turned things around by creating democratic systems in which the people chose (and sacked) their rulers. This reversal of roles clearly brought about a fundamental transformation in human history.

Democratic systems are still not universal. It will take some time, for example, before China and Saudi Arabia become democratic. However, even now they have accepted the reality that a new grain of human history has emerged: rulers are accountable to other people. They can stay in office only if they enjoy the support of their populaces. In theory, the Chinese political system is a Communist Party dictatorship. In practice, however, the Chinese Communist Party (unlike in the time Mao Zedong) knows that it has to earn its legitimacy daily. President Hu Jintao and Premier Wen Jiabao have emphasized that the role of the party is to serve the people. Wen Jiabao has urged government officials and Communist Party of China (CPC) members to better use their power and "serve the people wholeheartedly."[55] Wen has called on CPC members and government officials to be good public servants: "The word 'public' requires officials to prudently use their power for the benefit of the nation's people. The word 'servant' means that officials should make efforts to diligently serve the people."[56]

In a press conference on March 14, 2012, Wen also emphasized the need for the CPC to continue reforming:

> Although our party has made resolutions on a number of historical issues, after the implementation of reform and opening up, the mistakes of the Cultural Revolution and feudalism have not been completely eliminated. . . . As the economy developed, it has caused unfair distribution, the loss of credibility, corruption and other issues. I know that to solve these problems, it's necessary to not only enter into economic reform but also political reform, especially reform of the Party and the state's leadership system. . . . Reform has reached a critical stage. Without the success of political reform, economic reforms cannot be carried out. The results that we have achieved may be lost. A historical tragedy like the Cultural Revolution may occur again. Each party member and cadre should feel a sense of urgency.[57]

It is now increasingly clear that the governments that will survive and prosper in the twenty-first century are those that will respect this new grain of history. Any government today, no matter how powerful, faces great peril if it stops believing or accepting that it is accountable to its own people. Fortunately, the number of really bad governments that either oppress their people or ignore their wishes is diminishing. As a result, the human condition is improving, even in the most unlikely places. I remember vividly the conventional wisdom of the 1970s and 1980s that Bangladesh was a lost cause, the epitome of a society beyond hope. Yet few have noticed that its economy has grown at an annual pace of 6 percent during the past decade or so. Bangladesh's GDP more than doubled from 47.1 billion dollars in 2000 to 100 billion in 2010.[58] Even though Bangladesh has experienced some political instability as a result of the competition between two powerful leading politicians, Begum Khaleda Zia and Sheikh Hasina Wazed, this has not prevented the country's economic growth.

Africa is moving ahead too. It was truly striking when *The Economist* magazine, a traditional receptacle of conventional Anglo-Saxon wisdom, came out with a cover story on the rise of Africa in late 2011. The headline on the cover screamed, "Africa Rising." And in its editorial, *The Economist* boldly declared:

> Over the past decade six of the world's ten fastest-growing countries were African. In eight of the past ten years, Africa has grown faster than East Asia, including Japan. Even allowing for the knock-on effect of the northern hemisphere's slowdown, the IMF expects Africa to grow by 6% this year and nearly 6% in 2012, about the same as Asia. Africa now has a fast-growing middle class: according to Standard Bank, around 60m Africans have an income of $3,000 a year, and 100m will in 2015. The rate of foreign investment has soared around tenfold in the past decade.[59]

Since many in the West are unable to imagine an Africa rising, it may be useful to quote at some length from *The Economist*'s report:

> China's arrival [that is, China's increased investment in Africa] has improved Africa's infrastructure and boosted its manufacturing sector. Other non-Western countries, from Brazil and Turkey to Malaysia and India, are following its lead. . . . Africa's enthusiasm for technology is boosting growth. It has more than 600m mobile-phone users—more than America or Europe. Since roads are generally dreadful, advances in communications, with mobile banking and telephonic agro-info, have been a huge boon. Around a tenth of Africa's land mass is covered by mobile-internet services—a higher proportion than in India. The health of many millions of Africans has also improved, thanks in part to the wider distribution of mosquito nets and the gradual easing of the ravages of HIV/AIDS. Skills are improving: productivity is growing by nearly 3% a year, compared with 2.3% in America. All this is happening partly because Africa is at last getting a taste of peace and decent gov-

ernment. For three decades after African countries threw off their colonial shackles, not a single one (bar the Indian Ocean island of Mauritius) peacefully ousted a government or president at the ballot box. But since Benin set the mainland trend in 1991, it has happened more than 30 times—far more often than in the Arab world. Population trends could enhance these promising developments. A bulge of better-educated young people of working age is entering the job market and birth rates are beginning to decline. As the proportion of working-age people to dependents rises, growth should get a boost. Asia enjoyed such a "demographic dividend," which began three decades ago and is now tailing off. In Africa it is just starting.[60]

The second-most closed society of recent time, Myanmar (formerly known as Burma), in which the military regime had remained stubbornly in power since 1962 while refusing all entreaties to open up its economy and society, opened up on its own volition, without any sudden increase of external pressure. The rest of the world had virtually given up on Myanmar and assumed that nothing would change.

But it did. And what caused Myanmar to open up? Over time, the historians will uncover the exact triggers of change. But even without the benefit of historical perspective, it is clear that ASEAN's policy of continually engaging Myanmar while the West and the rest shunned it was a truly wise decision. The 1,000 ASEAN meetings a year that the Myanmar government officials attended exposed them to best practices in a variety of areas, from economic to environmental management, from health care to education, from agricultural to industrial development. Through this exposure, they were able to see firsthand how the ASEAN countries had moved ahead by accepting this new consensual cluster of norms. Through gradual, persistent exposure, the minds of Myanmar policymakers were turned. According to the *Wall Street Journal*, "When Western leaders deemed Myanmar a secretive pariah state and slapped on tough economic sanctions, many Southeast Asian investors and governments maintained good relations with the country—a policy that drew harsh criticism from human rights advocates across the world."[61] Malaysia's prime minister, Najib Razak, explained ASEAN's strategy in a 2012 editorial in the *Wall Street Journal*:

Myanmar was on the receiving end of very public diplomatic scoldings, often backed up by sanctions. Implicit in this stance was the idea that democratic nations such as Malaysia should shun their less-free neighbors, and that the only way to bring about improvements was to economically cripple those who had not yet embraced the ballot box. But Asean members took a more nuanced view, believing that constructive engagement and encouragement were just as effective, if not more, than sanctions and isolation in creating positive change. As such, Asean admitted Myanmar as a member in 1997 and extended an open hand of friendship.[62]

According to Singapore's foreign minister, K. Shanmugam, ASEAN's November 2011 decision to let Myanmar chair the regional organization was done to encourage Myanmar to pursue political reform. "Myanmar will be the external face of Asean," said Shanmugam. "The world will be watching. . . . I am confident it will be successful in the role." Just months later the military junta released Nobel Peace Prize winner, political activist, and now current chairperson of the National League for Democracy in Myanmar, Daw Aung San Suu Kyi, from house arrest.[63]

Multilateralism

This story of Myanmar also illustrates a fifth key element in this new consensual cluster of norms: multilateralism. It is one of the fastest-growing sunrise industries in our world. This rapid growth is demonstrated by the increasing number of multilateral conferences and multilateral agreements that are entwining a larger and larger number of countries in thicker and thicker webs of organizations. This surge toward multilateralism goes against the deeply rooted unilateral instincts of the American body politic. American policymakers' disdain for multilateralism manifested itself when John Bolton, who notoriously stated that there was "no such thing" as the UN, was appointed the American ambassador to the UN in 2005.[64]

Fortunately, this American distrust of multilateralism is not shared by the rest of the world. Tony Blair has proposed a blueprint for what he calls "muscular multilateralism," arguing that the only solution to deep-seated global problems is stronger multilateral institutions and a willingness to confront issues such as security, peacekeeping, and poverty.[65] Blair's explicit call for a stronger rules-based multilateral institution echoes Bill Clinton's implicit call for a rules-based global order, which was mentioned in the Introduction. Most reasonable people understand that the rising multilateralism is now irreversible. There is a good reason why other Western leaders do not advocate multilateralism. He or she would be greeted with derision.

Just as we have failed to notice that war among great powers has become a sunset industry, we may also have failed to notice that there may be a correlation between diminishing wars and rising multilateralism. Figures 1.7 and 1.8 suggest a correlation between multilateralism and declining war deaths.

The obvious question to ask is, why should there be a correlation between the two trends or between trade and war fatalities? The simple answer is that wars happen when two countries fail to communicate with each other. The lack of contact also allows each country to demonize the other. Multilateralism does the opposite. It brings people together and increases both communication and understanding. And it is particularly helpful when leaders meet face to face. This is why the proliferation of leaders' meetings is a positive global phenomenon that should be encouraged. In the Cold War, American and Soviet leaders rarely met each other even though a miscalculation by either could have destroyed the world. By contrast, the leaders of America and China meet regularly, especially in forums like the UN, the G-20, and the East Asian Summit. Neither the G-20 nor the East Asian Summit existed a decade ago.

I have served twice as ambassador from Singapore to the UN, from 1984 to 1989 and from 1998 to 2004. I experienced firsthand how a sense of community could develop among people coming from all over the world. Hence, I could develop close friendships with the ambassadors of Brazil and Saudi Arabia, Mongolia and Namibia, to name just four very different countries. The skeptic will immediately retort that ambassadors are functionally designed to make friends across borders. That is true. But it is equally true that these friendships produce benefits for the world.

The Law of the Sea Treaty is a case study showing how a sense of community developed among more than 180 ambassadors from all over the

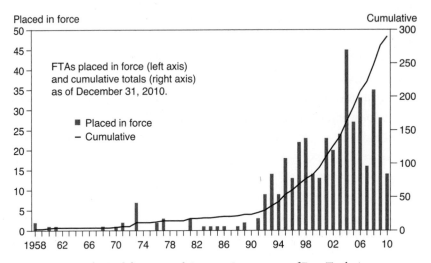

FIGURE 1.7 The Proliferation and Growing Importance of Free-Trade Agreements. *Source:* US Department of Agriculture, Economic Research Service, using data in the World Trade Organization Regional Trade Agreements database (http://rtais.wto .org/UI/PublicMaintainRTAHome.aspx). Reprinted with permission.

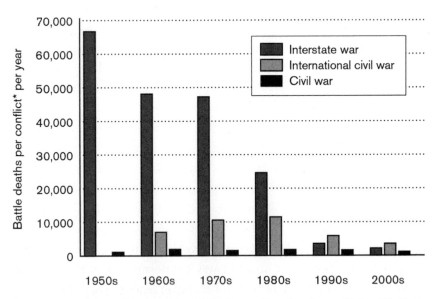

FIGURE 1.8 Diminishing War Casualties. *Source:* Based on Steven Pinker, *The Better Angels of Our Nature* (New York: Viking, 2011), p. 304.
*Deaths in state-based armed conflicts that involve army or militia on each side. (This does not include "one-sided conflict" or genocide.)

world can bring global benefits. The treaty defines the rights and responsibilities of all nations in their use of the world's oceans. It sets rules for businesses, the environment, and the management of marine natural resources. It was one of the most difficult treaties to negotiate. It took nine years from start to finish. There were bitter divisions between the coastal states, which wanted to claim most of the oceans for themselves, and the landlocked and geopolitically disadvantaged states, which felt that they were being deprived of the "common heritage of mankind" in the oceans. Differences seemed irresolvable. Yet over time a sense of community developed, even between the adversarial sides. Distrust diminished. Finally in 1982 the negotiations were concluded. Even though America failed to fulfill its obligations and ratify the treaty in the final instance (in what was seen as an act of betrayal by the rest of the world), America has respected the provisions of the treaty ever since. The oceans have become safer. The world has become more civilized.

Oceans cover 71 percent of the surface of the earth. If we can negotiate a good Law of the Sea Treaty, there is no reason that we cannot negotiate a Law of Planet Earth Treaty that spells out the obligations and benefits to each nation-state in taking good care of the remaining 29 percent of the planet, its minerals and raw material resources. If we succeed, it will be because of multilateralism in action.

Global Convergence

The phrase "consensual cluster of norms" sounds exquisitely and technically dull. It will not catch fire easily. It will never get its own hash tag. Yet this boring phrase may well provide the most accurate description of one of the most powerful forces ever seen in human history. For millennia, humanity as a whole has been divided by geography, history, religion, culture, verbal language, and body language. Today, despite this rich residue of differences, we are converging on a certain set of norms on how to create better societies. To put it simply, this global convergence is a big deal.

Other writers have also caught glimpses of the great global convergence that is taking place. Tom Friedman, with his usual insight, tried to describe convergence with the notion of the "flat world." After travelling around the world, he came to the conclusion that the "global economic playing field

[was] being leveled." He also said, using another memorable phrase, that for societies to succeed, they had to put on a "golden straitjacket" of Washington Consensus prescriptions.[66] (The Washington Consensus refers to the neoliberal economic policies imposed on developing countries by international financial institutions.)[67]

The good news is that the global convergence on a consensual cluster of norms has spread beyond the economic sphere. The five norms described here—acceptance of modern science, logical reasoning, free-market economics, a transformation of the social contract, and multilateralism—indicate that the consensus on norms is now flowing into a wider set of areas. More and more nations are behaving like each other and entering into the global mainstream comfortably. Anyone who doubts the existence of this great global convergence should take the time to attend a global gathering on any topic of his or her choice. Whether on water or on urban development, on higher education or on health, you will find a great meeting of minds emerging. When Singapore hosts the World Cities Summit (where New York City won the Lee Kuan Yew World City Prize in July 2012) or when Doha, Qatar, hosts the World Innovation Summit for Education, these global gatherings will see people flooding in from all corners of the globe, speaking a common language.

This is why the West should seriously reconsider its policy of trying to change recalcitrant countries by isolating them. Ironically, by imposing sanctions on Iran or Cuba, North Korea or Myanmar, the West is actually insulating them from this rising tide of common norms and protecting their regimes. By contrast, if their young people were encouraged to study overseas and if businesses were encouraged to foster trade and investment links between them and the rest of the world, change would come much faster to these countries. The Iranians, for example, would find it an eye-opening experience to visit the Infosys Campus in Bangalore or Tsinghua University in Beijing. They would provide a sharp wake-up call to Iranian policymakers.

The rising tide of common norms cannot be reversed. Too many minds all across the planet have become connected in a common discourse. However, even though the tide cannot be reversed, it can be accelerated with visionary institutions that try to bring together different cultures in an even closer embrace. Once such visionary initiative is the Yale-NUS College launched in Singapore in July 2012. It was not easy to launch this initiative. Some Yale faculty complained that the "pure" Yale traditions of academic freedom would be tainted by the "impure" traditions of restricted political expression in Singapore, forgetting, perhaps, that they are citizens of the first developed country to reintroduce torture. Although there was ample scope for misunderstanding in this bold effort to bring together the best traditions of Eastern and Western education, it went ahead. The project could yet fail. But if it succeeds, it will show that the rising tide of common norms is profoundly changing the human condition, creating a more peaceful and prosperous world embracing all humanity.

CHAPTER 2

A Theory of One World

WE NEED A THEORY OF ONE WORLD BECAUSE SO FAR GLOBAL THEORY has not kept up with global practice.

But why should this matter? It matters because the lack of such a theory prevents an effective global response to many pressing global challenges. Let us consider the words of four globally minded political leaders from the West: Bill Clinton, Al Gore, Tony Blair, and Gordon Brown. They continue to deliver brilliant speeches on the state of our global order. I have had the pleasure of listening to all of them in person. Many of their themes and global perceptions overlap.

Here are some excerpts from Clinton:

We share a common future on this planet of ours that is getting smaller and smaller and smaller.[1]

A world without walls is the only sustainable world. . . . If the world is dominated by people who believe that their races, their religions, their ethnic differences are the most important factors, then a huge number of people will perish in this century.[2]

The world has never truly had to develop an ethic of interdependence rooted in our common humanity. And if we do it, the 21st century will be the most interesting, exciting, peaceful era in history.[3]

You live in the age of interdependence. Borders don't count for much or stop much, good or bad, anymore.[4]

And this from Al Gore:

We are now in a Global Age. Like it or not, we live in an age when our destinies and the destinies of billions of people around the globe are increasingly intertwined. When our grand domestic and international challenges are also intertwined. We should neither bemoan nor naively idealize this new reality. We should deal with it.[5]

Our future is dependent upon increasing cooperation and interdependence in a world tied ever more closely together by technologies of communications and travel. The emergence of *a truly global civilization* [emphasis added] has been accompanied by the recognition of truly global challenges that require global responses that, as often as not, can only be led by the US—and only if the US restores and maintains its moral authority to lead.[6]

Tony Blair has the following to say:

Under the momentum of globalisation, the world is opening up and countries and cultures are coming closer together at an astonishing speed. In the 21st century the world is becoming ever more interdependent. Large communities of different nations and faiths now live cheek by jowl, whereas before oceans and continents separated them and individuals could go a lifetime without encountering anyone of another faith or tradition. In a shrinking world we must be global citizens as well as citizens of our own countries.[7]

We live in a completely new and different world today. This is not just a new century and a new millennium. There is a completely different complexion to the way that politics works today. If we want not just this administration to succeed, or this president to succeed, but also those of us who want to be supporters and partners in that to help, then we have to understand the nature of that different and changing world and what that means for policy.[8]

Gordon Brown remarks:

We now live in a world of global trade, global financial flows, global movements of people, and instant global communications. Our economies are connected as never before, and I believe that global economic problems require global solutions and global institutions.[9]

The new generation is in a position to solve some of the intractable problems that the world has faced for centuries. But we cannot do that unless global leaders recognize that there is now a category of problem that is not just a common problem or a shared problem, but a global problem that cannot be solved without all the nations of the world working together. We need a systematic approach as to how we as a global community can solve the problems that we face. There is an opportunity, because of the changes in technology and our ability to communicate and talk to each other that never existed in the previous generation, to make a huge difference in the way our society works. Global problems need global solutions.[10]

Significantly, while each of them could describe the state of our world well *after* they left office, none of them could adjust their countries' politics to reflect this global wisdom while they were in office. Clinton and Gore have become among the strongest advocates of global action against global warming. Yet in their eight years in office, they did little to prevent it. Several leading American figures, including Clinton, Gore, and Tom Friedman, have advocated a simple and effective solution to reducing global warming: a dollar a gallon tax on gasoline consumption. Yet neither Clinton nor Gore could even mention it, let alone advocate it, while they were in the White House. It would have been political suicide. There was no global theory of one world they could have used to back their arguments. All the arguments were focused on short-term national interests, not long-term global interests.

Gordon Brown has made powerful statements in support of stronger multilateralism. "'We are in a new situation in the year 2011,' Brown said. 'We now have problems that we can call global problems that are in need of global solutions.' Brown said global institutions such as the International

Monetary Fund and the World Bank, created in the 1940s, are no longer equipped to deal with the changing global landscape.... 'We have to build better global institutions ... for the future.'"[11] In creating these new institutions, countries around the world should agree on a "global ethic," Brown affirmed. The ethic should "enable people to see strangers as neighbors, [allow] people to believe in something bigger than just themselves ... [and] enable people to feel the pain of others however different, in countries they don't know much about."[12]

He has also said, "The post-1945 system of international institutions, built for a world of sheltered economies and just 50 states, is not yet broken but—for a world of 200 states and an open globalization—urgently in need of modernization and reform."[13] Yet when the IMF delicately approached the United Kingdom to "share" its sole seat on the IMF Executive Board, Brown unleashed a massive global diplomatic campaign to prevent this from happening. Even for a globally minded leader like Gordon Brown, national privileges (secured from a long-gone era of British imperial power) took precedence over global interests.

In short, the absence of a theory of one world prevents world leaders from taking effective global action because they don't know how to bring their citizens with them. There have been many visionary books on globalization. My three favorites are *The World Is Flat* by Tom Friedman, *In Defense of Globalization* by Jagdish Bhagwati, and *Why Globalization Works* by Martin Wolf. Both Bhagwati and Wolf have produced great definitions of globalization. Bhagwati says, "Economic globalization constitutes integration of national economies into the international economy through trade, direct foreign investment (by corporations and multinationals), short-term capital flows, international flows of workers and humanity generally, and flows of technology," and Wolf, quoting David Henderson, former chief economist of the Organization for Economic Cooperation and Development (OECD), says globalization is the "free movement of goods, services, labor and capital, thereby creating a single market in inputs and outputs; and full national treatment for foreign investors (and nationals working abroad) so that, economically speaking, there are no foreigners."[14]

Most books on globalization focus on the *processes* that are fundamentally transforming our world. While they do discuss some of the results of these processes, they do not try to put together a comprehensive theory of why our world has changed fundamentally. In short, we have a new world order, but we do not have a comprehensive theory that explains it. Yes, we have many metaphors that provide valuable insights. My favorite is the boat metaphor that I used in the Introduction. Kofi Annan also used to speak often of the "global village" we live in. But metaphors cannot provide a comprehensive theory. We have to investigate more deeply the various forces that are pushing humanity relentlessly toward a one-world order. Hence, to begin the process of searching for and elaborating on a new theory, this chapter will try to suggest four key pillars of convergence—environmental, economic, technological, and aspirational—that are driving humanity to acknowledge that we live in one world. I have deliberately looked at both tangible and intangible dimensions of these pillars to emphasize that this great dynamic of convergence toward one world is now unstoppable and irreversible.

The Environmental Pillar

Any theory of one world should begin with the environmental pillar as there is now a growing global awareness that the 7 billion occupants (the number will rise to 9 billion by 2050) of planet earth are *not* doing a good job of managing the only planet in the universe that we know to be capable of hosting human life. We do not have a second option, no planet to migrate to if we fail to preserve this one's environment. There is therefore a strong common interest that unites all 7 billion people: to preserve our one home.

Given this strong common interest, it is striking that while in other respects we have been climbing "the escalator of reason," we have not done so when it comes to preserving the earth for future generations. The one big contribution that the growing fear of global warming has made to our world has been to raise global consciousness that humanity has to come together to save our planet. There has been a remarkable proliferation of nongovernmental organizations (NGOs), both globally and nationally, that have raised environmental awareness all around the world. But partly as a result of the Western financial crisis of 2008–2009, governments are still far apart in finding a common global solution to global warming.

It is vital to emphasize here that global warming is not the only global environmental challenge we are facing. And in our information-rich universe, it is not difficult to track down the other challenges. I want to use Wikipedia's "list of environmental issues" to drive home the point that we all know, and can find out about, the slew of environmental challenges. We can no longer pretend that we do not know what these global environmental problems are. The list stares us in our faces:

Air pollution: environmental impact of the coal industry, indoor air quality, particulate matter, smog, tropospheric ozone, volatile organic compound

Climate change: environmental impact of the coal industry, fossil fuels, global dimming, global warming, greenhouse gas, ocean acidification, sea level rise, shutdown of thermohaline circulation

Conservation: coral bleaching, endangered species, Holocene extinction, invasive species, poaching, pollinator decline, species extinction

Consumerism: consumer capitalism, overconsumption, planned obsolescence

Energy: efficient energy use, energy conservation, environmental impact of the coal industry, renewable energy commercialization, renewable energy

Environmental degradation: eutrophication, habitat destruction, invasive species

Environmental health: air quality, asthma, electromagnetic fields, electromagnetic radiation and health, environmental impact of the coal industry, indoor air quality, lead poisoning, sick building syndrome

Fishing: blast fishing; bottom trawling; cyanide fishing; ghost nets; illegal, unreported, and unregulated fishing; overfishing; shark finning; whaling

Genetic engineering: genetic pollution, genetically modified food controversies

Intensive farming: environmental effects of meat production, irrigation, monoculture, overgrazing, pesticide drift, plasticulture, slash and burn

Land degradation: desertification, land pollution

Land use: habitat destruction, habitat fragmentation, urban sprawl

Logging: clearcutting, deforestation, illegal logging

Mining: acid mine drainage, hydraulic fracturing, mountaintop removal mining, slurry impoundments

Nanotechnology: nanopollution, nanotoxicology

Nuclear issues: high-level radioactive waste management, nuclear and radiation accidents, nuclear fallout, nuclear meltdown, nuclear power, nuclear weapons, nuclear safety

Overpopulation: burial, overpopulation in companion animals, tragedy of the commons, water crisis

Ozone depletion: CFC

Pollution: environmental impact of the coal industry, light pollution, noise pollution, nonpoint source pollution, point source pollution, visual pollution

Reservoirs: environmental impacts of reservoirs

Resource depletion: exploitation of natural resources, overdrafting

Soil: soil conservation, soil contamination, soil erosion, soil salination

Toxins: bioaccumulation, biomagnification, chlorofluorocarbons, DDT, dioxin, endocrine disruptors, environmental impact of the coal industry, herbicides, PCB, pesticides, toxic heavy metals, toxic waste

Waste: electronic waste, environmental impact of the coal industry, great Pacific garbage patch, incineration, landfill, leachate, litter, marine debris, medical waste, waste disposal incidents

Water pollution: acid rain, algal bloom, environmental impact of the coal industry, eutrophication, fish kill, marine debris, marine pollution, mercury in fish, microplastics, ocean acidification, ocean dumping, oil spills, ship pollution, thermal pollution, urban runoff, wastewater, water crisis[15]

Stewart Brand, the editor of the *Whole Earth Catalog* and a well-known environmentalist, notes the following speech by British environmentalist Mark Lynas, author of *Six Degrees*:

"About 74,000 years ago," Lynas began, "a volcanic event nearly wiped out humanity. We were down to just a thousand or so embattled breeding pairs. We've made a bit of a comeback since then. We're over seven billion strong. In half a million years we've gone from prodding anthills with sticks to building a worldwide digital communications network. Well done! But there's a small problem. In doing this we've had to capture between a quarter and a third of the entire photosynthetic production of the planet. We've raised the temperature of the Earth system, reduced the alkalinity of the oceans, altered the chemistry of the atmosphere, changed the reflectivity of the planet, hugely affected the distribution of freshwater, and killed off many of the species that share the planet with us. Welcome to the Anthropocene, our very uniquely human geological era." Some of those global alterations made by humans may be approaching tipping points—thresholds—that could destabilize the whole Earth system. Drawing on a landmark paper in *Nature* in 2009 ("A Safe Operating Space for Humanity," by Johan Rockström et al.) Lynas outlined the nine boundaries we should stay within, starting with three we've already crossed.[16]

This is a remarkable list of challenges. Any reasonable person looking at this should conclude that there is a need for coordinated global action to address most of these challenges. It would certainly help if the world's greatest economic power, America, could work with the world's greatest emerging economic power, China, to find common solutions. But this is not happening. Former US Treasury secretary Henry Paulson should be commended for setting up the Paulson Institute, "an independent center that will specialize in relationships involving the United States and China," which aims to encourage "progress in environmental protection and the development of alternative sources of clean energy, and promoting economic activity and cross-investment between the two countries, leading to the creation of jobs." "Every global concern—economic, environmental or security-related—can be addressed more effectively when the U.S. and China work together," Paulson has said.[17]

However, if Paulson is to succeed in his noble mission of bringing together America and China, he should be honest in his analysis of what divides America and China in the environmental area. The "inconvenient truth" (in the words of Al Gore) in this area is that, while the US leads China by a mile in the creation of environmental movements and consciousness, and the overall environmental record of the US is far superior to that of China, the US government is actually behind the Chinese government in recognizing the challenges of climate change. The growth of environmental movements in the US has been phenomenal. The *Boston Globe* notes that a new analysis from "the Urban Institute, an economic and social policy research group, shows that the number of nonprofit organizations dedicated to conservation and the environment rose faster than the number of nonprofit groups overall since 1995, growing by 4.6 percent per year compared to 2.8 percent per year for all nonprofits. Overall, the environmental movement has expanded in the number of organizations, members and total revenue almost every year since 1960."[18]

In China, the good news is that, even though China's political system has not changed, environmental NGOs have been allowed to emerge. There were no environmental NGOs as recently as 1994, but now, according to an article in *Discover* magazine, "more than 3,500 environmental organizations have legal status in China. While activists there are not as vocal as their counterparts in Europe or the United States, they have made an impact by encouraging transparency and pressuring local governments and industries to adhere to new national regulations. Through a program called the Green Choice Alliance, environmental groups publish lists of companies in violation of environmental regulations and offer to conduct a third-party audit if a company chooses to clean up its act."[19] According to the *China Daily*, "The number of NGOs in China has nearly doubled in the past 10 years with registered social organizations rising to about 460,000 by 2011. The sector is likely to see even stronger development as more friendly policies are in store."[20] Rather than providing money, international NGOs in China are repositioning themselves to shoulder more in terms of transferring their knowledge about capacity building and best practices in international development work.

Equally importantly, young people in China are starting their own NGOs. At the Rio+20 conference in Brazil in June 2012, a group of young Chinese who set up the China Youth Sustainable Development Action Forum shared their experiences. Du Yunpeng, one member, remembers that he and his classmates still had to do daily calisthenics on the roof of their school building when sandstorms (which will be exacerbated by climate change) hit the northern city of Tianjin many years ago. "It was a painful experience," he said.[21] Hence, this group of young Chinese decided to form a group to combat climate change; they went to Rio+20 on their own initiative, exchanged information with young people from America, and issued a joint declaration.[22]

The creation and proliferation of NGOs in China represent a significant opening of Chinese society, an opening that would have been inconceivable in the time of Mao Zedong and even Deng Xiaoping.

Since there is a lot of global despair on the environmental front, it may be useful here to acknowledge the massive efforts made by the Chinese government to improve the country's environment. The Yellow River— "the cradle of Chinese civilization"—has been silting for centuries. Using modern technology, the Chinese government has finally begun turning around the management of this hitherto unmanageable river. This is why the Yellow River Conservancy Commission won the Lee Kuan Yew Water Prize in 2010.[23] Even more impressively, China has begun a massive reforestation program in the long-deforested Loess Plateau. It has already planted forests in an area the size of Belgium. And when China is finished, it will have reforested an area the size of France.[24] Moreover, although China is the world's biggest emitter today, the Chinese government has announced that it will reduce the carbon intensity of GDP by 40–45 percent from 2005 levels by 2020.[25]

Given these developments, we need to find ways of doing objective audits of the contribution of countries to either improving or destroying the global environment. Despite all the incremental progress in some areas (with success, for instance, in chlorofluorocarbon management), the overall environment of the planet is deteriorating. The warnings about global warming continue to get more and more dire. Al Gore has said, "The warnings about global warming have been extremely clear for a long time. We are facing a global climate crisis. It is deepening. We are entering a period of consequences."[26] Larry Schweizer, president of the National Wildlife Federation, has said, "There will be no polar ice by 2060. . . . Somewhere along that path, the polar bear drops out."[27] Tony Blair has also warned that "global warming is too serious for the world any longer to ignore its danger or split into opposing factions on it."[28]

I am not an expert on global warming or climate change. Nor am I in a position to answer whether human activity is the principal cause for them. However, while there have always been skeptics, it is becoming clearer that

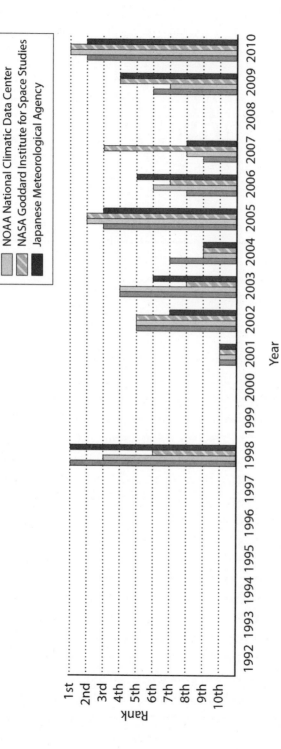

FIGURE 2.1 The Ten Hottest Years on Record. *Source:* Based on http://www.unep.org/geo/pdfs/Keeping_Track.pdf.

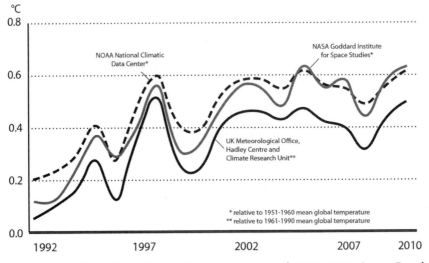

FIGURE 2.2 Global Annual Mean Temperature Anomaly, 1992–2010. *Source:* Based on http://www.unep.org/geo/pdfs/Keeping_Track.pdf.

in the scientific community there is a growing consensus that the world has to work together and deal with these profound global challenges.

In this regard, the story of Richard Muller is particularly telling. When he first announced that he was a climate change skeptic, the Koch brothers, who are known for their neoconservative credentials, decided to fund Muller's Berkeley Earth project with $150,000.[29] After just two years of research, Muller arrived at a conclusion that must have given the Koch brothers a heart attack. He confirmed that climate change was real in a July 2012 *New York Times* op-ed: "Last year, following an intensive research effort involving a dozen scientists, I concluded that global warming was real and that the prior estimates of the rate of warming were correct. I'm now going a step further: Humans are almost entirely the cause."[30]

But it is vital to emphasize that from the point of view of earth's 7 billion occupants, we do not need to reach total agreement that global warming is real. All we need to do is to reach agreement on whether global warming is a *possibility*. Even if the chances of global warming are assessed to be only, say, 1 percent, it would be logical and sensible to try doing something about the matter. This is probably why the hardheaded, tough-minded, and brutally realistic government of Singapore decided to join the campaign against global warming. Just the sheer fact that it was a possibility provided strong enough reason to take action to prevent it.

Good actions often require good theory, however. And this is where a good theory of one world would help. If there were universal agreement among 7 billion people that we need to work together to save our precious and fragile planet, then the burden would be fairly and equitably distributed and the burden on each individual would be limited. The most elementary principles of ethics and justice would dictate that the richer countries would have to bear a higher burden than the poorer countries. And we could easily find a formula to spread the burden.

So why, then, is no effective action being taken? Why have all the global environmental conferences essentially failed? The simplest answer here is that the global system rests on an antiquated theory of the world order. It rests on a nineteenth-century assumption: that the role of national leaders is primarily to defend their national sovereignty and national interests. These nineteenth-century mental maps again rest on another deeper assumption: that if each nation took good care of its interests and did not interfere in any other nation's interests, all this would lead to a more stable world order in the political sphere. No one has explicitly suggested that an "invisible hand" would operate in the political sphere just as effectively as it does in the economics sphere, with individuals looking only after their own interests. Yet it is also clear that no one has boldly suggested that the nation-state system, which may have worked well in the nineteenth and twentieth centuries, is clearly not the best system for the twenty-first century.

In an op-ed piece published in *The Globalist*, Yilmaz Argüden attributes the failure of environmental summits to the structure of global governance:

> The reason why the Rio+20 summit on sustainable development was a bust is simple: the summit's agenda did not include the right issues. Let me be more specific. The real issue is not being unaware of the situation or technological impediments, it is the way humanity has organized itself.
>
> The real issue, then, is the structure of global governance—the way in which incentive systems are organized and the lack of any credible

leadership on global issues that would have the authority and ability to impose remedies.

For example, who is in charge of carbon emissions? Who is in charge of the oceans? Who is in charge of poverty? And who is responsible for the millions of people who do not have access to electricity and clean water? When everybody is responsible, nobody is really responsible.

Therefore, the first agenda item for meetings such as Rio+20 should be how to consensually delegate sovereignty to global institutions and to make sure these global institutions have real legitimacy and jurisdiction over key global issues.[31]

This is precisely why we need a new theory of one world to capture new realities. In the absence of a new theory, leaders and policymakers are making decisions on the basis of old theories. John Maynard Keynes said it well: "The ideas of economists and political philosophers, both when they are right and when they are wrong, are more powerful than is commonly understood. Indeed the world is ruled by little else. Practical men, who believe themselves to be quite exempt from any intellectual influences, are usually the slaves of some defunct economist."[32] The most horrifying truth about our current planetary condition is that all our political leaders are making decisions on the basis of some defunct political ideas.

The Economic Pillar

When the G-20 leaders met in London in April 2009 to try to save the global economy, they should have made two big pronouncements. First, they should have announced that the only way to save the global economy from the financial crisis of 2008–2009 was through coordinated global action. This they did. Second, they should have announced that this crisis had clearly proven that we have, wittingly or unwittingly, created a single global economy. Hence, the only way to manage this single global economy was through continuous coordinated global responses. This they did not.

The failure to announce a single global economy was a fatal error. Having neglected to educate their own populations and the world, they reverted to old habits of focusing on their own national economies rather than on the larger single global economy. This also explains why the subsequent G-20 meetings in Pittsburgh, Toronto, Seoul, Cannes, and Los Cabos failed. In theory, the G-20 leaders had taken on the responsibility of managing the global economy. In practice, they focused only on their short-term and narrow national interests, not on global interests.

Why, if we are sailing in the high seas of global finance and our boat gets into trouble, do we all retreat into our cabins? This is what the G-20 leaders did after the London G-20 meeting, for two reasons. First, they are elected only by the occupants of their cabins. Hence, they are focused only on their cabins. Second, and this is an equally important reason, there is no theory of a single global economy to guide the decisionmaking of policymakers all over the world.

The absence of a theory may sound surprising. I checked on this lacuna with some leading professional economists. I asked them if they could refer me to a book or a series of essays that described how our single global economy worked. Paola Subacchi, an economist at Chatham House, replied:

> I have been thinking about your question and as far as I know there is no serious work on a single global economy. International economics looks at how two or more countries interact with each other, implicitly accepting the nation-state as the unit of analysis. Many books on globalisation address various aspects of this interaction. Perhaps the closest example of one single economy is the euro area, but in a very imperfect way, as the building of a single market and a single currency has not been matched by a congruent political structure.[33]

Subacchi also added:

> I think your piece does not appeal to economists because it is at odds with the discipline. International economics implicitly recognises nation-state as the unit of analysis. The key analytical point for international economists is not how a single economy performs, but how many economies, which are also nation-states, deal with each other. Global governance is the attempt to reconcile global markets and nation states—and persuade countries to slightly compromise on their interests for the sake

of public good. So we do not have a single global economy, but we surely have integrated markets.[34]

I am truly grateful to Subacchi for alerting me that most economists would not be comfortable with any economic theory that assumes a single global economy. Indeed, her warning to me was confirmed when I subsequently shared drafts of this chapter with other economists. They emphasized that the basic unit of analysis in economic theory was the "national" economy. But they acknowledged that a high degree of interdependence had been developed among national economies. However, this did not change the basic framework of economic analysis.

To emphasize the point that most prominent economists believe that the nation-state is the most important unit of economic analysis, let me now quote from an e-mail sent to me by another eminent economist after reading the paragraphs above. Eswar Prasad of Cornell University wrote, "The notion of a single global economy is a big step from the high level trade and financial integration we now observe. As we are seeing from Europe, however, you need an institutional framework that is truly global in nature to manage a global economy as a single unit. You would then need a unified political system or at least a high level of coordination at the political level." He added, "Economists don't have a theory of a single global economy because we (or at least I) have no idea what that means operationally in the absence of a political union. The US is a single economy, Europe is not (although it is clearly highly integrated)."[35] I consulted a colleague, T. N. Srinivasan, on the need for a theory of one world resting on the economic pillar. He replied as follows: "Obviously, no new economic theory is needed if the concept of a single *Global Economy* is one that is governed by a single Global Government elected by a *Global Polity* consisting of a Global Electorate and accountable to it. The objectives for the policies of the Global Government are set by a *Global Society* of which the *Global Polity* is a part. The Global Economy is one in which the dynamic process of integration among national economies has succeeded in fully integrating them in the sense of real and financial integration."[36] His point was that none of these global constructs currently exist. And yet our financial institutions are inextricably joined, whether economists prefer to recognize this fact or not.

The perspectives of economists differ dramatically from those of businessmen and businesswomen and other policymakers. Many of the latter consider a single global economy as part of their decisionmaking. They have to factor in global trends before making any practical decision to invest or not to invest in a venture. For example, many investing decisions are driven by calculations of energy, especially oil, prices. And energy prices are determined globally, not nationally. Any businessman who ignores this global dimension will come to grief. One of India's richest men, Vijay Mallya, enjoyed great success with Kingfisher Breweries and decided to set up Kingfisher Airlines. Initially, his airline was a great success. Then global oil prices went up. The cost of jet fuel sent his airline to the verge of bankruptcy, even though he had done all the right things within his country and company. A global force destroyed his business.

As I was writing the final version of this book in August 2012, the Eurozone remained intact. Neither Greece nor Spain had left. Yet even though the Eurozone was muddling through crisis after crisis, it was clearly facing unrelenting pressure from the rest of the world to find a solution that would not wreck the world. Major non-European leaders such as Barack Obama and Hu Jintao have strongly urged European leaders to resolve the crisis, for fear that a protracted recession in the Eurozone could slow the US economic recovery and China's growth. Numerous and disorderly sovereign debt defaults could even trigger a repeat of the 2008 financial crisis.[37] Otmar Issing, a distinguished German economist who had previously served as a member of the executive board of the European Central Bank, observed wryly that "it is more than strange when foreign politicians and experts are pressing Eurozone states to give up national sovereignty, out of fear that a collapse of monetary union might have severe consequences for their economies. Juvenal would have said: *Difficile est satiram non scribere* (It is difficult not to write a satire)."[38]

Issing is right. It is difficult not to write a satire about the Eurozone. The single European currency, the euro, was created by a constellation of brilliant European minds who believed that the euro would survive or fall on the basis of European decisions. They did not factor in how the rest of the world and the rest of the world economy would affect the euro. This lack of concern about how integrated the euro had become with the single global economy may have contributed to the challenges facing the euro. To put it bluntly, the euro can be saved only if the rest of the world believes that it can be saved. And if the rest of the world believes that it is doomed, the euro will collapse. To save the euro, Europe must learn to work more effectively with the rest of the world.

Indeed, the whole global economy has become so dense and intertwined that it may be a mistake to think of the "external" consequences or implications of national decisions as "externalities" anymore. After all, there is nothing external to the global economy. What used to be externalities have become deeply internalized in the new global economic system that we have created. And if policymakers do not understand that we now live and function within a single global economy, they could make hugely flawed decisions or take actions that could damage the world. The global economy could be pulled toward a cliff by shortsighted actions. This is not a theoretical possibility. The global economy came close to going off a cliff when a few Republican representatives, led by the Tea Party, refused to increase the debt ceiling of the US until barely two days before it would have been busted on August 2, 2011. Throughout the entire debate on this issue, not one of the representatives mentioned or discussed the possibility that their actions could damage the global economy. A cartoon in *The Economist* captured the situation exactly (see Figure 2.3).

Although the extent to which the US dollar impacts the world economy is an abstruse and contested argument, the policymakers of many of the world's major economies have come to realize that the world's dependency on the dollar is perilous. In 2012, more than 70 percent of global trade was still being carried out with the US dollar. Any sharp fall or appreciation of the US dollar could therefore have massive and often damaging consequences on many major national economies. Few in the West noticed that one of the biggest decisions that the five BRICS countries (Brazil, Russia, India, China, and South Africa) made at their summit in Sanya, China, on April 14, 2011, was to reduce their reliance on the US dollar:

> Recognizing that the international financial crisis has exposed the inadequacies and deficiencies of the existing international monetary and financial system, we support the reform and improvement of the international monetary system, with a broad-based international reserve cur-

FIGURE 2.3 Led by the Nose. *Source:* Kevin KAL Kallaugher, *The Economist*, Kaltoons
.com. Reprinted with permission.

rency system providing stability and certainty. We welcome the current
discussion about the role of the SDR [special drawing rights] in the existing international monetary system including the composition of SDR's
basket of currencies. We call for more attention to the risks of massive
cross-border capital flows now faced by the emerging economies. We call
for further international financial regulatory oversight and reform,
strengthening policy coordination and financial regulation and supervision cooperation, and promoting the sound development of global financial markets and banking systems.[39]

Similarly, in the subsequent BRICS summit in New Delhi on March
29, 2012, the member countries noted, "The build-up of sovereign debt
and concerns over medium to long-term fiscal adjustment in advanced
countries are creating an uncertain environment for global growth. Further, excessive liquidity from the aggressive policy actions taken by
central banks to stabilize their domestic economies have been spilling
over into emerging market economies, fostering excessive volatility in

capital flows and commodity prices."[40] These are dense statements, full of economic jargon. But the essence of their message is clear: economic policy decisions made by the US and EU are damaging them. In short, they are saying, "We live in a single global economy. Please factor in our interests too."

The BRICS countries decided to reduce their reliance on the US dollar because they were deeply troubled by a series of "unilateral" decisions made by the US government on the US dollar, even though the US dollar served as a global reserve currency. Their alarm grew out of the efforts of the US Federal Reserve to stimulate the US economy through quantitative easing (QE) measures in an effort to get the US domestic economy out of its slump. With QE1, which began in late 2008 and ran through early 2010, the Fed purchased $300 billion in Treasury securities, $1.2 trillion in mortgage-backed securities, and $175 billion in debt issued by federal agencies. The theory was that banks, flush with cash, would then lend the money out, stimulating the economy and creating jobs.[41] With QE2, which began in summer 2010, the Fed purchased $600 billion in Treasury securities. The brilliant euphemisms "QE1" and "QE2," chosen by the Fed, were designed to give the impression that the Fed was trying to remove the constraints on American economic growth by "easing" measures on the economy. Actually, without putting too fine a point on it, the US used its national monopoly on American printing presses to print more money.

So why should the world have worried if the US decided to stimulate its national economy in this way? The simple answer is that the money that the US printed to stimulate the US economy did not stay in the US. It flowed out into the rest of the world and generated a lot of financial volatility, which in turn negatively affected the livelihoods of billions of people. To understand the negative impact of QE1, QE2, and later QE3, let's return to the boat metaphor used in the Introduction. America, living in one of the cabins on our global boat, encountered some dirt in its cabin and decided to give it an almighty scrub by using a lot of soap and water. However, as it did so, it swept all its dirty water out of its own cabin and "allowed" it to flow into other cabins on the boat.

A report from the Chinese Xinhua news agency in October 2010 quoted Chen Deming, the Chinese commerce minister, saying that the

amount of American dollars flowing out the US was leading to an inflation assault on China: "Because the United States' issuance of dollars is out
of control and international commodity prices are continuing to rise,
China is being attacked by imported inflation. The uncertainties of this are
causing firms big problems."[42] The Brazilian finance minister, Guido Mantega, also said that the US was exporting its problems to the world: "If we
had expansionist monetary policy combined with more stimulative fiscal
policy in place, we wouldn't face this problem with the US economy."[43] He
argued that a more appropriate response would have been to use both fiscal and monetary weapons of stimulus. However, since the US Congress
was deadlocked on fiscal issues, the Fed had no choice but to use financial
instruments like quantitative easing.

Economics experts disagree about the impact of QE1 and QE2 on the
global economy. Some deny that global inflation was a result of QE1 and
QE2. Others, like Andy Xie, a former economist with Morgan Stanley, have
said that the unrest in Egypt, which began over rising commodity prices,
was a result of QE1 and QE2. In an article published in the *New York Times*,
he argued that the unrest in the Middle East was triggered by tensions
caused by inflation: "Loose money has caused the riots in Tunis and
Cairo."[44] It was no coincidence, Xie contended, that food and energy prices
started to rise right after the US floated the idea of injecting more money
into the markets through QE.

The real tragedy about the failure of the US legislators to understand
the global implications of their actions is that they may actually fritter away
one of the biggest assets that America has in the global economic system:
the key role of the US dollar as the main reserve currency. This is how two
American scholars, Robert Carbaugh and David Hedrick, describe the
benefits for the US:

> The United States realizes substantial benefits from the dollar's serving
> as the main reserve currency of the world. Americans can purchase prod-
> ucts at a marginally cheaper rate than other nations, which must ex-
> change their currency with each purchase and pay a transaction cost. As
> participants in the reserve currency country, the U.S. government and
> American businesses can issue debt denominated in dollars, and those
> assets are attractive to central bankers and foreign investors as ways to

hold their portfolio of international reserves. These features allow Americans access to a vast supply of credit and permit the public to borrow at lower interest rates for homes and automobiles and the government to finance larger deficits longer and at lower interest rates. Moreover, the United States can issue debt (securities) in its own currency, thus pushing exchange rate risk onto foreign lenders. This means that foreigners face the possibility that a fall in the dollar's exchange value could wipe out not only the value of the reserve currency that they hold but also the value of the U.S. assets that they hold in their international reserve portfolio. For example, if a Chinese investor realized a return of 5 percent on her holdings of U.S. Treasury securities, and if the dollar depreciated 5 percent against the yuan, she would realize no gain. With holdings of dollar-denominated assets of about $1.4 trillion in 2009, China has been especially concerned about the possibility of loss of purchasing power in the event of substantial dollar depreciation.[45]

Given this great advantage that the US dollar confers upon the US economy, it would have been natural to expect a more responsible management of the dollar. This has barely happened. Instead, as a result of the US political system becoming far more politically polarized, partisan interests trump both national and global interests in decisionmaking. The world as a whole is playing with fire here. If world markets and financiers ever conclude that the US government will not be able, whether for economic or for political reasons, to repay its debts, global money could flow as quickly out of US Treasury bills as it did out of Greek government bonds, if global money can find a safe haven elsewhere. It is, of course, in the rational interest of everyone to "pretend" that this could not happen. But while the probability of this happening was practically zero even a decade ago, it has now increased to 10, and may increase to 20, percent in the next decade or two. This is why in August 2011 the ratings agency S&P took away the triple A rating for US government securities.

To mitigate the potential catastrophe that would arise if the world lost faith in the US dollar as a global reserve currency, we should agree on a theory of a single global economy. The minds of leading policymakers must focus on the single global economy as the first priority. If they fail to do so, all their efforts to save their national economies could well prove to be futile. Even an economy as powerful as America's is not immune to global trends. Larry Summers has said, "It used to be said that when the U.S. sneezed, the world caught a cold. The opposite is equally true today."[46] Anyone who doubts this simple proposition that every economy is now subject to global economic discipline should study the Eurozone crisis in depth. Having created a single currency and the largest economy in the world in the form of the European Union, many European policymakers felt immune from global trends. Then confidence in Greece collapsed. Amazingly, the loss of confidence in one small European economy led inexorably to fears that the Euro itself might collapse. It has not happened yet (at the time of this writing), but the possibility has undermined the entire Eurozone. No country is safe from the consequences.

A significant part of the global economy is in manufacturing and trade. The *New York Times* carried a fascinating article on January 21, 2012, reporting a conversation between President Barack Obama and Steve Jobs (now deceased), the founder of Apple. Obama asked Jobs why he couldn't bring his manufacturing back from China to the US. Jobs's reply was clear and direct. "Those jobs aren't coming back," he said. The article listed a few reasons that the jobs would not return. One clear reason was available labor. "They [Apple] could hire 3,000 people overnight," said Jennifer Rigoni, who was Apple's worldwide supply demand manager until 2010 but declined to discuss the specifics of her work. "What U.S. plant can find 3,000 people overnight and convince them to live in dorms?"[47]

"Another critical advantage for Apple was that China provided engineers at a scale the United States could not match. Apple's executives had estimated that about 8,700 industrial engineers were needed to oversee and guide the 200,000 assembly-line workers eventually involved in manufacturing iPhones. The company's analysts had forecast it would take as long as nine months to find that many qualified engineers in the United States. In China, it took 15 days."[48]

The *New York Times* did not report how Obama reacted to Jobs's rebuff. We can guess that Obama would have been thinking, "My primary responsibility is to the American people. Surely Steve Jobs, as a fellow American, shares my interest in creating American jobs." Jobs, on the other hand, would have seen the situation differently: "My primary responsibility is to keep Apple competitive against any company anywhere in the world.

Hence, I have to look for opportunities anywhere in the world to keep Apple No. 1."

Their different objectives also amply demonstrate why we need a comprehensive theory of one world. National policymakers like Obama continue to believe that they can "fix" their national economies with national effort. Businessmen in practically any business know that they have to compete with all corners of the world. They know that every day they have to be sensitive to global trends. Any CEO of any major company—including blue-chip American companies like Coke and Pepsi, McDonald's and Apple—has to be acutely conscious of global supply-and-demand trends.

The fact of a single global economy is as incontestable as it is irreversible. The combination of more than fifty years of trade liberalization and the march of technology, which is shrinking our world at an enormous pace, has made global interdependence inevitable. There has been a great global convergence in one basic area of policy too: virtually all policymakers now accept that the only way to grow and prosper is to open up their economies. Even though Obama pleaded with Steve Jobs to bring back jobs from China to America, he did not try to resort to unilateral trade retaliation against China. Indeed, despite the massive economic crisis in both Europe and America, there has been little real backsliding toward protectionism. All sophisticated policymakers know that closing up economies is damaging. Hence the trend toward greater opening will continue. Consequently, interdependence will grow even more. A single global economy will continue emerging. The big question for our time is when theory will catch up with practice.

The Technological Pillar

When we say that technology is shrinking the world, most of us think of the ease and speed with which we can communicate across large distances via phone or e-mail. What we tend to skip over is technology's impact on human consciousness. There is no doubt that our primary identity remains with our nation-state. Yet there is now a growing awareness that we live in one world. If this tide of human consciousness continues to rise (and I believe that rapid technological change will make it rise even faster), a new global identity will surface in the next few decades.

To understand the forces driving it, we first need to understand how technology has dramatically changed the nature of human interaction across national boundaries. Our sense of who we are used to be tied to the village, city, or country we lived in. Today, many other layers of self-identification are being added because human beings everywhere are being rapidly connected to one world. A lot of this connection has happened only in the past decade or two. Among the technologies that are changing the world are cell phones, computers, and aircraft.

About twenty years ago, in 1990, only 11 million people had a cell phone subscription.[49] In 2000, the number was 500 million. Today, the number of cell phone subscriptions worldwide has passed 5.6 billion, with the number of fixed connections standing at 1.32 billion in 2011.[50] According to the analyst firm Gartner, global teledensity is now more than 100 percent; in other words there are more telecom connections than there are people. "While this figure does not imply 100% universal phone access, that goal is coming closer," reports John Tysoe, principal analyst at the Mobile World.[51] Twenty years ago, much of humanity was technologically disconnected. No longer.

The story of cell phone usage in China and India is particularly dramatic. According to the World Bank, India had zero subscribers in 1990 and 752 million subscribers in 2010. In 1990, China had 18,000 mobile subscribers, and by 2010, it had 859 million subscribers. Africa too has seen a similar explosion in cell phones, from 21,620 in 1990 to 539 million in 2010, surpassing the US (which had only 279 million subscribers in 2010).

A cell phone is not just a cell phone for local use. It now communicates effortlessly across frontiers. I grew up in an era in which we got very excited when an operator rang our home to say we had received a long-distance phone call from, say, India or London. Today, that same conversation can be carried out virtually free of charge via Skype, for example. And guess what? Hundreds of millions of people are communicating directly across vast distances at practically zero cost. It is hard to believe that we can experience this massive surge in human connectivity without any impact on the human condition.

Cell phones are getting smarter too. Phones are microcomputers. Since smartphones are all-in-one packages that allow people to surf the Internet, take notes, take photos, make phone calls, and watch videos, among other activities, there is less reason for people to get a traditional computer. It is not surprising that more Americans and Europeans are buying smartphones. A VisionMobile study pegs the number at 63 percent of all North American cell phone customers. As for Europe, VisionMobile found smartphone penetration to be at 51 percent.[52] What is truly surprising is how smartphone usage is surging outside the developed world:

> China has recently surpassed the United States in the smartphone market by volume, according to some estimates. China is also reported to have the highest number of cellphone users who actually own two or more mobile phones. Apple CEO Tim Cook said China is the company's second most important market, and iPhone purchases are an important reason for that. In Middle East nations like the United Arab Emirates and Saudi Arabia, mobile phone adoption is also exceedingly high, each over 150 percent as of mid-2010.[53]

Cell phones are now being accompanied by another technological device that is almost as mobile and is also growing rapidly in use: the iPad (and other tablet devices). It is absolutely amazing how the iPad can connect to virtually any information source almost anywhere in the world. Jack Dongarra, one of the computer scientists who tracks the world's five hundred fastest computers, has discovered that the iPad2, a tablet the size of a legal pad, rivals the Cray 2 supercomputer, the fastest computer in the world in 1985 and the size of a washing machine. The Cray 2 also required electronic cooling liquid to prevent overheating, while the iPad2 uses less than 10 watts of power and does not even require a fan.[54]

There would be no iPad without the World Wide Web. The Internet has exploded both the transmission and the sharing of information. It has changed human consciousness too. We all know that Wikipedia cannot be used as an authoritative source in any academic or scientific publication. Yet it is also true that laypeople all over the world now turn to Wikipedia as the *first* source of information. In the past, it cost a small fortune to own the *Encyclopedia Britannica*. I know because I yearned for it and could not afford it as a child. Today, the number of children who can access Wikipedia has grown by leaps and bounds. The statistics on Wikipedia's growth illustrate well how rapidly things are changing. It was launched in 2001 and grew to approximately 20,000 articles and 18 language editions by the end of that year. By 2010 it had grown to 21 million articles with 100,000 regularly active contributors. As of January 2012, there were editions of Wikipedia in 283 languages. It has become the largest and most popular general reference work on the Internet, with an estimated 365 million readers worldwide.[55]

I recall that when Wikipedia started, there was enormous skepticism that an open platform that could be altered by anybody could be a reliable source. The general assumption was that some pranksters or malevolent souls would try to distort the data in some way or another. Our old mindsets told us that unless there was a clear central authority, we could not trust the data. We were wrong: entrusting the integrity of the data to the largest possible number of custodians works better than a single world authority would. And what is amazing is that the contributors come from all over the world. No single nation owns Wikipedia, even though it was born and launched in January 2001 by Jimmy Wales in the United States. Wikipedia is therefore a cutting-edge example of the good that humanity can do by using new technological means to cooperate from all corners of the world. This would have seemed inconceivable barely two decades ago. Now the inconceivable has become real. This is how technology is changing the world.

Wikipedia is only the latest layer of what has been a growing global phenomenon. Increasingly, no matter which corner of the world we live in, we are beginning to live and breathe in a "single information universe." When Princess Diana died on August 31, 1997, or when Barack Obama got elected to the presidency in November 2008, the whole world knew instantly what had happened. When the World Cup soccer finals are held, we can see people watching them simultaneously in all corners of the world. When the Chilean miners were trapped underground for sixty-nine days in 2010, practically the whole world prayed for them and celebrated when they were rescued. One billion viewers—one-seventh of the world's population—watched the rescue live on TV and the Internet.[56]

The Chilean miners episode is worth considering further to understand how human compassion has begun to change. In previous eras, if the Chilean miners had been trapped, the news would have also traveled around the world fairly quickly. People would have reacted sympathetically to the miners, but they would have also been psychologically disengaged from the episode: the story belonged "over there" and not "over here." Now that sense of psychological disengagement is being replaced by a greater sense of psychological engagement. Over time, in place of various country-bound consciences, we will see the development of a global conscience. This is a process that we should be watching carefully to understand the great convergence the world is experiencing.

Open access to technology can also change hitherto closed societies. An awareness of backwardness can change human behavior significantly. One reason that China progressed rapidly after 1978 is that when Deng Xiaoping visited the US in January 1979, one of the bravest decisions he made was to allow Chinese television screens to show scenes of American middle-class homes with refrigerators, washing machines, TV sets, and two-car garages. Until Deng did that, the Chinese had been told China was a socialist paradise and America was a society where the workers were being exploited by their capitalist bosses. I know personally how shocked the Chinese must have been by this new information because I went through the same shock when I saw an American middle-class home for the first time in my life a few years earlier, in 1974. I could not believe that ordinary people (not the very rich) could live so well. Today, practically the whole world knows what a modern middle-class standard of living is like, and the whole world aspires to attain it.

One of the bravest things that Deng's successors did was to unleash the Internet in China. Today, the largest number of Internet users in any country can be found in China, not America. And open access to information is changing significantly the social and political climate in China. The Chinese government discovered this new reality when two high-speed trains had a collision on July 23, 2011. Altogether thirty-nine people died. Following their old political instincts, the authorities in the Railway Ministry tried to bury this incident as quickly as possible. Indeed, they literally tried to bury the evidence. The rescue effort concluded less than a day after the accident, and the damaged train cars were broken apart by backhoes and buried nearby. This is how Wikipedia documented what followed:

> The Railway Ministry justified the burial by claiming that the trains contained valuable "national level" technology that could be stolen. How-

ever, hours after the rescuers had been told to stop searching for survivors, a 2-year-old girl was found alive in the wreckage.

Chinese media was especially skeptical of the rescue efforts, particularly the burial of trains. In a press conference, the spokesman of the Railway Ministry, Wang Yongping, said that the burial was to facilitate the rescue work. His answer prompted heckling and gasps of disbelief from the journalists assembled. Wang then said to the press, "Whether or not you believe [this explanation], I believe it." This phrase eventually became an internet meme. There was no evidence that experts or officials entered the front car to investigate the cause of the accident when it was buried. Families of the victims of the crash were outraged at what they viewed was an inadequate investigation, as well as poor organization of the relief effort in the aftermath of the disaster. Images of the wreckage being shoveled into pits were circulated widely on the Internet, and led to speculation over a possible mishandling by the government or the concealment of evidence crucial for the ongoing investigation.

Despite reported directives from the Propaganda Department, Chinese media, both independent and state-owned, directly criticized the Ministry of Railways and voiced their skepticism of the government. Such challenges to officially-sanctioned orthodoxy were bold and rare, particularly on programs aired on China's state-owned television. In one instance, in response to Wang Yongping's assurance at the press conference that the Chinese railway system was running on "advanced technology," news anchor Bai Yansong retorted on CCTV, "The technology may be advanced, but is your management advanced? Are your standard operating procedures advanced? Is the supervision advanced? Is your respect for people advanced? Are all the minute details advanced? At the end of the day, is your overall operational capability advanced?" Similarly, Qiu Qiming of the CCTV program, *24-Hours*, launched into an on-air tirade about Chinese society: "If nobody can be safe, do we still want this speed? Can we drink a glass of milk that's safe? Can we stay in an apartment that will not fall apart? Can the roads we travel on in our cities not collapse? Can we travel in safe trains? And if and when a major accident does happen, can we not be in a hurry to bury the trains? Can we afford the people a basic sense of security? China, please slow down. If you're too fast, you may leave the souls of your people behind."[57]

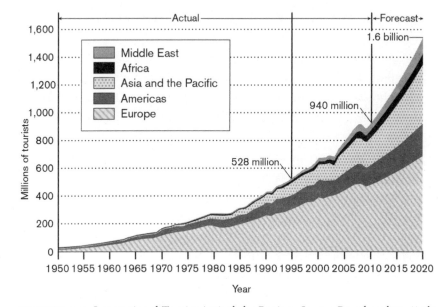

FIGURE 2.4 International Tourist Arrivals by Region. *Source:* Based on http://mkt
.unwto.org/sites/all/files/docpdf/unwtohighlights11enlr_3.pdf.

Western readers might be tempted to congratulate themselves for living
in open liberal democratic societies where cover-ups are rare and certainly
not as crude as the burial of the Chinese train. But liberal democratic societies are custodians of some "closed" global institutions, such as the UN Security Council and the IMF. Both function without paying much attention
to global accountability. Indeed, they behave and act as though they were
accountable to only a few key capitals. In fact, all global institutions should
get rid of the idea that they are accountable only to a few governments. Soon
they will be held accountable by an increasingly well-informed and ener-
getic global population. Technology will force closed societies, and closed
global institutions, to open up, as Chapter 7 will demonstrate.

One often-overlooked contributor to the opening of minds around the
world is tourism. The UN World Tourism Organization (UNWTO) notes
that, "in spite of occasional shocks, international tourist arrivals have
shown virtually uninterrupted growth: from 25 million in 1950, to 277
million in 1980, to 435 million in 1990, to 675 million in 2000, and the
current 940 million."[58] Figure 2.4 is worth studying carefully.

Despite several severe global crises (such as 9/11 or the SARS epidemic), global travel continues to grow. This too is an irreversible long-term secular trend that will bring the whole world together. It is estimated that international arrivals will hit 1.6 billion by 2020. In short, one in five inhabitants of planet earth will travel across an international boundary. It is hard to believe that this huge explosion in people-to-people contacts will have no impact on global consciousness.

In the past, most of the travelers who went long distance came from America and Europe. This is no longer true. There has been a huge surge of travel from Russia and China, Brazil and South Korea, to name just a few countries. China spent $55 billion on international tourism from 2001 to 2011—the third highest in the world. This trend is expected to continue. According to the World Travel and Tourism Council, China is expected to send an extra 125 million travelers abroad and generate an extra $100 billion in overseas spending between now and 2021. As *The Economist* puts it, "Chinese tourists seem to be everywhere, yet the Chinese tourist boom is only just beginning."[59]

As several hundred million Chinese travel overseas, will China remain the same or will it be transformed? It's hard to believe that there will be no impact on Chinese society. The pool of globally educated citizens will grow in China and in virtually every other society in the world.

The Common Aspirations Pillar

One of the good fortunes of my life may well have been the fact that I grew up in a tiny home in Singapore that had no flush toilet until I was about ten years old. Nor did we have a refrigerator, TV set, or, of course, a car. I mention all those items because they still represent the basic aspirations of all human beings, no matter where they live on the globe. As a result of information spreading throughout the world, people know what they have and what they don't have relative to other people. Most Americans and Europeans, of course, take all these material necessities for granted. What they don't realize is how many people still do not have access to many of these items and yearn for them. Of the 7 billion people on our planet, there are still 2.6 billion people—or half the population in the developing world—without access to a toilet or latrine.[60] An even larger number have no access to refrigerators. Globally, more than 1.3 billion people are without access to electricity, and 2.7 billion people are without clean cooking facilities. More than 95 percent of these people are in either sub-Saharan Africa or developing Asia, and 84 percent are in rural areas.[61] By contrast, TV sets have spread rapidly: 1.4 billion (or 79 percent of households) have a TV, although in Africa the figure is only 28 percent.[62]

It is truly good news that the vast majority of the world's people now have a common set of material aspirations. Once material aspirations become more important than differing ideological or religious aspirations, an overriding set of common interests will motivate the vast majority of the world's population to work together. Let me take a fairly extreme example of two societies that are sharply distrustful of each other: India and Pakistan. For the past sixty-five years, since partition, both have focused on their differences. Today, the aspirations of both populations are converging. The priority of both populations is economic development that will deliver a better material standard of living. The incentive to cooperate becomes greater and greater. Minorities in both countries may still want to emphasize their differences and perhaps even stimulate conflict. But the converging aspirations of the majorities make conflict harder and harder. The GDP per capita in India and Pakistan has increased from US $80 in 1960 in both countries to $1,500 in India and $1,000 in Pakistan in 2010.[63] A January 2011 article in Pakistan's largest English-language newspaper, the *News International*, declared:

> Despite a history of conflicts, mistrust and estranged relationship, an overwhelming number of Pakistanis and Indians want peace and friendship between the nuclear-armed South Asian nations, a survey conducted on both sides of the border has revealed. The survey—conducted by independent research agencies and sponsored by the Jang Group of Pakistan and The Times of India on the first anniversary of their joint peace initiative "Aman Ki Asha"—showed that 70 per cent of Pakistanis and 74 per cent of Indians want peaceful relations.[64]

India and Pakistan, like other traditional rivals such as Greece and Turkey, or Argentina and Brazil, are finding that their populations are being swept along each day by a strong global mainstream momentum that is becoming irresistible. Populations all over the world want their governments to focus on economic development, not on war. Hence, there is pressure on governments to build better infrastructure, better roads and railways, better sewage pipes and schools. We have, as a result, seen a greater improvement in the standards of living of populations in the last thirty years than we have in the last three hundred years.

These material aspirations are matched by similarly shared educational aspirations. A hundred years ago, getting into Harvard and Yale may have represented the aspirations of elites in America. Today, getting into Harvard and Yale represents the aspirations of elites all over the world. Parents in Santiago or Singapore, Tehran or Tokyo, Beijing or Budapest, jump for joy when their child gets admitted into Yale. I know this personally: when two of my children got into Yale, I was congratulated in all corners of the world because everyone knew what it meant. When people all over the world have common aspirations, we are clearly moving toward a one-world dynamic where our common aspirations are greater than our varying cultural or ethnic aspirations. It is true that very few, especially very few non-Americans, will get admitted into Ivy League universities. But the fact that the best minds all over the world have a common aspiration to get their children admitted there has an enormous unifying effect on global consciousness.

The explosion in the numbers of children going to primary and secondary schools is about to be accompanied by an explosion in the numbers going to universities. What is truly revealing is how the curricula of the best universities all around the world are converging. All the better universities know that they have to have strong science and engineering faculties to get any kind of global recognition. Equally importantly, the language of science and engineering is a global language. The laws of physics apply equally in all corners. Hence, the global spread of education in science and technology is another major driving force in the creation of one world.

Together these forces have created common values. Here again, without either a great plan or a common strategic map, humanity is moving toward creating a set of common values. This does not mean that humanity will become homogeneous. We will continue to worship different gods, enjoy different cultures, eat different foods, marry in different ways, and so on. Global diversity will not disappear. Indeed, with the resurgence of long-dormant cultures and societies, especially in Asia, cultural diversity will grow.

Yet even while we retain our different cultural and religious identities, we will converge on some important and fundamental values. Several philosophers have noticed this trend. Peter Singer has remarked that "the communications revolution has spawned a 'global audience' that creates the basis for a 'global ethics.'" Self-identification with the nation creates a national morality, whereas identification with the world would create a global morality. Amartya Sen has also made reference to our transborder "multiple identities—ethnic, religious, national, local, professional, and political."[65] The best example I can think of as a common value is the rule of law. Here, one of the biggest global revolutions of all time has taken place with scarcely a murmur: the substitution of rule by law with rule of law. And what is the key difference between rule by law and rule of law? Rule by law means that the general population obeys the laws of the land but the rulers (whether they are hereditary monarchies or absolute dictators) remain above and are not subject to those same laws. By contrast, under the rule of law, everyone in society, rulers and ruled, is subject to the same laws. There are no exceptions. The UN defines the rule of law as follows:

> The "rule of law" refers to a principle of governance in which all persons, institutions and entities, public and private, including the State itself, are accountable to laws that are publicly promulgated, equally enforced and independently adjudicated, and which are consistent with international human rights norms and standards. It requires, as well, measures to ensure adherence to the principles of supremacy of law, equality before the law, accountability to the law, fairness in the application of the law, separation of powers, participation in decision-making, legal certainty, avoidance of arbitrariness and procedural and legal transparency.[66]

To understand the impact of the transition from rule by law to rule of law, one society worth studying in some detail is Pakistan. In the West, the conventional wisdom is that Pakistan has become or is becoming a failed state led by corrupt rulers and a strong military and is infected with terrorist organizations. It is hard to think of a more unpromising environment for the emergence of rule of law, one of the most civilizing values of all time. Yet it was in Pakistan that a military ruler with almost absolute powers (and backed by the United States), General Pervez Musharraf, came to grief because he sacked Chief Justice Iftikhar Mohammad Chaudhry on March 9, 2007. It was in Pakistan that the High Court told the prime minister to remove the president's immunity from prosecution. If the rule of law can take hold in Pakistan, it must be spreading very widely around the world.

It's hard to tell what is behind the spread. Formal education helps. As more and more lawyers are educated to the best global practices, they naturally bring them home. But the rule of law can take hold of and transform a body politic only if the people of the society are in turn ready for these new regimes and welcome and support them. Even in the conservative and troubled society of Pakistan, the people were ready to support the chief justice over the political establishment because they had come to realize that their lives would be better off with greater rule of law.

If the rule of law spreads rapidly across the world, I have no doubt that it will in turn create a more stable and orderly world. The instinct to resolve problems and conflicts through rule of law at home should in turn lead to a habit of doing the same across borders, giving another reason that we might expect a continued decline in wars between states. Even in Southeast Asia, a relatively troubled region for decades, the governments of Indonesia and Malaysia and then of Malaysia and Singapore decided to resolve their territorial disputes by referring them to the International Court of Justice (ICJ).

Lee Kuan Yew, the first prime minister of Singapore, has said, "If a dispute cannot be resolved by negotiations, it is better to refer it to a third party dispute settlement mechanism, than to allow it to fester and sour bilateral relations. This was my approach and subsequent Singapore Prime Ministers have continued to subscribe to it."[67]

Commenting on the ICJ judgment that awarded sovereignty of the disputed island of Pedra Branca to Singapore, Barry Desker, dean of the S. Rajaratnam School of International Studies, observed that Southeast Asia was beginning to accept international legal norms. "In the past, the tendency in ASEAN was to try and resolve issues purely by mediation or negotiations between two parties. The result was that issues or disputes between parties in the region tended to go on and on without completion, without successful negotiation. I think we are now moving in the direction of accepting a turn to international law—a willingness to accept international arbitration and this bodes well for issues in which there are bilateral differences."[68]

Former ASEAN Secretary-General Rodolfo Severino has noted that "ASEAN has never been associated with international law and treaties. ASEAN has always been regarded as a group of sovereign nations operating on the basis of ad hoc understandings and informal procedures rather than within the framework of binding agreements arrived at through formal processes."[69] However, Kevin Tan suggests that "with the adoption of the ASEAN Charter at its 13th Summit in November 2007, ASEAN moved toward becoming a singular polity and has expressed its firm commitment to, inter alia, enhancing rule of law in terms akin to the use and definition of this expression by the UN. The ASEAN Charter has codified adherence to the rule of law—and its now familiar linkage to human rights and democracy—as a core ASEAN purpose and principle which all ASEAN member states have pledged to uphold."[70]

There is, however, one large paradoxical exception to this emerging rule that greater respect for rule of law at home leads to greater respect for rule of law globally: the United States. Few nations can match the record of the United States in implementing the rule of law at home. Powerful figures from Richard Nixon to Dominique Strauss-Kahn found that they were not immune to the domestic rule of law. But America as a nation has decided that it stands above the rule of law globally. In practice, the US has respected and abided by most international conventions and treaties. In theory, however, it continues to fight the constraints of international law. Although the Law of the Sea Treaty has been widely accepted as international law, and the US abides by it in practice, the US Congress still refuses to ratify it, insisting on its "sovereign" right to decide what is best for the national interest of the United States.

This exception of the United States—with its refusal to accept mandatory and binding international laws—shows more than ever the need to both create and spread the theory of one world. As long as policymakers continue to believe that "sovereign national interest" is the key consideration in deciding what to do, the world will remain a troubled place. And there are some distinguished minds who believe that the world is not yet ready to move from nation-states to the beginnings of a global order. Dani Rodrik, a Harvard professor, acknowledges that the world is changing. Yet he denies that the nation-state will be replaced soon: "[We] should not entirely dismiss the likelihood that a true global consciousness will develop in the future, along with transnational political communities. But today's challenges cannot be met by institutions that do not (yet) exist. For now, people still must turn for solutions to their national governments, which remain the best hope for collective action. The nation-state may be a relic bequeathed to us by the French Revolution, but it is all that we have."[71]

Rodrik is right in one sense. Our current global order is run by nation-states and by leaders of nation-states making decisions driven primarily by national interests. Yet this description of prevailing reality is also a description of the fundamental problem. The world has changed. Our way of managing it has not. This is why we urgently need to equip the minds of policymakers with new mental maps. National considerations will have to be balanced with global considerations, national interests with global interests, if leading policymakers are going to make wise decisions both for their countries and for the world at large.

Any national policymaker who has not understood that the theory of one world is driving global affairs will bring grief to his or her country. Even in a country as powerful as the United States, jobs will not return automatically unless policymakers realize that the manufacturing jobs lost to China will not return automatically and without considerable effort. To create new jobs in America, American policymakers will now have to study the global economy and figure out which sectors the US can now compete in. In the past, there was no need for American policymakers to do so. Now they will be unable to defend or enhance the nation's economic interests if they fail to understand the trends in the global economy.

Virtually every other nation has understood that the future of its national economic fortunes depends on global economic trends. Manmohan Singh, prime minister of India, has said, "All countries must compete in global markets and such competition is not inconsistent with cooperation nor is it adversarial."[72] Similarly, Premier Wen Jiabao of China has said, "China and India are cooperative partners instead of rivals. They have common interests in the global economic and trade system."[73] This is why all countries now pay attention to their relative rankings on the World Economic Forum (WEF) global competitiveness rankings. These provide a good indication of where a country is heading. I was in Istanbul, Turkey, when the WEF announced the 2012 competitiveness rankings, and the Turkish press was quick to highlight that Turkey had risen.

Supporting ethical arguments in favor of a theory of one world, which make the case that we live in a single moral community globally, is in the *rational self-interest* of the 7 billion people on our planet. We now have to recognize and accept that we live in one world. The same trends that are pushing us toward living in a single global community are also lifting billions of people out of poverty and improving the lives of hundreds of millions of people. This is why they deserve all our support. From time to time, there will be bouts of xenophobia as politicians try to play on fears of loss of national identity. The best way to neutralize any xenophobia is to create a theory of one world that explains how living in this one world creates a better world for all of us.

Global Irrationality

WHEN I REFLECT ON CERTAIN POLICIES OF THE US AND OTHER
Western powers post-9/11, I am reminded of an exchange in Robert Bolt's
play *A Man for All Seasons*. Bolt recreates a critical conversation between
Sir Thomas More and the much younger, more zealous Will Roper. Roper
wants More to arrest a wicked man, even though the man did not break
any law. Sir Thomas warns Roper of the dangers of such a view:

> Roper: While you talk, he's gone!
> More: And go he should, if he was the Devil himself, until he broke the
> law!
> Roper: So now you'd give the Devil benefit of law!
> More: Yes. What would you do? Cut a great road through the law to get
> after the Devil?
> Roper: I'd cut down every law in England to do that!
> More: (Roused and excited) Oh? (Advances on Roper) And when the
> last law was down, and the Devil turned round on you—where would
> you hide, Roper, the laws all being flat? (He leaves him) This country's
> planted thick with laws from coast to coast—man's laws, not God's—
> and if you cut them down—and you're just the man to do it—d'you re-
> ally think you could stand upright in the winds that would blow then?
> (Quietly) Yes, I'd give the Devil benefit of law, for my own safety's sake.[1]

Sometimes facts confirm fiction. Since 9/11, in pursuit of al-Qaeda (a cause as evil as the devil), the United States has decided that it can break existing international laws. As former US president Jimmy Carter put it:

> The United States is abandoning its role as the global champion of human rights. . . . While the country has made mistakes in the past, the widespread abuse of human rights over the last decade has been a dramatic change from the past. With leadership from the United States, the Universal Declaration of Human Rights was adopted in 1948 as "the foundation of freedom, justice and peace in the world." This was a bold and clear commitment that power would no longer serve as a cover to oppress or injure people, and it established equal rights of all people to life, liberty, security of person, equal protection of the law and freedom from torture, arbitrary detention or forced exile. . . . At a time when popular revolutions are sweeping the globe, the United States should be strengthening, not weakening, basic rules of law and principles of justice enumerated in the Universal Declaration of Human Rights. But instead of making the world safer, America's violation of international human rights abets our enemies and alienates our friends.[2]

What Sir Thomas More and Jimmy Carter both appreciated is that it is in the long-term interest of each one of us to promote stronger laws and stronger institutions, whether we are—at the moment—rich and powerful or poor and weak. Indeed, both these processes have contributed significantly to the success of Western civilization.

Against this historical backdrop, it is truly remarkable that few in the West are aware that when it comes to the global rule of law or global institutions, the West has been following the advice of Will Roper, not that of Sir Thomas More.[3] While there may have been a strategic rationale for this policy in previous decades, it has continued on autopilot even after the strategic rationale disappeared. All this creates massive global irrationality.

This irrationality may have been inspired or led by the West, but the acquiescence of the rest of humanity to it has also contributed to the problem. Since most of this chapter will consist of depressing stories of how we have ignored global interests in our global policies, let me begin with an important piece of good news: the long-term strategic interests of the 12 percent of the world's population who live in the West are now aligned with the 88 percent who live outside the West. We all live together in a small global village. Hence, we have a common interest to strengthen, not weaken, our global village councils.

Humanity claims to be the most intelligent species inhabiting this planet. We make this claim on the basis that humans, unlike other species, have made intelligent adaptations as our environment has changed and evolved. If we understood the new global environment and were trying to adapt to it, we would be working to strengthen global village councils in one way or another. Curiously, until as recently as 2011, we have been doing the opposite. We have been weakening them. All this was a result of key policymakers in key capitals using old mental maps and old policy assumptions long after the world had changed.

The UN System

Most of our key global village councils are in one way or another related to the United Nations (UN). Figure 3.1 shows clearly the pervasive impact of the UN system. A deep fissure exists between the dominant Western narrative and the narrative of the rest of the world. Most well-informed Western, especially American, citizens have come to believe that the UN system is just a vast, bloated, inefficient bureaucracy that does little good for the world. Hence the populations in many Western countries have little trust or confidence in the UN system. By contrast, and this is a great good fortune of our world at this point in history, the vast majority of those who live outside the West retain massive trust in the UN system. If the West understood global trends, it would immediately begin to take advantage of this trust to secure its long-term strategic interests. That would be a masterstroke of geopolitics.

To do so, the West, especially America, must realize that it has to change course. At one time, it may have made strategic sense for the West to keep global village councils weak. Since the West was so strong and could defend itself unilaterally, especially from military threats, it saw no strategic value in strengthening the UN system. Indeed, without declaring it as a Western policy, the West saw strategic value in *weakening* the UN system. And it did so successfully. However, the primary security threats to the West in the future

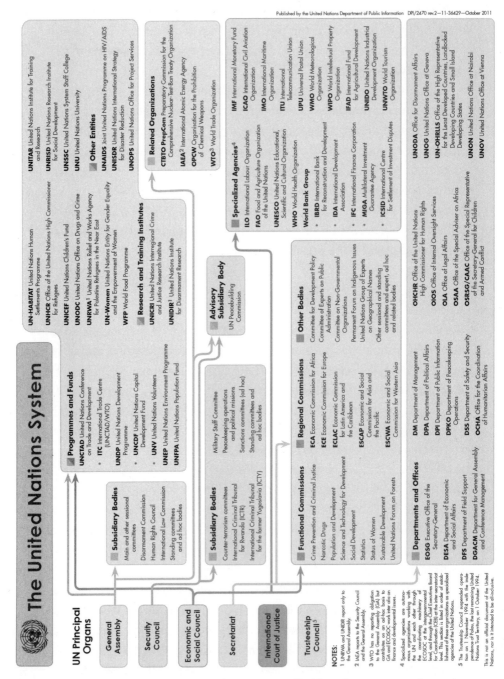

Published by the United Nations Department of Public Information DPI/2470 rev.2—11-36429—October 2011

FIGURE 3.1   The UN System. *Source:* UN Department of Public Information, April 2011.

will no longer be military. No armies of tanks are poised to invade any Western country. Instead, the main threats to the West, both in America and Europe, will be nonmilitary: from illegal immigrants to dangerous viruses, from new forms of economic competition to cultural isolation.

In this dramatically changed strategic environment, it would be absolutely foolish for the West to continue spending more on defense and less on global village councils. Yet even though this strategic folly becomes clearer every day, there is virtually no major voice in the West advocating a major change of course. The usual potent mix of ignorance and complacency, plus powerful vested interests that have much to lose from any change of course, leads to the perpetuation of outdated policies. This is why this chapter has to document in some detail the dangers of undermining the UN system, which is now of growing strategic value to the West.

As former Secretary of State Madeleine Albright bluntly put it, "Americans tend to dislike the word 'multilateralism'—it has too many syllables and ends in an 'ism.' The reality, however, is that the UN is the world's most visible multilateral organization and has the most members. No one country, even the United States, can tackle the bundle of issues the world faces—from terrorism to nuclear proliferation, economic inequality to environmental degradation." She goes on to say that "if we start thinking that the United Nations doesn't work, that we don't have to pay our bills, or that everything in diplomacy will turn out exactly the way we want it, we are leaving out an indispensable tool."[4]

The Problem of UN Budgets

Nothing illustrates the global irrationality of humanity, including the West, better than the absurd decision to *cut* the UN budget in December 2011 by 5 percent ($260 million). The current $5.41 billion two-year budget was slashed to $5.15 billion for 2012 and 2013. The pressure to cut the budget came primarily from the major Western countries, especially the US, which was among the first to praise the budget cut. US negotiator Joseph Torsella said, "This accord is the first time since 1998—and only the second time in the last 50 years—that the UN regular budget has declined in comparison to the previous budget's actual expenses." Torsella added that the new budget "saves the American taxpayers millions of dollars and sets the UN on the path of real fiscal discipline and continued reform."[5]

No one should oppose fiscal discipline and continued reform. At the same time, key departments and agencies need to be provided adequate resources when the demands on these agencies increase. This is common sense. And common sense tells us that the demand on the UN system will increase.

Since UN funding will be discussed a lot in this chapter, it may be useful to provide some technical classification to avoid confusion. The Better World Campaign website provides the following helpful classification:

> Funding for the United Nations and its agencies comes from two sources: assessed and voluntary contributions. Assessed contributions are payments made as part of the obligations that nations undertake when signing treaties. At the UN, assessments on member states provide a reliable source of funding to core UN functions through the UN regular and peacekeeping budgets, based on each country's ability to pay. Voluntary contributions are left to the discretion of each individual member state. These contributions, which make up nearly half of all UN funding, finance most of the world body's humanitarian relief and development agencies, including the UN Children's Fund (UNICEF), the World Food Program[me] (WFP), the UN Development Program[me] (UNDP), and the UN Refugee Agency (UNHCR [UN High Commissioner for Refugees]). The UN Regular Budget finances the General Assembly, the Security Council, the Economic and Social Council, the International Court of Justice, and the Secretariat as well as the UN's special political missions, the largest of which are the UN Assistance Mission in Afghanistan (UNAMA) and the UN Assistance Mission in Iraq (UNAMI).[6]

This technical distinction between assessed and voluntary contributions is an important one to understand because the West has tried to block the growth of the UN system by tightly controlling any increase in assessed contributions. These contributions are important to the UN system because they provide a predictable form of funding. The West does not like them because it cannot control the agenda of the activities supported by assessed contributions. Hence, the West prefers *voluntary* contributions because the West can then use its hitherto superior source of funding to influence the agenda of these UN activities. In short, the Western method of controlling the UN system was to starve it of assessed contributions and make it reliant on Western voluntary contributions. In line with this policy, the West, again led by America, has been promoting a policy of "zero-budget" growth for assessed contributions, which has now escalated, as indicated earlier, to "negative-budget" growth.

To understand the scope of human folly in dealing with the UN, all we have to do is to look at the ratio between the UN budget and the size of the global economy. All national budgets grow in tandem with the growth of national economies, as the increase in national economies indicates both rising resources and rising needs of the population. A rapidly growing global economy reflects the need for stronger global institutions. Since the US has traditionally been the biggest critic of UN budgets, it is useful to look at the comparative record of the UN and the US budgets since 1960.

In 1960, the US federal budget was $81.34 billion. By 2010, it had grown to $2.9 trillion. In short, it had grown thirty-six times. Meanwhile, the US economy had grown from $520.5 billion to $14.6 trillion, a twenty-eight-fold increase. As a percentage of the US economy, the US budget had grown from 15.6 to 19.9 percent.[7]

In 1960, the UN budget was $65.7 million. By 2010, it had grown to $5.41 billion for two years, or $2.7 billion per year. It had grown forty-one times. Meanwhile, the global economy had grown from $1.35 trillion to $63 trillion, a forty-seven-fold increase. Hence, as a percentage of the global economy, the UN budget had shrunk from 0.005 to 0.004 percent.[8] As we look at how the US budget has grown relative to the US economy and at how the UN budget has shrunk relative to the global economy, we have to ask only one simple question: has the demand for global public goods shrunk or increased in the past few decades? *Financial Times* columnist Martin Wolf has explained well the importance of global public goods:

> Public goods are the building blocks of civilization. Economic stability is itself a public good. So are security, science, a clean environment, trust, honest administration and free speech. The list could be far longer. This matters, because it is hard to secure adequate supply. The more global the

public goods the more difficult it is. Ironically, the better we have become at supplying private goods and so the richer we are, the more complex the public goods we need. Humanity's efforts to meet that challenge could prove to be the defining story of the century.[9]

He then adds:

Yet consider where we are now. The impact of humanity is, like the economy, increasingly global. Economic stability is a global public good. So, in the era of nuclear weapons, is security. So, in important respects, are control of organized crime, counterfeiting, piracy and, above all, pollution. So, even, is the supply of education or health. What happens anywhere affects everybody—and increasingly so. . . . Our states cannot supply them on their own. They need to co-operate. Traditionally, the least bad way of securing such co-operation is through some sort of leadership. The leader acts despite free riders. As a result, some global public goods have been adequately—if imperfectly—supplied. But as we move again into a multipolar era, the ability of any country to supply such leadership will be limited. Even in the unipolar days, it only worked where the hegemon wanted to provide the particular public good in question.[10]

The demand for global public goods has grown exponentially and will continue to grow as the world population increases from 7 billion today to 8 billion in the next ten years. This will result in a higher demand for food and energy and take a corresponding toll on the environment, exacerbating risks such as global warming. UN agencies help to mitigate these risks. For example, they help protect the environment (UN Environment Programme, or UNEP), promote development strategies (UNDP), address population concerns (UN Population Fund, or UNFPA), and protect the rights of the weaker members of our world, such as children (UNICEF) and refugees (UNHCR). If so, why are we shrinking the budget of the one global institution whose primary mission is to provide global public goods? What makes this observation even more painful is that the UN costs so little. The US spends $2,400 out of every $10,000 of its income to finance its national budget, but the global citizen spends 4¢ out of every $10,000 to finance the UN budget. This is global irrationality on a massive scale.

An obvious counterargument is that national budgets do a lot more than UN budgets: they pay for defense, homeland security, welfare payments, educational resources, and many other essential services. They cater to a lot of national needs. All this is true. I am not arguing that UN budgets should rise to the *scale* of national budgets. But I do think that a good case can be made that they should increase at the same *pace* as global needs have increased, especially as these have increased faster than national needs in some instances.

Few Americans (and indeed many others in the world) are keen to pay more to the UN General Assembly (UNGA) in New York since they perceive it to be a talk shop. I disagree vehemently with this perception. As Winston Churchill wisely said, "It is better to jaw-jaw than to war-war." The UN has contributed to reducing wars. However, even if it were true that the UNGA is a mere talk shop, this is certainly not true of other UN organizations, such as the World Health Organization (WHO) and the International Atomic Energy Agency (IAEA).

In the first decade of the twenty-first century, we saw the danger of global pandemics with the SARS virus in 2002–2003 and the H1N1 bird flu virus in 2009. Similarly, we all know that nuclear proliferation is a vital security issue worldwide. So are we providing additional resources to both these UN organizations? Instead, in another clear sign of global irrationality, we have effectively strangled both the WHO and the IAEA and prevented them from responding effectively to the challenges they face.

The World Health Organization (WHO)

As we move inexorably toward living in a more and more compact village, one clear common threat humanity faces is the rapid spread of new pandemics. Distances have disappeared. Viruses jump effortlessly across continents. Hence, we should be doing our utmost to strengthen the global health institutions, especially the WHO. Yet as Kelley Lee points out in her book *The World Health Organization (WHO)*, we have done the opposite. Lee dissects many flawed Western policies affecting the WHO. Lee did not set out to write a critique of Western governments' policies; she wanted to produce an objective diagnosis of the WHO. But her book reveals three major strategic errors that Western countries have made.

The first is to allow short-term and often sectional special interests to override enlightened long-term interests in developing stronger institutions. As the fastest-shrinking and most affluent members of the global village, the Western nations have the greatest vested interest in strengthening the WHO to improve global health conditions and to develop the capability and legitimacy (politically and organizationally) to fight major global epidemics. SARS began in a small village in China. From there it went to Hong Kong, and from Hong Kong it leapt to two cities on opposite sides of the global village: Singapore and Toronto. Similarly, Dr. Peter J. Hotez, dean of the National School of Tropical Medicine at Baylor University, has recently observed how diseases have spread from Latin America to the US. "Among the more frightening is Chagas disease. Transmitted by a 'kissing bug' that resembles a cockroach but with the ability to feed on human blood, it is a leading cause of heart failure and sudden death throughout Latin America. It is an especially virulent scourge among pregnant women, who can pass the disease along to their babies. Just last month [July 2012], the first case of congenital Chagas disease in the United States was reported."[11] To protect its long-term interests, the West should have spent the past few decades strengthening the WHO and providing it with more resources. Instead, it starved the WHO of resources just when it needed more to manage more complex health challenges.

Figure 3.2 describes Western folly in starving the WHO. In 1970–1971, the WHO received 62 percent of its budget from Regular Budget Funds (RBFs) and 18 percent from Extrabudgetary Funds (EBFs). By 2006–2007, the ratio had reversed to 28 percent from RBFs and 72 percent from EBFs. Why did this shift damage the WHO? The WHO can make long-term plans only from RBFs. EBFs can disappear overnight, at the whim of Western donors. The Western donors therefore engineered this shift to ensure that they could control the short-term agenda of the WHO even though they represented only 30-odd members out of 192 member states.[12]

To make matters worse, the "Geneva Group" of major donors introduced a policy of zero real growth to the RBFs of all UN organizations, including the WHO.[13] This zero-growth policy continued under both

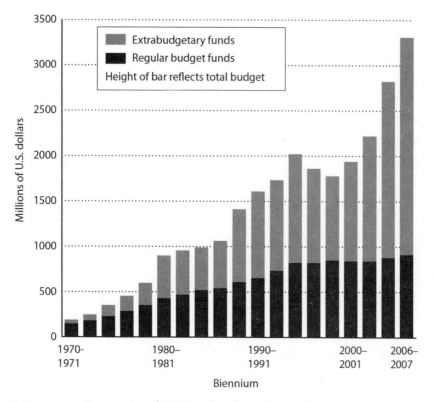

FIGURE 3.2 Proportions of WHO Budget from RBFs and EBFs by Biennia. *Source:* Based on Kelley Lee, *The World Health Organization (WHO),* (New York: Routledge Press, 2009), 40.

the more internationally minded Clinton-Gore administration and the less enlightened Bush-Cheney administration. In short, this decision to starve UN organizations was not driven by any ideology. It was driven by sheer geopolitical desire to control the global agenda. The biggest tragedy of the past few decades is that no major Western statesman has argued against the folly of weakening global institutions. Lee pays tribute to the heroic leadership of Halfdan Mahler as director-general of the WHO from 1973 to 1988. The US, unfortunately, opposed his reelection in 1988.

The second strategic error was to allow the traditional Western interest in biomedicine, with its focus on individual behavior and biology, to trump growing global interest in social medicine, with its emphasis on understanding and transforming social conditions underlying health and disease. Lee describes well how this tension "shaped the WHO's mandate, organizational structure and activities over the past six decades."[14] As Lee says, "Negotiations of the terrain between these two fundamentally different approaches, and their underlying values, remains a source of ongoing tension within the organization."[15] Since Lee is very polite, she does not want to say outright that US government policies toward the WHO are heavily influenced by the big pharmaceutical corporations. These corporations are interested in individual health spending, not in collective wellness or well-being.

The book makes abundantly clear that the American government never had any doubts about the superiority of its approach. Yet it does not take a genius to figure out that something has gone fundamentally wrong with American health care. The US spends 16 percent of its GNP on health care. Yet it has a poorer record in life expectancy and infant mortality than Singapore, which spends 4 percent of its GNP on health care. More significantly, Lee says, "the health gains achieved in low-income settings, notably Cuba and Kerala, India, also demonstrated the capacity to improve public health with limited resources."[16] Despite these successes in the developing world, Lee notes that "the rise of neoliberal-based fiscal policies brought even greater restrictions on public spending on health."[17] In short, ideology trumped real life-and-death experience. In Colombia, for example, only 9 percent of children were covered by the DPT vaccine in 1975. This increased to 87 percent by 1990. Despite the success of these relatively inexpensive public health efforts, the US opposed them.

Lee also documents how the US never hesitated to put pressure on the WHO whenever any US interests were affected. At the 2005 G-8 summit, world leaders pledged to work with the WHO and the UN toward universal access to antiretroviral drugs for AIDS by 2010, a goal later endorsed by the UN. Yet when a WHO official criticized a US trade agreement with Thailand that restricted such access, he was quickly removed. Lee describes the situation clearly: "The reported exertion of pressure by the US government on the WHO Director-General, which effectively silenced criticism of US bilateral trade agreements, was a reflection of the WHO's political impotence in the face of hard power."[18]

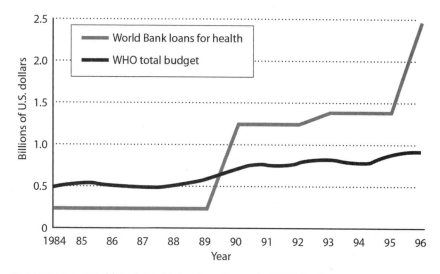

FIGURE 3.3 World Bank Health Lending Versus the WHO Budget, 1984–1996. *Source:* Based on Kent Buse and Catherine Gwin, "World Health: The World Bank and Global Cooperation in Health: The Case of Bangladesh," *Lancet* 351, no. 9103 (February 28, 1998): 665–669, cited in Kelley Lee, *The World Health Organization (WHO)* (New York: Routledge, 2009), 121.

The third major strategic error of the West has been to dilute the role of the WHO as the leading global health agency. It did this in many ways. First, it provided more resources to the World Bank for health projects. Figure 3.3 shows how World Bank lending on health went from roughly half of the WHO budget in 1984 to more than two and a half times bigger than the WHO budget in 1996. The West preferred to give money to the World Bank since it controlled its leadership and agenda. Second, the creation of large private foundations, especially the Bill and Melinda Gates Foundation, also undermined the central role of the WHO. Lee quotes Anne-Emanuelle Birn, research chair in international health at the University of Toronto, saying, "In part-funding selected initiatives, the [Gates] Foundation has influenced the decisions of other donor agencies, and thus global health priorities in general."[19] As a result, Lee concludes, "for the WHO, it has meant a substantial bypassing of its role as the lead UN health agency."[20]

How does the diminution of the WHO's role undermine long-term Western interests? As the most prosperous occupants of an ever-shrinking global village, the Western populations have the greatest vested interest in preventing the emergence of new epidemics that could hit their societies in a day or two, given the speed at which new viruses travel across the world. No Western state has the moral or political authority to investigate the internal health conditions of other states. The WHO does. Similarly, neither the World Bank nor the Gates Foundation has the authority or legitimacy to galvanize instant global cooperation to deal with an epidemic. The 6 billion people of the world who live outside the West will not allow the World Bank or the Gates Foundation to come into their countries and investigate their contributions, directly or indirectly, to any new global epidemic. But they will open their doors to WHO representatives because they perceive the WHO to be defending global, not sectional, interests. Hence, it has been an act of great strategic folly of the West to weaken the WHO.

During the SARS crises of 2002–2003, according to Lee, the "WHO's worldwide mobilization of scientists to identify and genetically sequence the infectious agent was especially impressive."[21] No other global agency can replace this indispensable role. It is therefore in the long-term enlightened self-interest of the West to strengthen the WHO instead of undermining it.[22]

Most people in the West are probably unaware that the West has endangered global health regimes by weakening the WHO. Indeed, it is more than likely that people in the West have probably heard of one or another broken initiative to address a major global health challenge. This impression would, in turn, reinforce the assumption that the West has been remarkably benevolent when it comes to helping humanity in the area of health.

The Lee Kuan Yew School of Public Policy of the National University of Singapore launched a major research project on global health governance led by the Centre on Asia and Globalisation (CAG), based at the university. As a result of this major study, CAG reached the following conclusion:

> In short, Global Health Governance suffers from an excess of institutions and mechanisms. Over the past several years, global health has risen rapidly on the agenda of global issues. Apart from traditional government and IGO [intergovernmental organization] action, non-state actors, from foundations to pharmaceutical corporations to NGOs, are actively experimenting with alternative ways to tackle health challenges. However, these initiatives are often driven by competing interests and values, un-

coordinated at best and mutually undermining at worst. The result is a cacophony of actors, largely unregulated, rarely transparent, and often acting at cross purposes. Despite all the new resources, domestic capacity to handle pandemics is weak or non-existent in most regions, leaving all parts of the world vulnerable to the next big outbreak. Even the most obvious global governance steps, such as a reliable and comprehensive global reporting system, have yet to be taken. These institutional gaps and lack of strategic coherence reflect not just the difficulties of global collective action, but also important tensions between the norms, principles and ethics driving various global governance efforts.[23]

Similarly, in a presentation delivered at the June 2010 Global Health: Together We Can Make It conference in Brussels, Ilona Kickbusch, director of the Global Health Programme at the Graduate Institute, Geneva, and chair of the Global Health Europe Task Force, argued, "As the determinants of health increasingly stem from collective problems that cannot be adequately addressed by the Westphalian model of independent nation states, national governments must increasingly look to the multilateral system for solutions." Kickbusch called for "a new commitment to the World Health Organization, and a clarification of its role." She remarked, "To move ahead in global health governance we need long term perspectives and long term investments. The uncoordinated venture philanthropy of recent years has developed what some call market multilateralism. This basically means a sector which should also produce a global public good has been driven from a results based perspective from the private sector." She concluded by saying that we have to rethink the direction this has taken us in. To improve our situation today, "we have to examine key elements of what it means to introduce those types of long term perspectives in global health governance, and then have a new kind of accountability—both of Member States of international organizations and of the other players."[24]

IAEA

The global contradiction we have seen in dealing with global health concerns is replicated in our approach to nuclear proliferation. On the one hand, there is no shortage of statements from world leaders warning us that

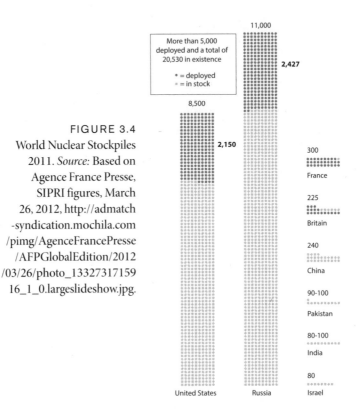

FIGURE 3.4
World Nuclear Stockpiles
2011. *Source:* Based on
Agence France Presse,
SIPRI figures, March
26, 2012, http://admatch
-syndication.mochila.com
/pimg/AgenceFrancePresse
/AFPGlobalEdition/2012
/03/26/photo_13327317159
16_1_0.largeslideshow.jpg.

a nightmare scenario would unfold if nuclear technology fell into rogue hands like those of al-Qaeda. (See Figure 3.4 for a graphic of nuclear stockpiles as of 2011.) In March 2003, Tony Blair told the British Parliament:

> I know there are several countries—mostly dictatorships with highly repressive regimes—desperately trying to acquire chemical weapons, biological weapons or, in particular, nuclear weapons capability. Some of these countries are now a short time away from having a serviceable nuclear weapon. This activity is not diminishing. It is increasing. . . . And the possibility of the two coming together—of terrorist groups in possession of WMD [weapon of mass destruction], even of a so-called dirty radiological bomb is now, in my judgement, a real and present danger.[25]

His was not the only voice. Many other Western leaders echoed his fears of nuclear proliferation. At the Nuclear Security Summit in April 2010, Barack Obama said:

Two decades after the end of the Cold War, we face a cruel irony of history—the risk of a nuclear confrontation between nations has gone down, but the risk of nuclear attack has gone up. Nuclear materials that could be sold or stolen and fashioned into a nuclear weapon exist in dozens of nations. Just the smallest amount of plutonium—about the size of an apple—could kill and injure hundreds of thousands of innocent people. Terrorist networks such as al Qaeda have tried to acquire the material for a nuclear weapon, and if they ever succeeded, they would surely use it. Were they to do so, it would be a catastrophe for the world—causing extraordinary loss of life, and striking a major blow to global peace and stability. In short, it is increasingly clear that the danger of nuclear terrorism is one of the greatest threats to global security—to our collective security.[26]

Obama also said, "At the dawn of the nuclear age that he helped to unleash, Albert Einstein said: 'Now everything has changed.' . . . And he warned: 'We are drifting towards a catastrophe beyond comparison. We shall require a substantially new manner of thinking if mankind is to survive.'"[27]

The logical consequence of this Western fear of nuclear proliferation should be to strengthen the main global council that deals with nuclear proliferation dangers, namely, the International Atomic Energy Agency. In December 2007, I accepted an invitation to become a member of the Commission of Eminent Persons to review the future of the IAEA under the chairmanship of a former president of Mexico, Ernesto Zedillo.

When I joined the commission, I expected to see a strong and healthy institution in IAEA since it was playing a vital role in the Western agenda of preventing nuclear proliferation. It came as a real shock to me to discover that, even though IAEA was already serving Western interests, it had been subjected to the same zero-budget-growth policies that the West had applied to all other UN organizations.

This experience with the IAEA commission was a real eye-opener for me. I had assumed that long-term Western policies toward international organizations were the result of careful, hardheaded, and tough-minded deliberations through which policies were designed to strengthen long-term Western interests. My assumption was an illusion. Short-term political calculations, propelled by the prejudices of the day, drove Western policies. In the process, long-term Western interests were damaged.

In regard to IAEA, one of its key roles is to inspect all nuclear power stations to ensure that they comply with international standards and to verify that there is no diversion of nuclear fuel for weaponization purposes. To fulfill this role, IAEA needs to keep on its regular payroll a strong and large team of dedicated nuclear inspectors. The best inspectors will stay with the IAEA only if they can be guaranteed good remuneration and good lifelong careers in the organization. IAEA can provide these good terms and conditions only from the funds it gets from reliable and predictable annexed contributions. It cannot guarantee good pay and careers from *voluntary* contributions because they come and go and are therefore unpredictable. Hence, to serve Western interests of having a strong team of nuclear inspectors, the West should be increasing the assessed contributions, not the voluntary contributions. Instead, amazingly, the West has been doing the exact opposite and thereby shooting itself in the foot.

Sadly, this is not the only way that the West has undermined IAEA. More dangerously, the West, especially America, has been infiltrating these organizations with intelligence-gathering spies. It has now been publicly revealed that many IAEA personnel sent to Iraq during Saddam Hussein's time were Western intelligence agents.[28] Even more dangerously, there have been reports surfacing that recently assassinated Iranian nuclear scientists were identified via intelligence provided by personnel infiltrated into IAEA teams. According to a *Christian Science Monitor* article on April 12, 2012, "Iranian officials say that nuclear inspectors of the UN's International Atomic Energy Agency (IAEA) have contributed to that toll, whether they are aware of it or not. They accuse the IAEA of breaking its own rules, by exposing secret information gleaned during inspections that, they charge, has been grist for hostile intelligence agencies seeking regime change in Iran. 'This has been proven to Iranians,' says Seyed Hossein Mousavian, a former member of Iran's nuclear negotiating team who is now at Princeton University."[29] If these stories prove to be true, they could undermine both Western and global interests as countries, including Iran, will progressively refuse to accept IAEA inspections on the grounds that they are infiltrated by Western intelligence agents.

Investing in the UN

This is why I emphasized at the outset of this chapter that the West should not underestimate the value of the trust that the UN enjoys in the hearts and minds of the rest of the world's population. And the UN can retain this trust only if it is clearly perceived to be serving global, not Western, interests. When I visited Beijing in May 2012, I got a firsthand experience of the value of this trust. For many years, the West had been trying to persuade China to pay more attention to its environment and to adopt sustainable development. Predictably, China reacted with suspicion to this unsolicited Western advice as it was seen to be a clever maneuver by the West to derail or slow down China's economic development. A Chinese policymaker told me that China finally accepted the wise advice when it was given to them by an independent UN agency, the UNDP. Furthermore, the Chinese government is clearly trying to formulate its positions to the various challenges of global governance discussed in this book. When it finally decided to organize a global seminar to address this issue, its partner of choice was the UNDP. Trust is an essential commodity as we go about restructuring the global system to handle new global challenges. We should try to retain as much as possible all the trust that the UN has accumulated in our world.

It is time for the US to constructively invest in the UN. If America were to terminate its zero-budget policies, the impact on the American economy and the American national budget would be truly inconsequential. The budget of the New York City Fire Department, which serves one city, is $1.5 billion a year. The budget for the UN's core functions—the Secretariat operations in New York, Geneva, Nairobi, Vienna, and five Regional Commissions, which serves the whole world—is $1.74 billion a year. Yet this financially inconsequential decision by the US government would bring enormous benefits if it led to the creation of more global public goods for our small global village. It would be good for America, and it would enhance global stability and trust. It would be a win-win investment.

The American delegation to the UN resents the fact that, even though the US pays 22 percent of the UN budget, it only has 1 vote out of 193 in the UN's decisionmaking processes. These American officials are right. There is a problem here that needs to be addressed. This is why Chapter 7 of this book will try to suggest a relationship between privileges and responsibilities in UN decisionmaking. But zero-budget growth is not the answer.

A Study in Irrationality: Nuclear Weapons Expenditures

To drive home the point that it is an act of massive global irrationality to cut or freeze UN assessed budgets of US $2.6 billion a year, let us compare the size of these budgets with money that we are spending in a completely irrational manner in another area: expenditures on nuclear armaments. It is estimated that the world will spend a combined US $1 trillion on nuclear weapons from 2011 to 2021. At roughly $100 billion a year (see Appendix 1), we are spending about forty times more a year on unnecessary nuclear weapons than on necessary UN expenses. All these confirm that humanity at large is behaving absurdly in many ways in managing our planet.

Spending more money on nuclear weapons than on nuclear prevention, among other necessary activities, is a monumental act of stupidity by any definition. Most of us look on with incredulity at images of terrorists who walk around with a huge belt of explosives tied to themselves, a walking arsenal of destruction. Most sane people think only "mad" people wrap themselves in deadly explosives. Yet humanity at large has done just that: we've tied a huge belt of nuclear weapons around the girth of planet earth, with enough explosives to destroy it several times over. How mad is that?

We comfort ourselves that, unlike the deranged terrorist, we have no intention of using those weapons. They are meant to provide deterrence. Yet while this deterrence capacity may have made some sense in the Cold War, when the US and USSR held off each other through the appropriately coined MAD (mutual assured destruction) doctrine, it no longer makes any sense in the post–Cold War era.

So are we heeding the voice of common sense in the field of nuclear weapons? There is good and bad news. The good news is that many leading global minds now realize the folly of accumulating nuclear weapons. The bad news is that, even though all thoughtful observers agree that the continued accumulation of nuclear weapons by humanity is sheer madness, the vested interests in key defense establishments in Washington and

Moscow, Islamabad and New Delhi, Tel Aviv and Pyongyang, cannot move away from their psychological reliance on nuclear weapons.

One of the wisest things that humanity at large can do is to create a stronger and stronger public consensus that we have to move slowly but steadily toward a nuclear-weapons-free world. In the past, this nuclear-free world was seen as an absurd, idealistic goal pursued by various kinds of fringe "peaceniks." But not anymore; now it makes sense.

When the final history of the nuclear weapons era is written (assuming humanity peacefully survives it), many tributes will be paid to four leading American statesmen who legitimized the idea of talking about a nuclear-free world in America and global dimensions: Henry Kissinger, Sam Nunn, William Perry, and George Schultz. They were known during the Cold War to be hardheaded and hard-line thinkers and policymakers. *New York Times* reporter Philip Taubman said in his book *Five Cold Warriors and Their Quest to Ban the Bomb* that when these statesmen broke ranks with other Cold Warriors and advocated nuclear disarmament, "it was roughly equivalent to John D. Rockefeller, Andrew Carnegie, J. P. Morgan and Jay Gould calling for the demise of capitalism."[30] (The fifth Cold Warrior mentioned in the book was renowned Stanford physicist Sidney Drell.)

After a meeting with policy experts to investigate safer, more comprehensive means of deterrence, these four men published an article to make the case against nuclear weapons. In part, they said:

> The doctrine of mutual assured destruction is obsolete in the post-Cold War era. . . .
>
> An unrestrained nuclear exchange between superpowers could destroy civilized life as we know it in days. . . .
>
> . . . With the spread of nuclear weapons, technology, materials and know-how, there is an increasing risk that nuclear weapons will be used. . . .
>
> For the United States and many other nations, existential threats relating to the very survival of the state have diminished, largely because of the end of the Cold War and the increasing realization that our common interests greatly exceed our differences. . . .
>
> Continued reliance on nuclear weapons as the principal element for deterrence is encouraging, or at least excusing, the spread of these

weapons, and will inevitably erode the essential cooperation necessary to avoid proliferation, protect nuclear materials and deal effectively with new threats. . . .

A world without nuclear weapons will not simply be today's world minus nuclear weapons.[31]

More recently, General James E. Cartwright, commander of American's nuclear forces from 2004 to 2007, was quoted in the *New York Times* in May 2012 saying that US nuclear deterrence could be guaranteed with a total arsenal of nine hundred warheads and with only half of them deployed at any one time. "The world has changed, but the current arsenal carries the baggage of the cold war," Cartwright remarked. "There is the baggage of significant numbers in reserve. There is the baggage of a nuclear stockpile beyond our needs. What is it we're really trying to deter? Our current arsenal does not address the threats of the 21st century."[32] Together with several senior national security figures, General Cartwright coauthored a global zero report on nuclear arms reduction. The others were Richard Burt, a former chief nuclear arms negotiator; Chuck Hagel, a former Republican senator from Nebraska; Thomas R. Pickering, a former ambassador to Russia; and General John J. Sheehan, who held senior NATO positions before retiring from active duty.[33] Civil society has also gotten involved. In October 2002, three Dominican nuns illegally entered an air force silo in Colorado that contained forty-nine nuclear warheads, each more destructive than the Hiroshima bomb. The nuns painted a cross on the silo in their own blood, hammered at the silo, conducted a liturgy, and were then arrested.[34]

American statesmen are not the only leaders advocating a world less reliant on nuclear weapons. Gareth Evans, a former foreign minister of Australia, has set up an influential group—the Asia-Pacific Leadership Network (APLN)—comprising thirty leading personalities from the Asia-Pacific countries, among them five former prime ministers and ten former foreign and defense ministers. I am a member too. At its first meeting in Japan in December 2011, APLN issued a statement that said, "We have joined together to support a nuclear weapons free world, believing that these weapons pose an existential threat to all nations and peoples."[35] The statement noted that recent statements challenging the utility of nuclear weapons provided "grounds of optimism" but concluded by saying that the momentum toward a nuclear-weapons-free world was "in danger of stalling."

If within in a decade or so, there is no serious reduction in nuclear arsenals and no new understanding among key policymakers that these weapons are both useless and dangerous, there will be real costs. In 2012, there was a lot of global press coverage on the Iranian nuclear issue, asking whether Israel or the US would attack Iranian nuclear sites and questioning the rationality of Iran's pursuit of its nuclear programs. Few noticed how ironic it was that Iran was accused of being "irrational" in trying to get nuclear weapons. In the world of nuclear weapons, we have actually created an "irrational" dynamic that treats nuclear nations as first-class powers and non-nuclear nations as second-class powers. Given this, it is perfectly "rational" for Iran to strive to get nuclear weapons, for Iranian leaders believe, rightly or wrongly, that Iran will finally be treated with respect only after it acquires or is *perceived* to have acquired a nuclear capability.

To persuade Iran to behave rationally on nuclear weapons, other nations should show the way by behaving rationally on nuclear weapons, demonstrating that the acquisition *or* modernization (and this is equally important) of nuclear weapons is a sunset industry. A world that is either devoid of nuclear weapons or is working toward eliminating them is an eminently achievable goal. Yet it is far from clear that we are moving in that direction anytime soon. The old nineteenth-century assumptions still cloud our ability to fashion new approaches to manage a new global situation appropriate to a new era.

The Dictatorial Power of the P5

The comparison that this chapter has made between the irrationality of reducing the UN budget while increasing expenditures on nuclear weapons may seem a little strong. Curiously, there is another connection between the five official nuclear powers (China, France, Russia, the UK, and the US) and the UN. These five powers are also the five permanent members (or P5) of the UN Security Council. In theory, they should act as the primary custodians of the UN system since they are literally and metaphorically kings upon the hill in the UN system. In practice, they have undermined the UN system. The real tragedy here is that they are undermining the legitimacy of the very organization that has given them a truly exalted status in the global system. In so doing, they also provide another powerful example of global irrationality that the world has to come to terms with.

The P5 clearly need a wake-up call. There was a major political eruption in 2011 that they should pay attention to because the lessons from it also apply to them. The Arab Spring blew across the Middle East and swept away leaders who had been in office collectively for 129 years: Zine al-Abidine Ben Ali of Tunisia and Husni Mubarak of Egypt, Muammar Gaddafi of Libya, and Ali Abdullah Saleh of Yemen.

The reactions of key Western capitals, including Washington, London, and Paris, were mixed. While all three lamented the loss of pro-Western dictators, especially Ben Ali and Mubarak, there was also some silent celebration, indeed even gloating, that the Arab Spring showed that the tide toward greater democracy and accountability in public institutions was nearly unstoppable. Hence, at the end of the day, Washington, London, and Paris were happy with the outcome. Of course, the Arab Spring was seen as a phenomenon that could happen over there but not over here. Let me suggest that Washington, London, and Paris engage in some deeper reflection as they too will experience some kind of Arab Spring over their international postures.

Why was Mubarak essentially overthrown? At the end of the day, he was overthrown because he saw himself as a supreme ruler who had a divine right to rule and who was not accountable to the people he claimed to be serving. In short, he was acting like a normal dictator. From time to time, some reformers in Egypt would urge him to open up the political and economic system. He steadfastly refused any kind of major political reform, causing political anger to build up over decades before it finally exploded. Clearly, it would have been better for Mubarak to allow and encourage minor reforms in order to defuse this anger against him.

Mubarak's lack of wisdom is now obvious. Ironically, there is a similar lack of wisdom in the capitals of the P5. They do not seem to be aware that in the global system they function like five dictators who steadfastly refuse to accept any kind of democratic accountability and transparency for their behavior in the UN system. Having served in the UN Security Council, I know how arbitrarily they exercise their power there and how steadfastly they refuse to change. This is why I wrote a chapter for a 2004 book warning that, while they would not lose their permanent seats in the council, they could progressively lose their global legitimacy if they did not intelligently adapt their behavior to demands for greater publicly demonstrated accountability and transparency.[36]

In 2012, the P5 were presented with a golden opportunity to demonstrate that they could support greater transparency and accountability. A group of five small nations (the S5)—Costa Rica, Jordan, Liechtenstein, Singapore, and Switzerland—proposed a resolution to be adopted by the UNGA to reform the *working methods* of the Security Council. I emphasize the phrase "working methods" to make the point that the S5 were not even questioning the P5's claim to "eternal" membership in the Security Council. They were only asking for a minimal improvement in the transparency of their working methods.

In concrete terms, the S5 made only one real request: that each time the P5 exercised their veto (and the S5 did *not* challenge their right to veto), they should "explain" the veto. The resolution called upon the P5 to do the following:

> 19. Explaining the reasons for resorting to a veto or declaring its intention to do so, in particular with regard to its consistency with the purposes and principles of the Charter of the United Nations and applicable international law. A copy of the explanation should be circulated as a separate Security Council document to all Members of the Organization.
>
> 20. Refraining from using a veto to block Council action aimed at preventing or ending genocide, war crimes and crimes against humanity.
>
> 21. Establishing a practice, in appropriate cases, of declaring, when casting a negative vote on a draft resolution before the Council, that such a negative vote shall not constitute a veto in the sense of Article 27, paragraph 3, of the Charter.[37]

This resolution was tabled for discussion in April and May 2012. In theory, the US should have supported the request for an explanation of its veto because Ambassador Susan Rice had reacted with fury to a February 2012 Russian and Chinese veto on a resolution condemning Bashar al-Assad's behavior in Syria. Using some strong language, she said the United States was "disgusted" and that the Security Council was being "held hostage by a couple of members."[38] "The international community must protect the Syrian people from this abhorrent brutality. But a couple members of this council remain steadfast in their willingness to sell out the Syrian people and shield a craven tyrant," adding, "Any further bloodshed that flows will be on their [Russia's and China's] hands."[39]

To prove to the Russians and Chinese that their views were not representative of the views of the broader international community, Rice tabled the same resolution (which had been vetoed by Russia and China) at the UN General Assembly. Her views were vindicated. This resolution received 137 votes in support and only 12 votes in opposition. Rice's message could not have been clearer: it was wrong of the Russians and Chinese to ignore the views of the international community when they vetoed Security Council resolutions.

Ambassador Rice's condemnation of the Russian and Chinese veto was in February. Hence, when the S5 resolution surfaced in April and called for greater public accountability of the use of the veto, Rice should have, in theory, supported this aspect of the S5 resolution. Instead, she reacted to the S5 resolution with the same fury that Mubarak displayed toward reformers in Egypt. She essentially told the S5 that the General Assembly had no business interfering in the work of the Security Council. Privately, she said that the council was superior to the assembly and hence not accountable to it. This was a strange statement to make since the UN Charter implies clearly that the accountability runs the other way.

Even though there had been a loud and public dispute among the P5 barely a few months earlier over the Russian and Chinese vetoes, all the P5 members reacted with total unity toward the S5 resolutions. There was absolutely no difference between the views of Western capitals (Washington, London, and Paris) and those of Moscow and Beijing regarding the S5 resolution. All five behaved equally as unelected dictators who did not tolerate any kind of democratic transparency or accountability for their actions. Using their combined political heft, they were able to crush the S5 resolution. Sadly, they were helped by nations such as Italy, Pakistan, and Argentina (who opposed Security Council reform to prevent the door opening for the entry of Germany, India, and Brazil) and by some African states that had adopted a politically unwise approach of all-or-nothing to any Security Council reform.

The absolute refusal of the P5 to brook even small reforms seems absurd in 2012. I do not know when the council equivalent of an Arab Spring will emerge to sweep away the legitimacy of the P5 in the global system. However, I have absolutely no doubt that a major political firestorm will break out in the next decade or two against the P5 if they continue to behave like Mubarak and refuse to accept any kind of even moderate reform. Sadly, the UN Secretariat Office of Legal Affairs (OLA) issued an opinion that the S5 resolution required a two-thirds majority before it could be adopted. It appears that the OLA was working behind the scenes with the P5 because, according to a reliable source, a P5 ambassador circulated the OLA opinion to all member states even before it was made public by the president of the UNGA.

A final anecdote will illustrate how opposed the P5 are to any kind of reform and how neurotic they can be about their supposed prerogatives. The Swiss ambassador to the United Nations, Paul Seger, served as the peace-building commissioner for Burundi. After briefing the council on Burundi (a fragile state), he asked whether he could sit in on the council's deliberations. The response of the Russian ambassador, Vitaly Churkin, was very telling: "No. We cannot open the council consultations to outsiders: it's never been done and it will never be done in the future."[40]

There have already been many warning signals that the P5 ignore global opinion at their peril. Hans Corell is a Swedish lawyer who served as under-secretary-general for legal affairs and the legal counsel of the UN for ten years, from 1994 to 2004. In December 2008, he proposed some modest reforms of the Security Council and warned members against violating international law. He explained, "My main concerns are that members of the Council sometimes violate the UN Charter and the tendency among some of its members to sometimes apply double standards and to manoeuvre looking to their own immediate interests rather than viewing things in a global and more long-term perspective. This does not meet the standards required by an international system based on the rule of law."[41]

Corell was always known to be a very courteous and temperate legal counsel, not prone to making any kinds of extreme statements. For him to openly call upon the Security Council not to ignore international law is a sign that a new "spring" is emerging that could sweep away the council.

Very few empires anticipate their demise. From the two-millennia-old Chinese imperial system, which vanished without a trace in the twentieth century, to the Soviet Union, which collapsed almost overnight, history is replete with examples of emperors with absolute power who could not conceive of the possibility of their extinction. The P5 should reread the famous poem "Ozymandias" by Percy Bysshe Shelley, which describes the fallen statue of Ozymandias (also known as Ramses II), a once-mighty Egyptian pharaoh:

> *And on the pedestal these words appear:*
> *"My name is Ozymandias, king of kings:*
> *Look on my works, ye Mighty, and despair!"*
> *Nothing beside remains. Round the decay*
> *Of that colossal wreck, boundless and bare*
> *The lone and level sands stretch far away.*[42]

This behavior of the P5 and other great powers suggests clearly that they are not aware that human history has altered fundamentally. Given that humanity at large is marching steadily and progressively up the "escalator of reason," it makes no sense to pursue policies that undermine the long-term interests of both the major powers and the rest of the world. The continuing efforts by the P5 to retain their absolute dictatorial power amounts to monumental folly. All such acts of global irrationality need to be fully understood and exposed.

Seven Global Contradictions

THE THEME OF THIS BOOK IS THE GREAT GLOBAL CONVERGENCE. THE subject of this chapter is global contradictions. How does one explain the clear dissonance between these two themes? A simple paradox may explain: convergence does create divergence.

As the 7 billion occupants of planet earth move inexorably and irresistibly toward living in a smaller and smaller global village, we are also creating a new phase of human history where societies and civilizations that used to exist in different pools of history are now being pushed together in close proximity. What used to be over there is now over here. Hence, new global contradictions are being created daily. At the same time, old fault lines, especially geopolitical fault lines, are finding a new resonance in an ever-shrinking global village.

Human history never moves forward smoothly or effortlessly. There are always bumps in the road or detours we have to navigate over and through. Hence, while I do wish to convey an optimistic message about the future in this book, I do want to tell the readers that there will be many disruptive events as we move ahead. Many of these disruptive events will be a result of the seven new and old global contradictions spelled out in this chapter. It is important to develop a deep understanding of these contradictions to grasp what is happening in the world around us. At the same time, as the conclusion of this chapter will try to demonstrate, there are complex trade-offs that policymakers will have to make between these contradictions. This is another reason why we have to understand them well.

Contradiction Number 1:
Global Interests Versus National Interests

This contradiction can be explained with a simple analogy. If we were passengers on a sinking Titanic, it would be absolutely foolish to rush down to save our cabins when the boat is sinking. If the boat sinks, our cabins will also sink. Hence, to save our cabins, we have to save the boat.

This is why this book began with the boat metaphor. In the past, when humanity lived in more than one hundred countries, it was like living in more than one hundred boats. All we needed were rules to ensure that the boats did not collide. Each boat had a captain or crew to take care of it. Today, with the shrinking of the world, 7 billion people live in 193 cabins on the same boat. We have captains and crews taking care of each cabin. But we have no captain or crew taking care of the boat as a whole.

This simple analogy explains well the contradiction between global interests and national interests. In our world of today, we have 193 governments working hard to protect their national interests. In so doing, they are protecting their cabins. However, it is equally important to protect the boat as a whole. But we have no established defender of global interests even though most of the new challenges are global in nature. Indeed, national governments that protect only their cabins on the boat cannot protect their populations from the perils that affect the boat as a whole: from global warming to global financial crises, from global pandemics to global terrorism. In short, whether we like it or not, we have to move toward creating institutions of global governance to protect global interests and deal with global crises.

One recent landmark event demonstrated what is needed to protect global interests. At the height of the 2008–2009 Western financial crisis, when the entire global economy appeared to be dying, the G-20 leaders met in London in April 2009 to try to rescue the proverbial global boat. And they succeeded. In so doing, they demonstrated clearly and powerfully that global institutions and processes are needed to deal with a rising tide of global challenges.

Sadly, as soon as the crisis was over, the G-20 governments retreated back into their own cabins and ignored global challenges. There was no one at the wheel. This behavior explained the failure of the subsequent G-20 meetings in Pittsburgh (September 24–25, 2009), Toronto (June 26–27, 2010), Seoul (November 11–12, 2010), Cannes (November 3–4, 2011), and Los Cabos (June 18–19, 2012). The rhetoric remained lofty, but the accomplishments were negligible.

Nobel laureate Joseph Stiglitz has explained well why G-20 meetings do not work. In his book *Freefall*, he says, "The G-20 has proposed a coordinated macroeconomics response—the United States increase its savings and Chinese reduce its—so that imbalances will be reduced in a way that maintains a strong global economy. The aspiration is noble, but each country's policies are likely to be driven by its own domestic agenda."[1] Governments are elected to take care of their national cabins, not of the boat as a whole. When any government has to make a choice between the short-term needs of the population within its cabin and the long-term requirements of maintaining a stable global order, the needs of the cabin will trump the needs of the boat. It is a major global contradiction that we will have to resolve. And if we do not resolve it soon, we will generate turbulence in the global order for decades to come.

Contradiction Number 2: The West Versus the Rest

The West provides only 12 percent of the world's population. The "Rest" provides 88 percent. If we were striving for a just, legitimate, and democratic global order, we would strive to ensure that the voices and interests of each human being are represented equally well in key global institutions. This is what all Western societies try to achieve domestically. Yet in the global order, the Western societies are doing the exact opposite. They insist on having a larger voice and a larger share of global power than their share of the global population would merit. This will, quite naturally, create a contradiction between the West and the Rest.

Three key institutions illustrate well how the West is severely over-represented in global institutions. The UN Security Council has, in theory, fifteen members. Yet as this book will document in Chapter 7, the UNSC is effectively dominated by the five permanent members: China, France,

Russia, the UK, and the US. Out of these five, three are from the West: France, the UK, and the US. In short, 12 percent of the population controls 60 percent of the most important seats in the most powerful international organization, the UNSC. Equally importantly, the West also dominates both the IMF and the World Bank. Here, the 12 percent of the world's population controls more than 50 percent of the votes of these two organizations. Even more perniciously, the West has insisted from the very beginning of the creation of these two organizations that the head of the IMF can only be a European and the head of the World Bank an American. Despite espousing rhetoric that the Western countries are ready to give up their domination of these two bodies, they effectively refuse to do so in practice.

Look at what happened in May 2011: on May 14, Dominique Strauss-Kahn, the head of the IMF, was arrested, handcuffed, and incarcerated on the basis of an accusation that he had sexually assaulted and attempted to rape a chambermaid in his hotel room. A few days later, on May 18, as a result of considerable political pressure, Strauss-Kahn resigned. Within a few days, the French government nominated Christine Lagarde, the French minister of economic affairs, to replace him, and on June 28, 2011, she was elected by the IMF to the post.

No better word can describe this episode than "chutzpah." The French leader of the IMF, Strauss-Kahn, had obviously disgraced himself and the leadership of the institution. Although the charges against him were later withdrawn and Strauss-Kahn resigned, the appropriate response of the French *and* other European governments should have been to apologize and widen the candidacy for a vital global institution. Instead, the European governments did the exact opposite. Dutch finance minister Jan Kees de Jager said Lagarde was "outstandingly suitable" to succeed Strauss-Kahn. Several other European governments, including Germany and Britain, quickly supported Lagarde too, making her the "frontrunner" for the job.[2]

There was no contrition or remorse on the part of the French or other Europeans over Strauss-Kahn's behavior. Instead, with astonishing hubris, they sought to retain control of the IMF. To add insult to injury, some Europeans actually argued that since the main crisis that the IMF was then engaged in was the European financial crisis, the leader of the IMF should remain European. If at the height of either the Latin American or Asian financial crises, anyone had argued that the head of the IMF should have been a Latin American or Asian, the Europeans would have guffawed. As the *FT* columnist Martin Wolf puts it, "The claim traditionally made by advanced countries is that their nationals should run international organizations, because they are relatively competent. Today's European disarray is, the critics note, a disproof of this proposition."[3]

Against this backdrop, how did Christine Lagarde win the democratic election to the IMF position? The answer is simple: the elections were rigged. The West's combined voting share in the IMF is more than 50 percent. The EU has 32 percent, the US has almost 17 percent, and Australia, Canada, and New Zealand combined have around 4 percent.[4] Hence, even if the rest of the world had produced a better candidate, it would have been mathematically impossible for the candidate of non-Western countries to win the election since they had less than 50 percent of the voting share of the IMF.

The only way to understand the reluctance of the West to give up its domination of global institutions is to compare it to the reluctance of reigning monarchs or dictators to give up their absolute powers. Ironically, French history provides the best illustration of what can go wrong when a ruling monarch refuses to share power. Against this historical backdrop, we should not once again be surprised if this profound Western reluctance to give up its domination of global institutions leads to global turbulence. Rulers who stay on long after their time has run out inevitably lose political legitimacy. The same is going to happen to all the global institutions dominated by the West, from the IMF to the World Bank, from the UN Security Council to the G-20. Charles Grant has described well this European over-representation:

> The London G20 summit in April 2009 highlighted a key factor that undermines the EU's credibility: it is over-represented in virtually every international institution. At the G20, in addition to the countries that are formally members (Britain, France, Germany and Italy), the EU was represented by the [European] Commission, the Czech Republic (as EU president), Spain and the Netherlands, not to mention the heads of the World Trade Organization, the International Monetary Fund and the Financial Stability Forum, who are also European. The surfeit of Europeans is even more evident at G8 meetings, when six Europeans (including the

EU presidency and the Commission president) sit beside the US, Canada, Japan and Russia. One reason why the "quartet," which is supposed to manage the Middle East peace process, is not more effective is that it is in fact a sextet. Alongside the UN, the US and Russia, the EU often has three representatives: Solana, the commissioner for external relations and the rotating presidency. The EU is similarly over-represented in many other international organizations.[5]

This European over-representation is not confined to a few international organizations, like the IMF and the World Bank. It permeates the international system. For example, in the International Olympic Council, 47 out of 106 members are European. However, even in sports organizations, things are beginning to change, as demonstrated by the International Cricket Council (ICC). The ICC was founded in 1909 by England, Australia, and South Africa as the Imperial Cricket Conference and was originally open only to countries under the British Empire. It was renamed the International Cricket Council in 1965 and was opened to all countries, though ICC governance was still dominated by England. The president of the famed Marylebone Cricket Club (MCC) also presided over the ICC, and the MCC secretary was also the ICC secretary. After South Africa's withdrawal in 1961, England and Australia enjoyed founding member status, meaning that any changes to the ICC membership or organization had to be approved by both countries. In 1993, with the ascendance of Asian cricket, England and Australia lost their veto power, allowing for a more democratic ICC. That same year, Sir Clyde Walcott from Barbados was elected as the first nonwhite, non-British ICC chairman.[6]

What has happened to the ICC in the past decade or so may provide a foretaste of things to come. It was assumed that London would never give up its control over the ICC. Then the advertising market for cricket shifted dramatically from the UK and Australia to South Asia, especially India. Since India had the biggest audience for cricket, it saw no reason to adhere to a cricketing organization controlled by the British. The shift of economic power in the field led inevitably to a shift of the political control. As the share of the West in both the global population and global GNP shrinks steadily, the West will inevitably have to learn to share power in global institutions, as it has with the ICC.

Contradiction Number 3: The World's Greatest Power Versus the World's Greatest Emerging Power

This is not a new contradiction. Since the dawn of geopolitics, there has always been tension between the world's greatest power and the world's greatest emerging power. No great power likes to cede its number one spot. One of the few times the number one power ceded its position to the number two power peacefully was when Great Britain allowed the United States to take the number one position in the late nineteenth century. Many books have been written on why this transition happened peacefully. One reason was that one Anglo-Saxon power was giving way to another.

Today, the situation is almost the exact opposite of this British-American transition. The number one power is America, a Western power. The number two power rapidly catching up on number one is China, an Asian power. Indeed, if and when China becomes the number one power in the next decade or two, it will be the first time in two centuries that a non-Western power has emerged as number one.

The logic of history tells us that such power transitions do not happen peacefully. Indeed, we should expect to see a rising level of tension as America worries more and more about losing its primacy to China. It would have been quite natural to see America carrying out various moves to thwart the rise of China. That's how America faced the Soviet Union. So why isn't this happening? Indeed, why are we seeing an unnatural degree of geopolitical calm between the world's greatest power and the world's greatest emerging power?

It would be virtually impossible to get Beijing and Washington to agree on the answers to these natural questions. There are two distinct and sometimes competing narratives in the two capitals. The view in China is that the calm in Sino-American relations is a result of the extraordinary patience and forbearance shown by China. Chinese leaders believe that they have followed the wise advice of Deng Xiaoping and decided not to challenge American leadership in any way or in any area. And when China felt that it was directly provoked, it also followed Deng's advice and swallowed its humiliation. Few Americans remember any instances of provocation. Chinese leaders remember many. In May 1999, during the NATO bombing of Yugoslavia, an American plane bombed the Chinese Embassy in Belgrade. America apologized for this "mistake," but no Chinese leader believed it was a mistake.[7] Similarly, a Chinese fighter jet was downed when it crashed into an American spy plane near Hainan Island, China, in April 2001. Here, too, China felt humiliated. In Chapter 5, I will describe in detail the great humiliation Premier Zhu Rongji suffered in April 1999 when he went to Washington, DC, to negotiate China's entry into the WTO. Hence, in the leading Chinese minds, there has developed a great conviction that China has been responsible for the low tension in the US-China relations because China has swallowed bitter humiliation time and again. Indeed this is what the great Chinese leader Deng Xiaoping advised China to do. The Chinese are also quietly aware that the geopolitical incompetence of America has helped them a lot, but they are wise enough not to trumpet this. China has shown a careful long-term strategy of emerging peacefully without ruffling feathers and, with the exception of a few mistakes that will also be documented in this volume, successfully executed its strategy.

The view in Washington is almost exactly the opposite. Few Americans believe that China has been able to rise peacefully because of China's geopolitical acumen or America's geopolitical mistakes. Instead, the prevailing view in Washington is that America has been remarkably generous to China and allowed it to emerge peacefully because America is an inherently generous country. There can be no denying that America has been generous to China in many real ways: allowing China's accession to the World Trade Organization (WTO) (under stiff conditions, it must be emphasized, but stiff conditions that ironically benefited China); allowing China to enjoy massive trade surpluses; allowing China to join the Asia-Pacific Economic Cooperation (APEC); and, perhaps most importantly of all, allowing hundreds of thousands of Chinese students to study in American universities. These are generous acts.

But it is also true that America allowed China to rise because it was so supremely self-confident that it would always remain number one. China's benign rise was a result of American neglect, not a result of any long-term strategy. China acted strategically; America did not. I can speak about this from personal experience. In February 2009, Hillary Clinton visited China on her first overseas visit as US secretary of state. I wrote at the time:

There's little evidence Clinton has engaged in any serious strategic think-ing about U.S.-China relations. If she had, she would have asked some big questions. Traditionally, relations between dominant powers and emerging powers have been tense. This should have been the norm with China and the United States. Yet China has emerged without alarming Americans. That's close to a geopolitical miracle. Who deserves credit for it? Beijing or Washington? China seems to have a clear, comprehensive strategy. The United States has none.[8]

Officials in DC reacted angrily to this column. A senior official at the National Security Council (NSC), Jeff Bader, called up the Singapore Em-bassy in Washington to complain. I was puzzled by this complaint on three counts. First, Jeff Bader was a friend of mine with whom I had worked at the UN. Why didn't he call me directly? Second, America believes in free speech and the marketplace of ideas. So why was it trying to censor an ac-ademic like me? Third, I was trying to help America by suggesting that a clear long-term strategy was needed to manage the rise of China. How was that unhelpful to America? But I learned a valuable lesson from Jeff Bader's protest: when it comes to geopolitical issues, great power interests trump great power values, including values of free speech.

I also tell this story about the NSC protest over a single column to il-lustrate how sensitive the establishment in Washington has become to any discussion on the nature of Sino-American relations. The real truth about this relationship is that, while there is a lot of calm on the surface, tension is brewing below. I am convinced that there is a lot of simmering anger in China about the country being pushed around callously by Washington. Similarly, the tolerance for any criticism of the US-China relationship is very low in Washington. Two distinguished scholars from China and America, Wang Jisi and Ken Lieberthal, may have done both countries a favor by pointing out how fragile the relationship has become. In a report issued in March 2012, they said:

Both Beijing and Washington seek to build a constructive partnership for the long run. U.S.-China relations are, moreover, mature. The two sides un-derstand well each other's position on all major issues and deal with each other extensively. . . . This history and these extensive activities have not, however, produced trust regarding long-term intentions on either side, and arguably the problem of lack of such trust is becoming more serious. Distrust is itself corrosive, producing attitudes and actions that themselves contribute to greater distrust. Distrust itself makes it difficult for leaders on each side to be confident they understand the deep thinking among leaders on the other side regarding the future U.S.-China relationship.[9]

Given the many simmering tensions, it would be unwise to assume smooth sailing ahead for America and China in their geopolitical relationship. The need for the US and China to cooperate is therefore rising each day. Yet the potential for a major US-China misunderstanding is rising as well. In November 2011, Secretary of State Hillary Clinton announced loudly and boldly a "pivot" to Asia, signifying a turning point in American foreign policy that would reduce the focus on the Middle East and shift it to Asia.[10] The Obama administration did not say that this was America's response to a rising China, but the whole rest of the world, including China, saw it as such. Other nations saw it as a clear signal that Sino-American geopolitical competition was heating up. The logical consequence is therefore not difficult to figure out. We should be prepared for global turbulence if the US-China relationship follows the millennial old patterns and no longer remains on an even keel.

Contradiction Number 4:
Expanding China Versus a Shrinking World

The fourth global contradiction is between an expanding China and a shrinking world. In January 2010, I had the pleasure of attending a small private dinner in Singapore with a senior Chinese figure on foreign affairs. What I told him in private is what I have written publicly: that China should prepare itself for greater difficulties in its relations with the rest of the world. He asked why. I borrowed Kofi Annan's metaphor about the global village to point out two major changes: the global village was shrinking rapidly, yet in its middle one home was getting bigger and bigger. That home was China. It was inevitable that the 5.7 billion people who lived outside China in this global village would feel squeezed between a rapidly expanding China and a rapidly shrinking global village.

To illustrate my point, I provided several examples from different parts of the world. I mentioned that I had visited Suriname, a tiny country in Latin America, a few months earlier. Traditionally, there had been very few Chinese living in Suriname. However, in recent years there had been an explosion of Chinese migrants to Suriname. China's embassy put the number at about 40,000, nearly 10 percent of the entire Suriname population, including legal and illegal migrants.[11] This sudden upsurge of Chinese migrants, which had also resulted from an increase of Chinese dealings with Latin America, had naturally led to political resistance to the Chinese presence in Suriname. Suriname was not the only country to be affected in this way. Several other Latin American countries had seen a similar increase in the Chinese presence.

Around that time, several news reports had also surfaced of difficulties between Chinese companies and the populations that hosted them in other parts of the world. The most dramatic was the case of Zambian miners who had gone on strike over the wage and living conditions in Chinese-owned copper mines in 2006 and 2008. The issue proved to be a political opportunity in the 2006 Zambian general election. Opposition leader Michael Sata capitalized on workers' resentment of the Chinese presence to muster votes, even publicly calling for the recognition of Taiwan, which China maintains is a renegade province. Though Sata lost the national election, he produced wins in Lusaka and Copperbelt, two prosperous provinces where there were significant numbers of Chinese. He said, "[The] Chinese don't bring in any equipment or create any sensible employment. In fact, to every Zambian in a Chinese company, there are about 15 Chinese. I have done my intelligence research and it is devastating to know that all Chinese companies are paying an average of $50 per month to Zambian employees."[12] Several other African leaders had also expressed concern over the nature of the growing Chinese presence in Africa. Bagudu Hirse, the minister of state for foreign affairs for Nigeria, the biggest country in Africa, said this: "We accept what China is doing and we welcome their investment, but they must understand that we are very sensitive to good governance and democracy. We cannot start thinking of imposing sanctions on Guinea or Niger for bad governance, and then China goes behind us and strikes some other deals. We suspect that they do that anyway. China will never confirm it but we read the newspapers and we know what is going on."[13]

Another criticism came from Egypt, traditionally the most important country in the Arab world. Mustafa al-Gindi, an independent member of parliament, remarked, "Whatever they say, it is a fact that the Chinese come to Africa not just with engineers and scientists, they are coming with farmers, it is neo-colonialism, there are no ethics, no values from the Chinese."[14] The foreign minister of Libya, Musa Kusa, was equally critical: "When we look at the reality on the ground we find that there is something akin to a Chinese invasion of the African continent. This is something that brings to mind the effects that colonialism had on the African continent. Therefore we advise our Chinese friends not to follow in this direction—bringing thousands of Chinese workers to Africa under the pretext of employment, for at the same time Africa is suffering from unemployment."[15]

Difficulties between China and the West could have been predicted. There has been a long and troubled history between China and the West since the nineteenth century. By contrast, China has traditionally enjoyed good relations with Africa and Latin America. At the height of its power, China did not colonize Africa. In the fifteenth century, Admiral Zheng He sailed around the Horn of Africa and followed the coast down to the Mozambique Channel, aiming to signal Chinese strength. He brought gifts and granted titles from the Ming emperor to the local rulers, with the aim of establishing a large number of tributary states. In his seven naval expeditions, carried out between 1405 and 1433, Admiral Zheng's fleets visited Arabia, Brunei, East Africa, India, Maritime Southeast Asia, and Thailand, dispensing and receiving goods along the way. Zheng He distributed gold, silver, porcelain, and silk; in return, China received such novelties as ostriches, zebras, camels, ivory, and a giraffe. Moreover, throughout history, Africans traveled to China. One of the most famous, Moroccan traveler and scholar Ibn Battuta, reached China in April 1345.[16] He wrote of that country, "China is the safest, best regulated of countries for a traveler. A man may go by himself on a nine-month journey, carrying with him a large sum of money, without any fear. Silk is used for clothing even by poor monks and beggars. Its porcelains are the finest of all makes of pottery and its hens are bigger than geese in our country."[17]

Unlike the traditional adversarial history between the West and the Rest, there is no such adversarial history between China and the rest of the world. This is why China needs to reflect deeply about the implications of the discontent at Chinese presence around the world. Even if all the overseas Chinese officials and businesses behaved impeccably and correctly, this sudden upsurge in the Chinese presence is bound to lead to an inevitable rise of resentment.

However, given the size of the overseas Chinese presence, it is practically impossible for all the Chinese officials and businesses to behave impeccably. Mistakes will be made. And with the growing importance and impact of the Chinese economy, it is not just the physical presence of the Chinese overseas that will lead to resentment. The sheer impact of the Chinese economy can also be enormous. Interestingly, even though China has been cooperating actively with Brazil in the new BRICS format, there have been a lot of critical statements by Brazilian officials about China's economic performance, especially on the valuation of its currency.

In March 2012, Brazil's finance minister, Guido Mantega, warned that Brazil would not "sit idle in the face of the currency war. . . . We have, and we are ready to use a whole arsenal to prevent or neutralize the excessive appreciation of our currency," referring to the flurry of capital controls imposed this year to repel foreign capital. His comments echoed those of a top IMF official who singled out China as a principal culprit in causing destabilizing capital flows. Nicholas Eyzaguirre, the IMF's Western Hemisphere director, said China's closed capital account and managed currency were responsible for export-damaging currency appreciation and global distortions. "There is a correlation [between] the fact that China pegs its currency and pressures on the exchange rate of Brazil or Peru," Eyzaguirre said.[18]

Arvind Subramaniam, a senior fellow at the Peterson Institute for International Economics, also warned in a *Financial Times* article in April 2012 that "China poses competitive problems for other developing countries, because it is these countries that are China's main competitors. In recent research with Aaditya Mattoo of the World Bank and Prachi Mishra of the IMF, we show that China's exchange rate has a substantial effect on the exports of other developing countries that compete with China in third-country markets. For example, a 10 per cent appreciation of the renminbi could increase exports of competitors by between 2 and 6 per cent." Advocating reform, he noted that "about a decade ago, Mr Zhu shrewdly used accession to the WTO as a way of furthering domestic and external liberalisation, often against public and political opinion. Today's reformers can similarly harness the lever of international co-operation to help liberalise China's exchange rate and financial sector policies."[19]

Overall, China has been remarkably competent geopolitically, but it is not immune to mistakes, as it showed in 2010 and 2011. It completely mishandled an episode in which a Chinese fishing boat collided with Japanese Coast Guard patrols near the disputed Senkaku Islands on September 7, 2010, an error that could potentially set back Sino-Japanese relations for several decades.[20] It was unwise for China to demand an apology from Japan after having publicly humiliated Japan into releasing the fishing boat. This further angered Japan.

Similarly, China also mishandled the Korean crisis of 2010. In November 2010, North Korean artillery shelled the South Korean island of Yeonpyeong and killed two South Korean civilians as well as two South Korean Marines. North Korea has had a long track record of taking aggressive, reckless actions. The main restraining force on North Korea has been China, and, to be fair, China's overall record has not been bad. But after the artillery shelling, China did not condemn North Korea's actions. One of the biggest diplomatic coups for China in recent decades was its ability to establish diplomatic relations in 1992 with South Korea, a defense ally of the US. Indeed, relations between China and South Korea have blossomed, with trade rising from US $5 billion in 1992 to US $186 billion in 2008.[21] Against this backdrop, the South Koreans were clearly disappointed with China. To signal their displeasure, the South Korean government decided to send its ambassador in Oslo to attend the Nobel Peace Prize ceremony for Chinese dissident Liu Xiaobo in December 2010, even though the Chinese government had strongly lobbied the South Korean government not to do so.

To make matters worse, China began to make more aggressive statements and take more aggressive postures on the South China Sea in 2010 and 2011. China published a map of the South China Sea with dotted lines that seemed to show that China claimed around 80 percent of the sea (see Figure 4.1). When China submitted to the UN Commission on the Limits of the Continental Shelf a map including the nine-dotted-lines territorial claim in the South China Sea on May 7, 2009, the Philippines lodged a diplomatic protest against China. Vietnam and Malaysia followed. In-

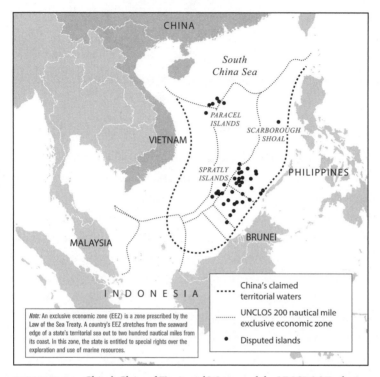

FIGURE 4.1   China's Claimed Territorial Waters and the UNCLOS Exclusive Economic Zone. *Source:* Based on http://newsimg.bbc.co.uk/media/images /45552000/gif/_45552694_south_china-sea_466.gif and data from UNCLOS and the CIA.

donesia also registered a protest, although it had no claims on the South China Sea. In the face of this opposition, Chinese officials refused to back down. In March 2010, they told US officials that they considered the South China Sea to be a "core interest" on a par with Taiwan, Tibet, and Xinjiang.[22] In July 2010, an editorial in the *Global Times* stated, "China will never waive its right to protect its core interest with military means."[23] The same month, a Chinese Ministry of Defense spokesman said that "China has indisputable sovereignty of the South Sea and China has sufficient historical and legal backing" to underpin its claims.[24]

All these aggressive Chinese postures on the South China Sea created a geopolitical opportunity for America, to which China reacted angrily. This was understandable. But such immediate angry responses also had to be followed by more thoughtful reflections by China on where it had gone wrong.

China will have to work very hard to keep its relations with the rest of the world on an even keel. And if it does not, it should not be surprised if its adversaries and competitors seize the advantages provided by China's mistakes in handling the impact of China's rise on the rest of the world.

Contradiction Number 5: Islam Versus the West

The fifth major global contradiction is between Islam and the West. It may well be the most dangerous. Since the tensions between America and China are geopolitical they can be managed or resolved through rational discourse or rational actions. While there are misunderstandings created by cultural differences, there is no clash of religious views or values involved. Indeed, one of the most surprising developments of recent times is how much the Chinese admire and respect Western civilization. More amazingly, the Chinese (whose music is so very different from Western classical music) have fallen in love with Western classical music. Thousands of young Chinese are studying the violin, the piano, the harp, and the cello. And they are flooding Western orchestras with new talent. In short, there is not even a whiff of a clash of civilizations between China and the West. Samuel Huntington was wrong here.

By contrast, there is more than a hint, indeed a very strong hint, of a real clash of civilizations between Islam and the West. Even though the West and Islam, especially Europe and North Africa, live together in close proximity, there is a growing gap in understanding between these two civilizations. These two societies seem to be sailing past each other, traveling in opposite directions, and staring at each other with mutual incomprehension. The sources of misunderstanding are many.

The first is historical. Both sides have cultural memories of the Crusades. And there is no doubt that both sides have completely different narratives of the same events. In Western mythology, brave Christian knights traveled long distances to save the Holy Land from the infidels. They fought courageously. The Muslim narrative is one of defending holy Islamic territory from marauding bands of uncivilized Western barbarians who raped and looted wherever they went. The facts hardly matter anymore. When the myths are so deeply imprinted in both cultures, they are not going to be gainsaid by facts, even if these could be unequivocally established. For instance, few in the West remember how Cordoba was reclaimed from the Moors. By contrast, Osama bin Laden consistently referred to it to reignite Islamic passions. If this myth had no resonance in the Islamic world, he could not have used it.

The second source of misunderstanding is religious. That Christianity and Islam are different religions is obvious. What is less obvious is that most Christian societies, with the possible exception of America, are becoming more secular, whereas most Islamic societies are becoming more religious. I have seen this firsthand in Islamic societies in Southeast Asia. Until a few decades ago, few Islamic women in Malaysia or Indonesia wore the hijab. Now many more do. The same trend can be seen in Egypt or Turkey. The declining religiosity of the West and the rising religiosity of the Islamic world are a potentially significant source of misunderstanding. In the secular society of Denmark, for instance, where any religious figure can be made an object of satire, it seemed perfectly natural and civilized to draw a cartoon of the Prophet Muhammad. In the Islamic world, Denmark was encouraging blasphemy, hence the explosion of anger there. It was a classic case of mutual incomprehension.

When the Arab Spring protests erupted in January 2011, the Western world celebrated the burst of freedom in Egypt and Tunisia. They naturally expected that with freedom, the Egyptian and Tunisians would naturally elect modern secular parties, similar to those in the West. Instead, political Islam emerged powerfully. Why? These parties captured better the hopes and aspirations of the Egyptian and Tunisian people. They need not portend reactionary behavior: political parties based on political Islam can modernize their societies, as demonstrated by the Justice and Development Party (AKP) in Turkey. As long as modernization is not perceived to be Westernization, political Islam can push for modernization. But an acceptance of modernization coupled with a rejection of Westernization in the Islamic world baffles many in the West.

The third source of misunderstanding is psychological. Both sides feel a deep sense of victimhood. Both sides are unaware of the depths of the other's feelings. Muslims feel victimized because for two centuries and more until the late 1940s, virtually all Islamic countries, stretching from Morocco in the West to Indonesia in the East, were colonized. Even after decolonization, Western power trampled over all their interests. The ongoing inability of 1.3 billion Muslims to liberate the West Bank and Gaza from Israel sticks like a very painful bone in their throats. It is immensely humiliating. The sense of victimhood is only increased by the knowledge that during the last decade Western bombs have fallen only on Muslim populations.

By contrast, especially since 9/11, the West has developed its own powerful narrative of victimhood. Many Americans believe that 9/11 was a completely irrational attack on innocent civilians by dangerous Islamic terrorists. The subsequent attacks in Madrid on March 11, 2004, and in London on July 7, 2005, only reinforced the Western belief that fanatical Islamists want to destroy Western civilization. The average American and the average European believe "We do the Muslims no harm. Why are they killing us, especially killing innocent people?" The West feels itself the unjustly aggrieved victim of several horrendous attacks.

I am not a Muslim or a Westerner, though I have known many of both. My mother was almost killed by a Muslim mob when she fled during the partition of India and Pakistan in 1947. But was she most at risk from Pakistani Muslims or the effects of Western colonialism? Clearly, both aspects combined to threaten her life. Her example reminds me personally how dangerous the divide has become between the West and Islam.

In the next chapter, I will discuss some potential solutions to the contradictions spelled out in this one, including between Islam and the West. They require political and moral courage from Western politicians. I say Western politicians because at this point the Western world is far more powerful in economic, political, cultural, and military terms than the Islamic world. The stronger must show magnanimity and wisdom toward the weaker.

Contradiction Number 6:
Global Environment Versus Global Consumer

The sixth contradiction is between the global environment and the global consumer. Two completely contradictory trends are emerging in the world. There is a growing global consensus that humanity is now seriously threatening the fragile environment of our planet. Global warming is the most obvious threat, but the global environment is being threatened in many other dimensions: rainforests, fishery stocks, water supply, to name just a few. All over the world, there is now a growing awareness that we all need to work together to save our planet. The 2010 Seoul G-20 leaders communiqué, which is supposed to represent the views of twenty of the most powerful nations in the world, summarized this outlook well: "Addressing the threat of global climate change is an urgent priority for all nations. We reiterate our commitment to take strong and action-oriented measures and remain fully dedicated to UN climate change negotiations."[25]

Similarly, at the conclusion of the 2005 UN summit, the General Assembly passed a resolution that summarized this outlook well:

> We recognize that climate change is a serious and long-term challenge that has the potential to affect every part of the globe. We emphasize the need to meet all the commitments and obligations we have undertaken in the United Nations Framework Convention on Climate Change. . . . We acknowledge that the global nature of climate change calls for the widest possible cooperation and participation in an effective and appropriate international response, in accordance with the principles of the Convention. We are committed to moving forward the global discussion on long-term cooperative action to address climate change, in accordance with these principles.[26]

Both the G-20 communiqué and the General Assembly summit resolution should demonstrate a high degree of global consensus that global warming needs to be addressed. So far, so good.

The other piece of good news is that hundreds of millions of people are being rescued from poverty. The global middle classes are exploding, especially in Asia. As the previous chapter documented, the number of people in the middle class has increased from several hundred million in 1990 to approximately 1.8 billion in 2010, and it is projected to increase to 4.8 billion by 2050.[27] All those new entrants into the global middle class are going to become major global consumers. They will demand regular electricity supplies, purchase all kinds of "white goods" (refrigerators, washing machines) and cars, and travel more frequently. Their carbon footprints will leave very deep impressions.

The Chinese middle class has undergone a massive expansion in the past twenty years, growing from 174 million people to more than 800 million. Though China is the standout case, the ranks of the middle class are swelling all across the major emerging economies of the world. The Indian middle class grew from 147 million in 1990 to 264 million in 2009. The Latin American and Caribbean middle class has expanded by 84 million people and in the Middle East and Africa by more than 150 million.[28] The US National Intelligence Council projects that the global middle class will encompass 2 billion people in 2030, doubling in size from 2012.[29]

The paradox the world faces now is that the combination of these two pieces of good news—awareness of environmental vulnerability and a growing middle class—contains a danger. We cannot have both global public goods. We can either take care of our planet, or we can rapidly expand our global middle classes. But which? It is ethical to save our planet. It is equally ethical to elevate people from poverty. Look at India, for example. Even with all the development in India, there are still 400 million people who live without electricity.[30] In today's world, electricity is a necessity, not a luxury. To provide these 400 million people with electricity, India will have to build many more power plants to make up for a shortfall in its energy production of almost 10 percent. A McKinsey survey has projected that this shortfall will rise to 25 percent by 2017. In other words, only 75 percent of all demand for electricity will be met.[31] Most of these new power plants will be coal fired. No Indian politician would survive if he were to argue against power plants. Jairam Ramesh, the minister of rural development, has captured well the Indian dilemma. "The paradox of economic growth is that ecological devastation benefits one section of society," Ramesh says. "On the environment, the track record of Indian industry is not much to write home about." As it stands, the corporations and the wealthy of India are reaping financial dividends on the destruction of the environment, while the poor bear most of the burden but do not experience any of the rewards.[32]

The only ethical solution is to spread the burden equitably throughout the world, with the rich populations bearing the most sacrifice. It is clearly ethically wrong to deny a poor Indian access to electricity while allowing an average middle-class American family to maintain two SUVs. The carbon footprint of each American is more than twelve times higher than the carbon footprint of each Indian.[33] We should start with the wealthiest citizens. Here, quite amazingly, there is a simple $1 solution that would help the world enormously. If the US could levy a $1-a-gallon tax on gasoline consumption, it would reduce American consumption significantly. The revenues from the tax could be invested in green technology to further reduce the carbon footprint of the average American. In short, solutions are available. Sadly, they remain politically out of reach.

This is why Al Gore should seriously consider returning his Nobel Peace Prize to the Norwegian Nobel Committee. While he has done a great job of educating the world on global warming, he has been unable to make even a minor dent on the American political system in trying to persuade it to do something reasonable to save the planet. Not one American politician dares to echo his call for a $1-a-gallon tax. Moreover, America still has not ratified the Kyoto Protocol. Al Gore could make a truly noble gesture of offering to return the Nobel Peace Prize to draw attention to his country's failure to make equitable sacrifices to save our global environment. That is the inconvenient truth.

Until America changes course, the moral burden of saving the planet is being passed on to the newly emerging middle classes in Africa, Asia, and Latin America. So far there has been no real outrage there because they have not yet been asked to make sacrifices. But if and when they are asked to do so, the global contradiction between the need to save our planet and the desire of the new middle classes to improve their lives will emerge sharply.

Contradiction Number 7: Governments Versus Nongovernmental Organizations

The seventh major global contradiction is between state and nonstate actors on the world stage. In theory, international life is driven by national governments. In practice, nongovernmental organizations and forces, in various stages and forms, are also driving international life across the world. They are influencing, in a powerful fashion, norms, perceptions, and practices that travel all around the world.

In the area of norms defining which actions are legitimate or illegitimate, the NGOs have had a major impact. In theory, what countries do within their own territories are their own "internal" affairs. The UN Charter, the defining document of international affairs, has also made the principle of noninterference in internal affairs sacrosanct. "Nothing contained in the present Charter shall authorize the United Nations to intervene in matters which are essentially within the domestic jurisdiction of any state."[34]

However, in many areas, this principle of noninterference in internal affairs has been undermined by NGOs. The area of human rights, for example, has been completely transformed by global human rights organizations such as Amnesty International and Human Rights Watch. Countries do not have to respond to negative reports by these international NGOs, but they ignore them at their peril.

The work of these human rights NGOs has also been supplemented by the work of other nongovernmental networks. In *A New World Order*, Anne-Marie Slaughter describes how lawyers and judges, accountants and bankers, have developed borderless global networks by regularly working with each other. Although global governance is traditionally perceived as the result of states pursuing national interests, Slaughter argues that global governance manifests itself in the decentralized, and less visible, activities of judges, regulators, and legislators working with foreign counterparts and NGOs on specific issues. In response to the question of how to make these networks accountable, she suggests that norms of inclusiveness and transparency can help make them responsive to the public will.[35]

From time to time, the texture of international life has changed in the face of opposition from national governments. In theory, if the governments of, say, the US, China, and Russia opposed an international convention, the international convention would not materialize. But this is exactly what did *not* happen with the Convention on the Prohibition of the Use, Stockpiling, Production and Transfer of Anti-Personnel Mines and on their Destruction. The US, China, and Russia opposed it. Yet it was adopted by the UN on December 3, 1997, because of the dedicated work done by the International Campaign to Ban Landmines, comprising more than 1,400 groups, including Human Rights Watch, Medico International, Handicap International, Physicians for Human Rights, Vietnam Veterans of America Foundation, and the Mines Advisory Group. A prominent supporter was Diana, Princess of Wales. The organization and its founding coordinator, Jody Williams, jointly received the 1997 Nobel Peace Prize for their efforts to bring about the Mine Ban Treaty (Ottawa Treaty).

Similarly, the creation of the International Criminal Court (ICC) was vociferously opposed by the US, India, and China. Surprisingly, some of the most vociferous criticisms that came from the US were from one US Supreme Court justice. Former UN Secretary-General Kofi Annan's upcoming memoir, *Interventions: A Life in Peace and War*, even suggests that Justice Antonin Scalia called the ICC a "kangaroo court."[36] Yet as of September 2011, 116 states were states parties to the Statute of the Court, including all of South America, nearly all of Europe, and roughly half of Africa. The US tried to use the UN Security Council to undermine the ICC, but despite this ferocious opposition, the ICC came into force on July 1, 2002, and has progressively gained legitimacy and acceptance all round the world. Even the US has begun using the ICC as an instrument in UNSC resolutions.

With the establishment of transnational organizations, more and more people are becoming aware that we live in a small global village and that we should try to behave appropriately. One NGO that has played an exceptionally powerful role in shaping global perceptions has been the World Economic Forum. The annual WEF meetings in Davos in January each year bring together powerful personalities from governments and corporations, the media, and academia.

I have attended more than ten UN General Assembly meetings where government representatives meet every year to discuss the state of the world. I have also attended more than ten WEF Davos meetings where government and nongovernment representatives meet each year to discuss the state of the world. The UNGA meetings have the advantage of passing resolutions that are perceived to represent the will of the international community. The WEF meetings have the advantage of global press coverage that shapes global perceptions profoundly.

Strikingly, while the UN has often proved incompetent in bringing together long-standing adversaries, the WEF has been able to do so from time to time. For example, in 1988 Turkey and Greece signed a declaration at Davos to dispel the risk of war. More historic encounters took place at subsequent Davos summits, including unprecedented meetings in 1989 between representatives from North and South Korea, and a discussion between the East and West German leaders on reconciliation. In 1992, Nelson Mandela and South African president F.W. de Klerk made their first international appearance together at Davos.[37] Israeli foreign minister Shimon Peres and PLO chairman Yasser Arafat constructed a draft agreement at the 1994 meeting.[38]

Gideon Rachman, in a *Financial Times* article, described well the virtues offered by Davos:

> At Davos, political leaders from all over the world tacitly agree to set aside their differences and to speak a common language. Closeted together in a mountain valley, they restate their commitment to a single, global economy and to the capitalist values that underpin it. They mingle cheerfully with the same multinational executives and investment bankers. They campaign to attract foreign investment and trade. For five days, the world's leaders seem to agree on a narrative about how the world works. At Davos, even the most intractable differences are temporarily smothered by the globalization consensus.[39]

In the theory of international affairs, world leaders should have a preference for attending UNGA meetings, where they can address all the governments of the world in one room. In the practice of international affairs, many prefer Davos. It has no formal role, but it works.

Some NGOs, such as al-Qaeda, can do a lot of damage. Many of the major global drug cartels are technically NGOs. They too have taken advantage of all the modern means of communication to establish global networks. Some of these NGOs can also change perceptions significantly. In short, we have to recognize both the positive and negative impact of the work NGOs do. They are not inherently morally superior to governments. At the same time, we have to recognize that they have become an indispensable part of international life.

The next chapter will discuss how we can manage some of the major geopolitical fault lines of the world. NGOs can play a helpful role. For a long time, for example, relations between America and India were marked with distrust and suspicion because the two countries had been on opposing sides in the Cold War. Then, in 2001 the Confederation of Indian Industry (CII), led by the highly respected Tarun Das, partnered with the

Aspen Institute to sponsor a meeting in Udaipur, India, between Indian and American thought leaders. "We started talking about defense, about energy," recalled Tarun Das, the former head of the CII. "We started talking about H.I.V./AIDS. The dialogue went into: 'What else can we do? How can we build trust between the two countries?' There was only mistrust after 50 years."[40]

The CII has sponsored fourteen more such meetings between Indian and American leaders, which have produced tangible results. The two countries are now strategic partners and cooperate extensively on defense and security. The most significant contribution of the initial CII exchanges was laying the foundation for the landmark United States–India Civil Nuclear Agreement, which was signed and ratified by both countries in 2008.[41]

Similarly, the Lee Kuan Yew School of Public Policy of NUS (where I am the dean) has sponsored some track 1.5 meetings between Indian and Chinese think tank and nongovernmental representatives. Track 1.5 meetings are meetings endorsed by governments but with no governmental representatives present, though both governments are subsequently briefed on the discussion and the outcome. There is some evidence that such meetings outside the traditional intergovernmental discussion framework have helped to improve relations.

One last point is worth explaining here. This explosion of human interaction across borders facilitated by nonstate actors has changed the chemistry of our planet. In previous centuries, most of the elites in any society interacted primarily with the citizens of their own countries. Now they are just as likely to interact with the citizens of other countries. The net result of this, to end with a paradox, is that the "foreign" is becoming less "foreign." Indeed, the "foreign" is becoming familiar. This is clearly a positive development contributing significantly to the great convergence discussed in this volume.

In conclusion, let me emphasize one key point: convergence also creates complexity. In this new world of ours, no one can claim to be a world leader or world thinker if he or she fails to understand the major global contradictions of our time. Nor can he or she make a significant difference to improve our global order without working out how to make complex trade-offs among these global contradictions.

Paradoxically, the contemporary Western mind, which has until recently been more open than other minds, may have more difficulty grasping this complexity. Through a tangled combination of having to be always politically correct and never admitting to Machiavellian calculations, most Western commentators have fallen into a black-and-white mind-set. In their minds, there are right or wrong solutions. In the real world, most solutions are right *and* wrong solutions wrapped together.

Let me illustrate this point with a controversial example. Most Chinese intellectuals I speak to are genuinely convinced that Mao Zedong did more good than harm for China. It is conventionally said in China that Mao was 70 percent right and 30 percent wrong. Most Western intellectuals find this judgment to be inconceivable. Yet most Asians find this Chinese judgment to be perfectly conceivable because Mao inherited a China that had been almost completely broken after having been trampled and humiliated by several major powers. He inherited a broken nation and made it stand tall. It is true that he made horrible mistakes toward the end of his rule, especially with the Great Leap Forward and Cultural Revolution. His rule is believed to have caused the deaths of 40 to 70 million people. But if Mao had not picked up the mighty nation and made it stand tall, China would have been far worse off. Mao brought about many positive changes. These included promoting the status of women, improving popular literacy, doubling the school population, providing universal housing, abolishing unemployment and inflation, increasing access to health care, and raising life expectancy significantly. In fact, China's population almost doubled during the period of Mao's leadership, from around 550 to more than 900 million. Several Chinese intellectuals have also told me that Deng could not have lifted China to greater heights without the platform of national unity he had inherited from Mao.

Equally importantly, even after Mao made his famous statement in 1949 that "the Chinese people have stood up!," he faced two great geopolitical challenges. First, he had to fight a massive war against the vastly superior American forces in the Korean Peninsula in 1950–1951. Second, he found himself in an equally dangerous confrontation with the world's second-most powerful superpower, the Soviet Union. In 1969, there were major direct military clashes between Chinese and Soviet military forces at the Sino-Soviet border near the Ussuri River. These clashes could have easily escalated. Mao was acutely aware that the Soviet Union was capable of using nuclear weapons against China. Mao did not blink. Instead, he always took advantage of the prevailing "contradictions" of his time to steer China into safe waters. It is possible that only a leader like Mao with his extraordinary strategic gumption and skills could have succeeded in steering China through these great challenges.

The era of strong leaders like Mao is over. The grain of human history has changed irrevocably, and we probably will never see again such dominant rulers like him. But the era of global contradictions is not over. Instead, as this chapter has tried to document, there will be more, rather than fewer, global contradictions. Victory in any sphere will go to those who master and use these global contradictions rather than opposing them. And to succeed in a world of so many contradictions, all nations will have to make complex trade-offs.

Let me take another provocative example. To put the dilemma for the West plainly and simply, as the relative power of the Western world continues to recede steadily in the twenty-first century, Western leaders will have to learn once again to be careful and pragmatic in their foreign policies. Black-and-white postures will have to be replaced with nuanced policies. In this regard, the best test case for the West to demonstrate a capacity to master complexity would be to begin a thought experiment with the Iranian challenge. Can the West conceive of the possibility that the best way to engender change in Iran is to slip Iran into the story of the great convergence that this book has been documenting? China is a different China today because millions of Chinese have studied in Western universities. Would Iran also change if millions of Iranians were admitted into Western universities? Can a nation like Iran ignore the logic of the great convergence of the world if it is plunged into this global maelstrom of human history?

The tragedy of our contemporary world is that the dominant Western discourse is still incapable of mastering such intricacy. When the military regime of Myanmar suddenly and inexplicably opened up in 2011 and released Aung San Suu Kyi from twenty-one years of house arrest and various other forms of harassment, the West celebrated and embraced her enthusiastically in her moment of celebration. She fully deserved this embrace. But to keep the Myanmar experiment of openness going, it was equally important to open doors to those military leaders who showed courage in releasing Aung San Suu Kyi. Of course, this would have been politically incorrect. And because it was politically incorrect, no Western leader invited President Gen Thein Sein to visit. And in so doing, Western leaders demonstrated that they remain victims of a black-and-white mind-set that will prove to be a huge competitive liability as we sail into a world of complex geopolitical contradictions.

CHAPTER
5

Will Geopolitics Derail Convergence?

ALTHOUGH GEOPOLITICS HAS BEEN AROUND FOR A FEW THOUSAND years, there may not be an agreed meaning of the word. The *Oxford English Dictionary* defines it as follows: "politics, especially international relations, as influenced by geographical factors."[1] For a long time, this definition held: the difference between politics and geopolitics was the geodimension—the intersection between geography and politics. The old adage was "Geography is destiny." New Zealand and Lebanon are both small states. New Zealand is geographically blessed. Lebanon is not.

But the term "geopolitics" has now grown to encompass far more than geography. It also refers to relations among great powers, regardless of their geographical connections. America and China are separated by a vast ocean, but there is no doubt that the most important geopolitical relationship in the world is the one between them.

There are two principal schools of geopolitical strategy: broadly, the liberal-internationalist school and the realist school. The liberal-internationalist school argues that something fundamental has changed in human history. In the past, geopolitics was a zero-sum game. Today, these games have been replaced by nations working together within larger cooperative global frameworks. The geopolitical contest can be a win-win game. Robert Jackson and Georg Sørensen describe this school: "Liberals generally take a more optimistic view of human nature. They have an inherent

145

belief in human progress. For liberals, international relations are not about power struggles between nation states. Societies are able to cooperate for the common good."[2] Scholars such as Anne-Marie Slaughter and John Ikenberry are associated with this school.

The realist school argues the opposite: that nothing fundamental has changed in human history. The geopolitics of today is the same as the geopolitics of a thousand years ago. Nation-states are always competing for influence and power in a contest that can in the end produce only one winner. According to Jackson and Sørensen, "Basic realist ideas and assumptions are: 1) a pessimistic view of human nature; 2) a conviction that international relations are necessarily conflictual and that international conflicts are ultimately resolved by war; 3) a high regard for the values of national security and state survival; and 4) a basic scepticism that there can be progress in international politics that is comparable to that in domestic political life."[3] Scholars such as Robert Kagan and Aaron Friedberg are realists.

I have found myself wondering if our transitional era is characterized by the truth of both schools. States have begun to cooperate more and more, as suggested by the liberal-internationalists. But despite the cooperation, sometimes-aggressive competition continues, as suggested by the realists. When the Yugoslav war broke out in the 1990s, the European states competed for influence in the former Yugoslavia, but they also cooperated to put the fires out. Many Asians see merits in both viewpoints. It will take some time—maybe a century or more—before we understand the full difference between Asian and Western minds. After several decades of dealing with Asian and Western minds, I have come to believe that some of these differences are significant. Westerners tend to work within Cartesian frameworks and tend to have a black-and-white view of the world. One side is right, and the other is wrong. The Asian mind is more comfortable with contradictions and paradoxes. Both sides of a contradictory proposition can be correct.

To understand contemporary geopolitics, we have to assume that there are two streams of geopolitics flowing simultaneously through our time. One stream is pushing the nation-states to cooperate; the other stream is pushing the same nation-states to compete. Both streams jockey for influence in the minds of policymakers. When Barack Obama and Xi Jinping met in the White House on February 14, 2012, their minds were constantly calculating how America and China could both compete and collaborate with each other. Competition between major powers may not disappear for another century or two. To understand how both of these streams operate, including the forces at play within each one, let's analyze in-depth four of the most difficult geopolitical challenges currently facing the world. These are the relationships between America and China, China and India, and Islam and the West, and the evolving geopolitics of Southeast Asia. There will be a bumpy ride or two before optimists like me can be certain of happy outcomes.

The America-China Relationship

In geopolitics, the most important relationship is always between the world's greatest power (today America) and the world's greatest emerging power (today China). For most of history, when one great power tries to supplant another one, that has almost always been accompanied by war. The only recent historical exception was when America replaced the UK as the world's greatest power almost one hundred years ago. That transition may have been easier because one Anglo-Saxon power replaced another, and there were many ties, practical and financial, between the two. In the mid-nineteenth century, Britain was the biggest investor by far in America. When China achieves the largest GDP in the world (*one* of the key indicators of great-power status), probably before 2020, it will be the first time in two hundred years that a non-European power will have the largest economy in the world.

Still, the prospects of a war between America and China are very low. Before stepping down as secretary of defense—a post he had served in for almost five years—Robert Gates told reporters on July 1, 2011, "We [America and China] are both going to continue to be interested in protecting our interests in the Pacific, and East Asia particularly. But I would regard the chances of military conflict between the two countries as quite low. . . . I can't imagine either power being that stupid."[4] Many factors explain this low prospect of war: the danger of mutual assured destruction by nuclear weapons, the growing interdependence between the Chinese and American economies, the growing awareness that China and America have to manage many global challenges together, and, equally importantly, the deft management by both sides of geopolitical differences. Reflecting the importance of good management of America-China relations, one of the greatest statesmen of our times, Henry Kissinger, argued in 2011 that a cooperative United States–China relationship is "essential to global stability and peace." Kissinger went on to warn that were a cold war to develop between the countries, it "would arrest progress for a generation on both sides of the Pacific" and "spread disputes into internal politics of every region at a time when global issues such as nuclear proliferation, the environment, energy security and climate change impose global cooperation." He concluded that "relations between China and the United States need not—and should not—become a zero-sum game."[5]

If Henry Kissinger were forced to choose between describing himself as a realist or a liberal-internationalist, there is virtually no doubt that he would prefer to be called a realist. That a realist like Kissinger is emphasizing the enormous interdependence that has developed between America and China provides confirmation that we need to factor in both the realist and liberal-internationalist points of view to understand our dominant global dynamic. Hence, the America-China relationship demonstrates how two streams of geopolitics can operate simultaneously. There are many factors pushing China and America to cooperate. China relies on the American market to import its manufactured products. America relies on China to buy its Treasury bills to ensure that American interest rates do not shoot up. America relies on China to help keep the volatile North Korean situation stable. China in turn relies on America to keep the Persian Gulf region stable as it still imports a lot of oil from there. China and America often cooperate in the UN Security Council to manage the "hot" issues of the day.

Geopolitical Opportunities

Yet, even while they collaborate with each other, each keeps a wary eye on the other to exploit any geopolitical opportunity that comes along. Both sides have been good at seizing geopolitical opportunities. The 9/11 attacks were clearly a seismic geopolitical event. A decade later, it is clear that China has emerged as the biggest geopolitical beneficiary, which was by no means inevitable given the initial outpouring of shock and sympathy for America. China seized the opportunity almost immediately. The Chinese president, Jiang Zemin, was among the first world leaders to call to offer support to George W. Bush, even though barely a few months earlier, China and America had been publicly squabbling over a downed American spy plane that had crash-landed on Hainan Island. Eighteen months later, George W. Bush discovered a big problem on his hands when his "illegal" invasion of Iraq prevented him from exporting Iraqi oil. Bush needed an enabling UN Security Council resolution to facilitate Iraqi oil exports. The country that helped him the most was China. After the bruising battles with France, Germany, and Russia in the UN Security Council over the legality of the declaration of war, there was no guarantee that America would succeed. In the end, however, Washington prevailed through Resolution 1483, adopted on May 22, 2003. A senior US diplomat told me without hesitation that the most helpful country in securing this resolution for America was China.

In helping America, China obtained both short-term and long-term geopolitical dividends. An immediate short-term benefit was that Bush pressured President Chen Shui-bian of Taiwan not to pursue his covert "independence" strategy for Taiwan. This helped China enormously. But the long-term benefit was even more significant. By legitimizing the presence of American armed forces in Iraq, China consciously or unconsciously ensured that the US would be fully taken up with the occupation and would have very little time to focus on China's slow and steady rise as a geopolitical competitor.[6] A well-known Hong Kong journalist, Frank Ching, wrote a column ten years after 9/11 saying, "Bin Laden's attack on the United States was a heaven-sent opportunity for China. . . . It's not going too far to say that China owes a huge debt of gratitude to Osama bin Laden."[7]

Just as American geopolitical mistakes helped China, Chinese geopolitical mistakes have helped America. On September 7, 2010, the Japanese Coast Guard arrested the captain of a Chinese fishing boat that had collided with two patrol boats in disputed territorial waters near the Senkaku (Diaoyu) Islands and held him for fourteen days. Both the Chinese media and the Chinese government went ballistic in response. Even after Japan released the fishing boat and captain, China demanded an apology from Japan. This was unwise. The Japanese public was truly shocked by this strong Chinese reaction. A well-known Japanese journalist, Yoichi

Funabashi, was asked if, for Japan, the Senkaku shock was bigger than the Nixon shocks, meaning when in the summer of 1971 Richard Nixon normalized relations with China without informing Japan and stopped gold convertibility of the dollar, which caused the yen to appreciate drastically. He replied, "It will be much bigger. Problems that arise between Japan and the United States can, in the end, be resolved within the framework of the alliance. The alliance is the ballast. However, that cannot be said of the Japan-China relationship. There is always the danger it will roll completely out of control due to even the slightest accident. Japan and China now stand at ground zero, and the landscape is a bleak, vast nothingness."[8] With one big mistake over a fishing boat, China helped to strengthen the American-Japanese defense alliance.

China made other mistakes, the first one in reacting passively to the North Korean shelling of a South Korean island on November 23, 2010, which killed two South Korean Marines and two civilians. This undid much of the hard work China had put into courting South Korea. Hence, somewhat unusually, despite strong lobbying by the Chinese government, the South Korean ambassador decided to attend the Nobel Peace Prize ceremony honoring Chinese dissident Liu Xiaobo on December 10, 2010.

Earlier, China had taken unusually aggressive postures on the South China Sea issue. China announced a unilateral ban on fishing in the Gulf of Tonkin and detained Vietnamese fishing boats. China had declared that it viewed the South China Sea as a "core interest." China also objected strongly to Vietnam and Malaysia's joint submission to the UN on extended continental shelf claims in the South China Sea. Christopher Joyner explains the importance of these South China Sea disputes: "The Spratly Islands are considered strategic, economic, and political assets for littoral states in the South China Sea because they can serve as legal base points for states to project claims of exclusive jurisdiction over waters and resources in the South China Sea. They hold strategic importance for all states in the region, because they straddle the sea lanes through which commercial vessels must sail en route to and from Southeast Asian ports."[9]

All these actions offered Secretary of State Hillary Clinton an opportunity to exploit the potential divisions between China and ASEAN at the ASEAN Regional Forum in July 2010. In a well-orchestrated move that appeared to have the backing of many Southeast Asian nations, Clinton called the dispute "a leading diplomatic priority" for the United States and voiced her country's willingness to mediate a resolution. "The United States has a national interest in freedom of navigation, open access to Asia's maritime commons and respect for international law in the South China Sea," Clinton said. She added that the United States supported "a collaborative diplomatic process by all claimants for resolving the various territorial disputes without coercion."[10]

This statement infuriated Beijing. The Chinese foreign minister, Yang Jiechi, was visibly taken aback and described Clinton's remarks as orchestrated, "virtually an attack on China," and he asserted, "Nobody believes there's anything that's threatening the region's peace and stability." Greg Torode reported that Yang was shocked and accused his US counterpart of unleashing an anti-China plot. "Yang left the closed-door meeting," Torode wrote,

> and later gave a rambling speech in which he threatened economic punishment for Southeast Asian nations that sought to stand up to Beijing. John Pomfret collaborates [sic] this account: "Foreign Minister Yang reacted by leaving the meeting for an hour. When he returned, he gave a rambling 30-minute response in which he accused the U.S. of plotting against China on the issue." . . . On 1 August Yang stated, "What will be the consequences if this issue is turned into an international or multilateral one? It will only make matters worse and the resolution more difficult. International practices show that the best way to resolve such disputes is for countries concerned to have direct bilateral negotiations."[11]

It would be wise for China not to underestimate the disquiet that its huge claims over the South China Sea have created. Using dotted lines on a map that was first published in the 1940s, China has claimed more than 80 percent of the South China Sea. That claim has been met with incredulity. Lee Kuan Yew, a former prime minister of Singapore, observed that it is "clear that territorial claims [are] more complex than producing a map with dotted lines and saying: 'All this is mine.' I mean who produces this map? What is the authenticity of this map? Who kept it? And even if you can prove its antiquity, what does it show?"[12] A commentary in the *Asia Times* on October 5, 2011, put that matter succinctly: "It would be rather absurd if England were to try to claim sovereignty over most of the English Channel, Iran the Persian Gulf, Thailand the Gulf of Thailand, Vietnam the Gulf of Tonkin, Japan the Sea of Japan, or Mexico the Gulf of Mexico. But that is exactly what China is trying to do by claiming most of the South China Sea."[13]

This mutual exploitation of each other's mistakes shows that, even while China and America continue to collaborate in many important areas, they are also constantly competing with each other. Both are aware of this competition. Both sides take equal pleasure when they notch up a victory or two. This game in itself is not dangerous. But it can become dangerous when either side crosses a "red line" that tramples on a key national interest of the other side. Right now, the danger of America crossing such a red line is higher than that of China doing so as China is still much militarily weaker than America. This is not because China is an inherently more benign great power than America. The one irrefutable lesson of thousands of years of geopolitics is that no great power is benign. It will always seek to pursue or secure its interests. The only question is whether that power will act wisely or unwisely. Right now, America faces the danger of acting unwisely in two areas.

China's Red Lines

The first is military. America remains far more powerful than China. Hence, the big strategic question that Washington should be asking is whether it wants to stimulate a major arms race. Simple geopolitical wisdom suggests that it is in America's long-term interest to avoid one. With China, America cannot try the same gambit that worked successfully with the Soviet Union: it could outspend the former Soviet Union several times over. Now with China's economy on the verge of becoming bigger than America's and the American economy facing the prospect of remaining weak for another decade or so, it would be wise for Washington to avoid such outlays. China may have far deeper pockets for the foreseeable future.

Sadly, Washington is nowhere close to achieving "wisdom" in the military arena. In a *Washington Post* column in August 2011, Fareed Zakaria pointed out that American defense expenditures remain at an all-time high:

Between 2001 and 2009, overall spending on defense rose from $412 billion to $699 billion, a 70 percent increase, which is larger than in any comparable period since the Korean War. Including the supplementary spending on Iraq and Afghanistan, we spent $250 billion more than average U.S. defense expenditures during the Cold War—a time when the Soviet, Chinese and Eastern European militaries were arrayed against the United States and its allies. Over the past decade, when we had no serious national adversaries, U.S. defense spending has gone from about a third of total worldwide defense spending to 50 percent. In other words, we spend more on defense than the planet's remaining countries put together.[14]

It is true that President Obama was forced to announce major defense cuts on January 5, 2012, to reduce American budget deficits, but America will still continue to vastly outspend its nearest competitor. Why is this necessary? And is it wise?

The enormous military spending may also encourage a pattern of relatively aggressive behavior. The US Navy has been aggressively patrolling close to the coast of China for several decades. Under international law, the navy has a right to sail or fly surveillance aircraft in international waters, which are twelve miles away from Chinese shores. However, I wonder whether any American policymaker has seriously asked himself or herself some searching questions about the wisdom of continuing these patrols. First, was it sensible for the US Navy to continue its old patterns (which it knew would aggravate China) while Washington was implicitly seeking China's help through the financial crisis? Second, even though China has passively accepted the patrols, how much longer will it continue to do so? Third, if the US Navy insists on the right to patrol twelve miles away from Chinese shores, will it also allow Chinese naval vessels and surveillance aircraft to do the same twelve miles from American shores when China develops the capability to do so?

Similarly, an incipient arms race is beginning between America and China in outer space. I recall vividly expressions of alarm in the American media when a Chinese missile successfully destroyed a satellite in outer space in January 2007. Yet in all this media coverage, I saw little analysis of the military capabilities America has already accumulated in outer space.

If both sides do not restrain themselves, the danger is that both America and China will lock each other into an expensive arms race from which they will not be able to extract themselves. Hence, the time has come for both China and America to have an open and frank dialogue about the incipient arms race.

Fortunately, such a discussion isn't hard to envisage. Chinese and American leaders are meeting frequently: between 1990 and 2010, there were almost forty face-to-face meetings between the American president and his Chinese counterpart. America and China, unlike America and the USSR, belong to several "multilateral" organizations, including APEC and the G-20. Each of these annual meetings provides an opportunity for face-to-face discussion. Even so, America-China dialogue often lapses into a formalistic conversation structured and focused on short-term issues, not long-term challenges and opportunities, as evidenced by the US-China strategic and economic dialogues since 2009. Despite the unprecedented high level and size of delegations from both sides, the dialogues rarely mention any long-term strategic issues—addressing climate change, restructuring the world financial system, reforming the world institutions (e.g., UN), rearranging the world security system, achieving energy security, and so on—in which both powers have vital interests as well as inescapable responsibilities. Instead, the dialogues are entangled with China's "core interests" and America's "vital interests" on issues such as China's internal stability, the trade balance, and the currency issue.

The second red line that America could cross inadvertently is over China's political stability. This is also the area where the gaps in perception are the greatest. From the point of view of Chinese leaders, China experienced almost continuous political instability and turbulence from the First Opium War of 1839 to the Cultural Revolution, which ended in 1976. After almost 140 years of instability, the Chinese people have experienced more than thirty years of continuous economic growth and relative political stability. The two are linked. Without political stability, the Chinese people would not have enjoyed economic growth and a rapid improvement in living standards. Chinese leaders believe fervently that at the present stage of China's development, China's political stability would vanish without a strong Communist Party of China in charge. They are equally aware that the CPC has to transform itself. In some ways, it already has done so. Yet the CPC's staying power is essential to keep China going. Polls have shown that a majority of Chinese citizens accept that the CPC should stay in power as long as the CPC continues to deliver good economic results and social benefits. There is an implicit social contract between the CPC and the Chinese people. The following exchange between a Chinese Central Television anchor and a reporter captures it well:

Anchor: To follow up his investigation of how satisfied people are with the Party, our reporter Wang Guan, now joins us in the studio. So Wang Guan, I learned that we have done an opinion poll on the Communist Party. What do the results tell us?

Wang Guan: Yes, we have done an independent opinion poll, through Sina Weibo, which is China's very own Twitter, and other social media. We asked Chinese citizens to rate the performance of the Communist Party, on a one to five scale, with one being the lowest, and five the highest. The interviewees come from across all sectors, with vastly different economic and educational backgrounds. The youngest person was 18, and the oldest 71. The average score is 3.87. From the poll, we can see three unique trends here. One is that older people are generally more satisfied with what the party has done—people in their 50s, 60s, and 70s have a combined average score of 4.1. Younger-generation Chinese, or those born in the 1980s and after, scored relatively lower. Their medium score is 3.34, well below the average, which means they think the performance of the Party is not bad, but in many aspects, it could certainly have done better.

Anchor: So what exactly do the people think about the CPC's performance, and in what areas could the Party do better?

Wang Guan: The vast majority of people (84%) believe the biggest legitimacy of the ruling Communist Party comes from the economic success it helped create in the past few decades. More Chinese than at any point in the country's history, can decide what to eat, where to live, what to think, and how to live their lives. Secondly, more than 70 percent (72%) of those interviewed, said the Party should be credited with fighting off Western imperialism back in the early years of the 20th Century. They think this victory saved the war-ravaged nation and, for the first time, gave the Chinese a sense of belonging and self-esteem. On the challenges the Party faces, 89 percent of our interviewees pointed to rampant corruption, which, in turn, fuels social inequality, and undermines the reputation and credibility of the Party. Over 60 percent (64%) said they are saddened by the loss of traditional Chinese culture and values. Many people only seem to care about making money and climbing up the social hierarchy. Finally, half of the people (46%) said they are disappointed in the fact that the rule of law is only written on the paper, but in many instances, not well implemented.[15]

I have quoted this exchange at some length as many in the West will be surprised to learn of such open discussion. Mitt Romney captured well the American perception in his *Wall Street Journal* article of February 16, 2012, where he said, "A nation that represses its own people cannot ultimately be a trusted partner in an international system based on economic and political freedom."[16] He added, "We should not fail to recognize that a China that is a prosperous tyranny will increasingly pose problems for us, for its neighbors, and for the entire world."[17] Romney may have expressed his views more directly and bluntly than most other American leaders, but there is no doubt he represents much of the American establishment: China is a tyranny that cannot last and cannot work in the long term.

China and America need to avoid incautious rhetoric over tyranny or stability. There is no doubt that the Chinese government becomes very aggravated whenever America raises human rights issues. Yet it has also learned to manage these instances as "irritations," not threats. At the same time, America should also consider whether it is wise to push for political change. On the one hand, if, indeed, China is a political tyranny, it will eventually perform badly and self-destruct. On the other, America should pause and ask what a more "democratic" government might do at home, in the region, and in the world at large. A more democratic government in China could be more populist and more nationalistic. To get a glimpse of what a more nationalist voice in China would sound like, we should read the editorials and articles in the *Global Times*. Its point of view reflects a strong stream within the Chinese body politic. If it became the dominant voice in China, it is not clear that China would behave in as restrained a fashion as it has in recent years. Contrary to Romney's observation, the sudden emergence of a more democratic China could pose even more problems for the region and for the world.

Nevertheless, a more democratic China will eventually emerge. The ultimate political destination for China is not in doubt. It will be an unavoidable choice, especially once China has developed the largest middle class in the world. The only question is whether America or any other power will help by interfering in China's domestic processes. The temptation to interfere is strong in America. A wiser course is to allow China to develop at its own pace. By not crossing the red line in this area, America would also help to preserve geopolitical stability.

Both the leaders of America and of China were reminded of the fragilities of the Chinese political system when the police chief of Chongqing, Wang Lijun, suddenly took refuge in the American Consulate of Chengdu on February 6, 2012. Wang was basically trying to get out of the clutches of his boss, then-rising political star Bo Xilai. He feared for his life. If this incident had not been carefully handled, relations between America and China could have been badly damaged. Fortunately, Wang decided to surrender himself to police from Beijing. A major diplomatic problem was averted. Similarly, the Chen Guangcheng affair also demonstrated deft diplomacy and an unexpected flexibility on the part of Chinese leaders. Although allowing blind dissident lawyer Chen Guangcheng to leave China implied a loss of face for them in the short term, in the long term it was a wise decision as it showed a more cooperative face of the Chinese government to the world. This concession also avoided the derailment of the Sino-American relationship.

However, the Wang Lijun incident, which eventually led to the removal of Bo Xilai, demonstrated to Chinese leaders how vulnerable the Chinese political system is. In the end, they collectively decided that Bo had to be removed because he was trying, like Mao Zedong in the Cultural Revolution, to gain power by appealing directly to the masses. This could have endangered the rule of the CPC. Hence, with great delicacy and great care, Bo was sidelined without the party suffering a major trauma. Nonetheless, the whole episode demonstrated once again to the Chinese leadership the importance of political stability at home. Given this core interest, it would be helpful for the American establishment to develop a greater sensibility to China's concerns in this area.

The Crisis of Becoming Number Two

Finally, it does not take a geopolitical genius to predict when a major crisis point will emerge in the America-China relationship. It will happen sometime in the decade after 2016. Why 2016? That will be the year when, by some estimates, the US economy will no longer be number one in the world. In a short letter to the *Financial Times* on February 9, 2012, Jeff Sachs stated the following: "In 1980, the US share of world income (measured in purchasing power parity prices) was 24.6 per cent. In 2011, it was 19.1 per cent. The IMF projects that it will decline to 17.6 per cent as of 2016. China, by contrast, was a mere 2.2 per cent of world income in 1980, rising to 14.4 per cent in 2011, and projected by the IMF to overtake the US by 2016, with 18 per cent. If this isn't a world-altering shift, it's hard to imagine what would be."[18]

Some economists will challenge the use of PPP prices as the measurement of the size of an economy. However, even in "nominal" terms, America's relative economic size is going to shrink steadily. Edward Luce, who wrote the book *Time to Start Thinking: America in the Age of Descent*, states the following: In 2000, America had about 31 percent of the global economy, just under a third. By 2010, it was down to 23.5 percent just under a quarter. By 2020 or so, America's share could decline to about a sixth.[19] If these facts do not confirm that America is firmly headed to becoming number two in the world, what facts could do so?

When Americans finally wake up to the realization that their economy is number two in the world, it is more than likely that an acrimonious debate will begin with the famous question "Who lost America's number one spot?" America has had debates like these before, like "Who lost Vietnam?" or "Who lost Iraq?" Such acrimonious debates are rarely enlightening. Instead, they will be full of scapegoating. China will, of course, be scapegoat number one.

The reason I worry a great deal about this debate on "Who lost America's number one spot?" is that I have had firsthand experience of the reluctance of high-ranking Americans to confront an undeniable hard reality that is about to hit America in the face. In January 2012, I was asked to chair the panel discussion "The Future of American Power in the 21st Century" at the Davos meeting. The panel members were truly distinguished

American citizens. In fact, Michael Froman said that his fellow panelists were "three of the most internationalist legislators in our country." There were two Republicans, Senators Saxby Chambliss (Georgia) and Bob Corker (Tennessee), and two Democrats, Michael Froman, deputy assistant to the president and deputy national security adviser for international economic affairs, and Congresswoman Nita M. Lowey (New York). My opening question was an easy one: "What do you see as the future of American power?" Their answers were predictable: America would always remain number one. My second question was posed more delicately. I said that I had seen some projections that America could have the second-largest economy within a decade or so. Hence I asked whether America could adjust to being number two in the world.

I am not easily shocked, but I must confess that I was shocked by the reactions of the four pundits. Not one of them could say or imply that America could ever be number two. The most interesting response came from Senator Corker:

> If people in China do well, if you look at the demographics, the size of their economy is going to be very large. And so, I think all of us can do the math, we all look at the growth rates. And yet I'll stop there, because I'm not going to take your—I'm not going to buy that whatever it is you're trying to get me to buy, and tell you. But I'll agree exactly, that the American people absolutely would not be prepared psychologically for an event where the world began to believe that it was not the greatest power on earth. . . . I'm not going to say that's the way it's going to be. But I will tell you that the American psychology certainly is not prepared to deal with that.[20]

From their responses, it was clear that "America as number one" was a sacred cow. I was not the only one to be shocked. The president of Carnegie Mellon University, Jared Cohon, was in the room. He was equally shocked.

These four high-level American representatives are not alone in refusing to confront the reality that America could be number two sometime soon. President Barack Obama would also like to broadcast the message that America will always be number one. In his State of the Union address in January 2012, he quoted a well-known American scholar, Robert Kagan, who has written a book called *The Myth of American Decline*. "The renewal of American leadership can be felt across the globe," Obama said, echoing Kagan's thesis. "From the coalitions we've built to secure nuclear materials, to the missions we've led against hunger and disease; from the blows we've dealt to our enemies, to the enduring power of our moral example, America is back. . . . Anyone who tells you otherwise, anyone who tells you that America is in decline or that our influence has waned, doesn't know what they're talking about," Obama maintained. Similarly, Mitt Romney recently declared, "This century must be an American century." It is no wonder that Charles Kupchan commented, "The main contenders for the Oval Office are knocking themselves out to reassure Americans that their nation remains at the pinnacle of the global pecking order."[21]

Given this clear reluctance to prepare the American people for an inevitable reality, it is quite natural that American politicians will be tempted to blame China. In one way or another, American politicians will accuse China of "cheating" either by manipulating its currency to keep it low or by forcibly keeping the wages of its workers low. Romney provided an early indication of how this China blame game will play out in a *Wall Street Journal* article of February 16, 2012:

> Should the 21st century be an American century? To answer, it is only necessary to contemplate the alternatives. One much bruited these days is that of a Chinese century. With China's billion-plus population, its 10% annual average growth rates, and its burgeoning military power, a China that comes to dominate Asia and much of the globe is increasingly becoming thinkable. The character of the Chinese government—one that marries aspects of the free market with suppression of political and personal freedom—would become a widespread and disquieting norm. . . . Unless China changes its ways, on day one of my presidency I will designate it a currency manipulator and take appropriate counteraction. A trade war with China is the last thing I want, but I cannot tolerate our current trade surrender.[22]

To avoid an unproductive and potentially dangerous debate, thoughtful Americans should begin to educate the American people that America and China are where they are today not because of the decisions they made in the last one or two years but because of the decisions they made in the last one or two decades. On January 20, 1993, a bright young new American president, Bill Clinton, assumed office. His administration showed great promise. Clinton had gathered a very talented team around him. Despite his personal shortcomings, there is no doubt that Bill Clinton is one of the most intelligent and possibly one of the wisest leaders of our time.

Yet despite his intelligence and wisdom, it can be argued that many of America's contemporary problems may have begun during his administration. It is unlikely that during his presidency Clinton allowed himself to wonder whether the US economy might falter sometime in the following decade or two. Success was taken for granted. When Clinton and his team aggressively promoted globalization, they genuinely believed that America would be the ultimate beneficiary because America would always be the most competitive economy.

It is true that Clinton often gave speeches telling the American people that America needed new directions. Indeed, the theme for his first State of the Union address in January 1993 was "Our nation needs a new direction." He pointed out correctly the challenges America would face: jobs, health care reform, education, welfare, strengthening of families, crime, reform, deficit reduction, budget, defense, taxes, Medicare, and Social Security. Yet what was truly remarkable about this speech were the glaring omissions. At the beginning of his speech he said, "Nations, like individuals, must ultimately decide how they wish to conduct themselves—how they wish to be thought of by those with whom they live, and, later, how they wish to be judged by history. Like every man and woman, they must decide whether they are prepared to rise to the occasions history presents them."[23]

Yet even though Bill Clinton wisely declared that nations must respond to the challenges of their times, he completely failed to warn the American people that as a result of massive globalization, they would have to adjust and adapt or they would be left behind as the rest of the world moved ahead. The American people needed to hear this advice, but it was politically impossible for Bill Clinton to deliver it. Instead, American leaders and the American people were told they had reached the End of History, as if it were a race to be won, and that they had certainly come in first. This supreme self-confidence in turn led to many strategic errors.

Sadly, Clinton made some flawed short-term decisions. He must have known that they were flawed, but he must have also been convinced that they would do no real harm to the US economy. I say he must have known that his decisions were flawed because he was one of the most outspoken advocates of globalization.[24] Clinton supported global trade negotiations and global trade liberalization. Yet when he hosted a WTO meeting in Seattle in November 1999, he caved in to street demonstrators and labor unions and abandoned a global trade round to pacify a few thousand port and other workers in Seattle. A Reuters report of December 4, 1999, described the failure: "So much for the Clinton round. Touted as one of President Clinton's top foreign policy goals, a new round of global trade talks that might have carried his name collapsed before it even got started. . . . Clinton may curry favor from labor unions and other U.S. groups, but in the process, undercut U.S. leadership at the talks, some diplomats said. 'It was the Americans,' said a European Union official. 'They were so determined to drive through their own agenda that they were blind to where this would lead.'"[25]

Clinton's decision to cave in did a lot of long-term harm to the US economy because it helped to sustain the perception that America could do whatever it wanted and would suffer no long-term change, even when it indulged in semiprotectionist measures and gestures. By not making the hard decisions to prepare the American population for new global competition, Clinton missed a valuable opportunity to prepare America for the world ahead. In the first decade of the twenty-first century, the Bush administration made a comparable error when it ducked making hard decisions about budget deficits. Both administrations seemed to suggest that America could do whatever it wanted vis-à-vis the global economy and would suffer no fallout. America the powerful need not adapt. In so doing, both administrations had postponed and increased the pain of these necessary adjustments.

By contrast, while Clinton's inauguration was the day when America looked to the future with great confidence, China looked ahead with great uncertainty and even despair. January 1993 was barely three-and-a-half years after the Tiananmen Square catastrophe, which had led to global isolation and great uncertainty about the future prospects for the Chinese economy. And China was desperate to get out of its isolation. It was so desperate to do so and find a means to reconcile with America that it decided to swallow a very bitter pill. America said that it would allow China to join the APEC forum of economies if both Taiwan and Hong Kong were allowed to join at the same time, knowing that China believed that both Taiwan and Hong Kong were integral parts of China. The "fiction" that this was a forum of "economies" and not "countries" made this bitter pill swallowable for China.

The admission of Taiwan and Hong Kong to APEC was not the only challenge China faced. In the 1990s, China, under the leadership of Zhu Rongji, was determined to get into the WTO. Zhu knew that the only way to make the Chinese economy strong and competitive was to get China into that organization as this would force the Chinese government to destroy many of the special interests and vested interests that were determined to keep their special privileges.

Zhu famously said, "I've prepared 100 coffins. 99 for corrupt officials and one for myself."[26] It is hard to think of a more courageous statement. It came in the very year that Bill Clinton demonstrated his cowardice. The US was clearly aware that Zhu was taking big political risks in pushing for WTO membership. WikiLeaks released a Congressional Research Service report that describes well the challenges that Zhu Rongji faced in April 1999:

> Even though Zhu Rongji may be willing to make significant concessions to assure China's WTO accession, the more important question is whether he will be able to make them. Although he still appears to be in a strong position politically at home, the domestic reforms Zhu has pushed for are painful, cutting across a wide group of constituencies that have vested interests in the status quo. Zhu remains potentially vulnerable to resistance and criticism from these groups, many of whom are potential victims of the kind of international competition that WTO obligations could bring. Almost exclusively, the entities with something to lose from WTO accession are part of the official state sector; the private and entrepreneurial parts of the Chinese economy, already competitive, stand to be the chief beneficiaries of WTO membership.
>
> This official concern about the state sector is a serious complication in Premier Zhu's efforts to gain support for substantive and meaningful

economic concessions on WTO. Zhu's support for a decision requiring the PLA [People's Liberation Army] to sell off its money-earning corporate interests, for instance, has won him few friends in China's military establishment. Indeed, a key military leader, a vice-chair of the crucial Central Military Commission, has been described in one press account as an unexpected leader in the "say no to Zhu" contingent in China. There are others who may want to say no to Zhu: ministers of state government bureaucracies faced with massive cuts in personnel and resources; demobilized soldiers; and workers at state-owned-enterprises [SOEs] who may lose their jobs, housing, and medical care as a result of SOE reform. Some Chinese and U.S. economists also wonder whether such key, protected sectors in China as telecommunications and agriculture can absorb the economic shock of an influx of highly competitive foreign imports without resulting in massive bankruptcies and widespread unemployment. Despite these constraints, Zhu is thought to be exerting enormous pressure at home to gain support for enough concessions to gain WTO access on what U.S. officials have insisted must be "commercially viable" terms."[27]

Despite this massive opposition, Zhu Rongji was prepared to push for the right thing. Clinton, despite all his fine rhetoric about keeping the world open, couldn't match Zhu's courage:

But even as Premier Zhu was en route to the United States, President Bill Clinton was making decisions that would prevent a deal from being consummated. Over the weekend of April 4-5, President Clinton met with his advisors. His foreign policy advisors, National Security Advisor Samuel Berger and Secretary of State Madeleine Albright, along with United States Trade Representative (USTR) Charlene Barshefsky favored clinching a deal that was better for American business than any had dared to hope only a few months earlier. However, Clinton's domestic advisors, Treasury Secretary Robert Rubin, National Economic Council head Gene Sperling, and domestic political advisor John Podesta, argued that unless there were guaranteed protections for labor unions and industries that compete directly with their Chinese counterparts, Congress would vote to kill the deal—and that would be worse for U.S.-China relations than no deal.

President Clinton sided with his domestic advisors and requested that USTR go back to the negotiating table to ask for extended protection for textiles and added assurances against large-scale increases in imports. On the morning of April 7, President Clinton declared that it would be wrong to walk away from a good agreement with China, but then, in a two-and-a-half-hour meeting with Premier Zhu at the White House that evening, he did exactly that. Although an agricultural agreement was quickly signed the next morning, Zhu was sent back to China virtually empty handed.[28]

To make matters worse, the difficulties in the trade negotiations were compounded by cultural misunderstanding. A *Washington Post* article by Steven Mufson and Robert Kaiser describes well this dimension:

> In the annals of cross-cultural misunderstanding, the meeting between President Clinton and Chinese Premier Zhu Rongji at the White House on April 7 may have been a classic.
>
> Zhu, ready to take on the most powerful and entrenched interest groups in China by letting foreign companies compete in his country, expected Clinton to welcome Beijing into the World Trade Organization. But the president—distracted by war in Kosovo and worried about a surge in anti-Chinese sentiment in Congress—had decided to put off a final decision, despite a flurry of concessions offered by the Chinese.
>
> On the day Zhu landed here, the Chinese sensed that their hopes might be dashed. They sought one last opportunity for the premier to speak directly to Clinton. Clinton put his arm around the considerably smaller Zhu, according to a Chinese diplomat's account, and told him: "If you really need this now, we can do it. It's hard for me to do it now, it's a bad time politically, but if you really need it, we can do it. Do you really need it now?"[29]

Zhu, dismayed but unwilling to be a supplicant, said he didn't. The Chinese official who provided this account added, "How I wish I could have had a cultural translator in that room at that moment to explain to both men what they were hearing each other say."[30]

Clinton did not see any great dangers for America with his decision to cave in to the anti-WTO demonstrators because he assumed that the American economy was an open and connected one. He saw the setback as temporary. The root cause of Clinton's optimism that America would do all right was a strong and deeply held belief that America was on the right side of history in handling the challenges of globalization.

By contrast, Zhu knew that China had been on the wrong side of history in dealing with those same challenges. China had suffered for almost two centuries because the previous emperors and rulers believed that China as a large and long-standing empire need not open itself to the world in any way. They had resisted all efforts to open up to the global economy. Zhu and many other senior Chinese leaders learned a powerful lesson from two centuries of suffering. They knew that China had to reposition itself on the right side of history by opening itself up to global competition.

China's Embrace of Globalization

Surprisingly, on the issue of sovereignty, China has also proved to be more forward-looking that the US. Superficially, China bristles whenever there is any "interference in the internal affairs" (a key aspect of sovereignty) of China, whether it is about Tibet or Xinjiang, human rights violations or religious protest movements like the Falun Gong. By contrast, the US, as an open society, freely accepts criticism from the rest of the world as it believes that the "marketplace of ideas" should determine what is right or wrong in any description of an internal situation. But although China is still a somewhat politically closed society, it is a closed society with an open mind. America may be an open society, but it is an open society with a closed mind. In theory, China cherishes sovereignty more than America does. In practice, China has been steadily ceding its sovereignty, especially its economic sovereignty, and opening itself up to the world in the very period that America has progressively become more closed to the world.

In fact, many experts have made the same observation. Susan Jacoby, the author of *The Age of American Unreason*, argues that "Americans are increasingly close-minded and unwilling to listen to opposing views."[31] Ann Lee of New York University has penned a book entitled *What the U.S. Can Learn from China: An Open-Minded Guide to Treating Our Greatest*

Competitor as Our Greatest Teacher. "Lee looks mainly at the Chinese governance system, suggesting, among other things, that the US make politicians pass competency tests, incorporate the Special Economic Zone model and use the 50 states as economic laboratories, and restrict banks to traditional banking activities." In addition, "Lee [has] pointed out that according to an independent survey, more than 80 percent of Chinese think their government is doing a good job, while President Obama's approval rating is less than 50 percent among Americans and Congress is at record low rating of 13 percent."[32]

The fundamental reason that China and America have been going in opposite directions is because the Chinese tried the isolated "Middle Kingdom" approach. It failed. It made China weak. China now wants to engage the world and its international organizations. A study by the Economic Strategy Institute reveals, "The one over-arching objective which informs and drives (China's) conduct is the need for stability. Chinese leaders need—above all else—to ensure the existence of a benign and conducive global environment for China to continue to grow economically at a fast but sustainable pace—in short, to continue its 'peaceful rise.'" In addition, the report notes that within these international organizations, "China's growing role not only supports its strategic interests, but, it should be acknowledged, is also frequently constructive and helpful for the organizations in which it participates."[33]

These contrasting attitudes of America and China to international treaties and conventions and international organizations may surprise a lay reader. Much of the international fabric that provided the foundations for these treaties and organizations rested on ideas generated in America. Yet China has a better track record than America in the field of ratifying international treaties and conventions, as well as in joining international organizations. China has signed and ratified international agreements that the US has refused to sign or ratify, including the Biodiversity Convention, the Kyoto Protocol, the Hazardous Wastes Convention, and the Law of the Sea Treaty.[34]

China has learned powerfully that engagement with international organizations can improve China's conditions significantly. There is a direct correlation between China's membership in the WTO and the rapid expansion of its external trade, as demonstrated in Figure 5.1.

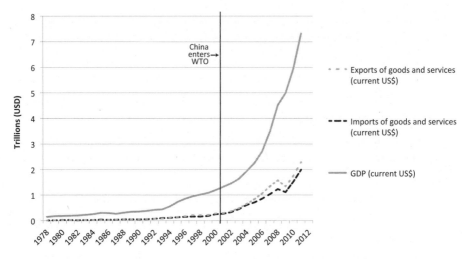

FIGURE 5.1 China's Imports and Exports, 1978–2010. *Source:* World Bank data from World Development Indicators Data Bank.

By contrast, while China has been embracing the WTO and opening itself up to more and more international trade, American policymakers have progressively turned away from the WTO, even though the WTO is essentially an American creation. George W. Bush launched the Doha Round in November 2001 but failed to complete it in his eight years as president. Today, free trade has become so toxic a subject in American political discourse that President Obama hardly mentions it anymore. According to a CNN article written on January 25, 2008:

> A large majority—68%—of those surveyed in a Fortune poll says America's trading partners are benefiting the most from free trade, not the U.S.... Fortune's poll, a survey of 1,000 adult Americans taken Jan. 14–16, shows that voters have identified winners and losers in the free-trade agenda. Nearly half of those polled believe that growth in international trade has made things better for consumers (though nearly as many think it has made things worse), but 55% believe American business has been harmed, and 78% think it has made things worse for American workers.... [Therefore,] "the Democratic mantra is now "fair trade, not free trade."[35]

These contrasting attitudes and performances suggest that countries need to examine in a deeper fashion what their real attitudes are toward sovereignty and a rapidly changing world order. Hermit kingdoms, even very large ones, will collapse. I published an article in the spring 2009 *Wilson Quarterly* entitled "Can America Fail?" I picked this provocative title because I knew that such an idea was unthinkable to most American minds. I put across a simple argument: American society could stumble and fall back if it did not force itself to conceive of failure. It suffers from three systemic challenges: groupthink, the erosion of individual responsibility, and an inability to see how its abuse of power has contributed to many of the problems it now confronts abroad. Many Americans are oblivious to the structural failures within their system of governance (dominated by special interests), their social contract (characterized by a widening gap between rich and poor), and their response to globalization (increased protectionism). Deep structural reform is necessary in America to avert an otherwise inevitable failure. The most dangerous condition afflicting America today is that it has developed a dangerously distorted discourse about the real challenges it is facing.

Truth-telling does not come easily to politicians, especially democratically elected ones. They have a structural incentive to pander to the wishes of the voters, not to make them uncomfortable with hard truths. There is, for example, one hard truth that no American politician dares to tell the American people: America is still the most powerful country in the world, but even the most powerful country has effectively lost a lot of its economic sovereignty. By creating an open economy and encouraging global interdependence, the US policymakers of the 1960s and 1970s essentially made America's economy contingent on the world economy.

With this effective loss of economic sovereignty, American politicians have a duty to lead people to adjust and adapt. There is no substitute for working harder, studying harder, cutting wasteful subsidies, reducing and eliminating budget deficits, and going through several years of economic sacrifice. Tom Friedman puts the matter succinctly: "Our country faces a big choice right now. We can either have a hard decade or a bad century."[36]

When the debate finally explodes in America over who lost America's economic supremacy, China will face two dangers. The first danger is scapegoating by America. The second will be smugness in China. In practical terms, China can do little to stop scapegoating in America. Indeed, China experiences this regularly every four years whenever a new American presidential election campaign begins. From Bill Clinton's famous 1992 pronouncement that he will not "coddle the butchers of Beijing" to Mitt Romney's statement in 2012 that he will declare China a "currency manipulator," it has been traditional for American presidential candidates to attack China in an effort to look tough and strong. So far, China has wisely followed Deng Xiaoping's advice and kept a low profile in response to these provocations. However, as Chinese society progressively opens up and China's population grows more sensitive to American insults, this continued scapegoating of China in America could derail Sino-American relations. All that China can do now is to progressively educate the American public that this tactic is unwise, even though China is unlikely to succeed.

Fortunately, China can do more in response to the danger of smugness. To change the course of China's economy, Zhu Rongji had to fight against the odds and confront thousands of vested interests. When Zhu stepped down on March 16, 2003, he followed the rules of the Chinese political system and disappeared completely from public view. Unlike Bill Clinton and Tony Blair, who could use their global stature to travel around the world and earn handsome speaking fees, the Chinese political system obliged Zhu to stay at home and remain silent. This tradition of silencing past leaders may have been a strategic error by China. Zhu's successors would have been better off listening to his advice. Over the past few years, several rumors have suggested that Zhu has been dissatisfied with their performance.

In theory, his successors agree that China should continue to reform. Indeed, at the National People's Congress in March 2012, Chinese premier Wen Jiabao described China's growth process as "unbalanced, unsustainable and uncoordinated," a remarkable statement since Wen has been in charge of China's economic policies for a decade or more. In response to this speech, Yukon Huang, a former World Bank official who had advised China in the past, said, while he gave China's leaders an "A" for good intentions, he gave China's leadership an "F" for not turning these intentions into reality. This is quite an indictment for a leadership that has delivered a decade or more of steady economic growth. However, his grades might be fair in terms of judging how well China's leadership has used the first decade of the twenty-first century to prepare China for the future. Zhu Rongji brilliantly prepared China's future partly because he was willing to discard the mental maps that had guided decisionmaking in the past. After three decades of success, China may also have to slaughter some new sacred cows. Hence, in the next decade or so, both America and China will have to engage in some deep reflection on how to prepare for a future that will be very different from the past.

The China-India Relationship

The second most important geopolitical relationship in the world is between the world's two emerging superpowers, China and India. Goldman Sachs has forecast that by 2050 or earlier, the number one and number two economies in the world will be China's and India's. Hence, even though the American-China relationship is the most important geopolitical relationship today, the China-India relationship will be the most important one tomorrow.

Competitive Elements

In trying to understand how this relationship will evolve, we must recognize that both forms of geopolitics are at play in this relationship. There are elements of collaboration and of competition. The competitive dimensions are not difficult to unearth. The two countries have an unresolved border dispute, over which they went to war in 1962. They were on opposite sides during the Cold War, with China leaning toward America and India leaning toward the Soviet Union. A residue of that Cold War legacy remains in China's continued support for Pakistan, which is read by many observers in New Delhi as anti-India. In addition, some Indian strategic analysts have said that China is now trying to "encircle" India. "Through increased incursions, China is seeking to pin down the Indian Army along the Himalayas. Beijing uses border talks with New Delhi as a cover to step up military pressure on India and strategically encircle it," says analyst Brahma Chellaney.[37] He also asserts, "The countries around India have become battlegrounds for China's moves to encircle India. From a military invasion in 1962 and a subsequent cartographic aggression, China is moving towards a hydrological aggression and a multipronged strategic squeeze of India. China's damming of rivers flowing from Tibet to India are highlighting Indian vulnerability on the water front even before India has plugged its disadvantage on the nuclear front by building a credible but minimal deterrent."[38]

"There is a method in the madness in terms of where they are locating their ports and staging points," reports Kanwal Sibal, a former Indian foreign secretary who is now a member of the government's National Security Advisory Board. "This kind of effort is aimed at counterbalancing and undermining India's natural influence in these areas."[39]

There have also been some recent incidents that have marred bilateral relations. Some of them may seem petty, but they left a large political signature. India canceled a visit by its senior Indian Administration Services (IAS) officers in May 2007 when China refused to give a visa to an IAS officer born in Arunachal Pradesh because China claimed that Arunachal Pradesh was part of its territory. China also refused to issue a visa for General B. S. Jaswal, a top Indian army general, because he controlled Jammu and Kashmir, disputed territory between India and China. India retaliated by denying permission to two Chinese officials seeking to take a course at the National Defence College of India and canceling an Indian military delegation's Beijing visit.

Overall, it is not difficult to find elements of competition between China and India. Western media tend to highlight areas of competition rather than collaboration. Some of this clearly reflects wishful geopolitical thinking in the West, especially in America. Just as America gained a significant geopolitical advantage when China leaned toward it in the Cold War, America could gain a similar geopolitical advantage if India leaned toward America. There can be no doubt that China has become a key factor in the American-India relationship. George W. Bush conferred a huge geopolitical gift to India by effectively "legitimizing" the Indian nuclear program, both through the bilateral nuclear accords signed in October 2008 and through lobbying in the Nuclear Suppliers Group (NSG) in August 2008 to grant a waiver to India to commence civilian nuclear trade. The forty-five-nation NSG granted the waiver on September 6, 2008, allowing India to access civilian nuclear technology and fuel from other countries. Bush signed the legislation on the Indo-American nuclear deal, approved by the US Congress, into law, now called the United States–India Nuclear Cooperation Approval and Nonproliferation Enhancement Act, on October 8, 2008. The agreement was signed by Minister of Indian External Affairs Pranab Mukherjee and his counterpart, Secretary of State Condoleezza Rice, on October 10. As a result, Prime Minister Manmohan Singh has declared publicly that Bush has been a "great friend of India." "When history is written, I think it will be recorded that President George W. Bush played a historic role in bringing our two democracies closer to each other," he has added.[40]

While there is no doubt that it would serve American interests for India to lean toward America in any conflict between America and China, it is not so clear that it would serve India's long-term interests to do so. In January 2010, I delivered a speech in New Delhi entitled "Will China and India Grow Together or Grow Apart?" Somewhat unusually, two Indian officials of Cabinet rank, Montek Singh Ahluwalia and Shiv Shankar Menon, joined me on the stage to comment on my remarks. The main message I put across was a simple one. Both China and India were entering into one of the most promising periods of their economic growth and civilizational rejuvenation. It would be sheer folly for China and India to waste this precious moment by engaging in zero-sum geopolitical competition. The only beneficiary of such competition would be the established Western powers, especially America, which would love to use India as a foil to thwart the rise of China. National Security Adviser Menon essentially agreed with me and said that with a few thousand years of strategic culture of its own, India would never allow itself to be used as an instrument by other powers.

Collaborative Elements

Many in the West who focus on the competing interests of China and India fail to realize that they share some fundamental common interests as well. These common interests have led to a significant degree of collaboration and cooperation between these two rising powers in key global forums.

Many of these common interests stem from the fact that they are adopting a common strategy to reemerge as great powers: economic liberalization at home and integration with the global economy. As a result, China and India also share a common interest in sustaining and strengthening the global economic system. Both need a strong WTO and an open rules-based trading order to continue exporting and growing. They also have a common interest in restructuring the global financial system.

Equally importantly, China and India share a very fundamental interest in not being asked to take on too big a burden in responding to global warming. As I explained in my previous book *The New Asian Hemisphere*,[41] global warming is not just happening because of the new "flows" of greenhouse gas emissions from China and India. It is also happening because of the "stock" of greenhouse gas (GHG) emissions put up by the Western industrialized countries during the past two centuries. Since 1850, China has contributed less than 8 percent of the world's total emissions of carbon dioxide, whereas the US is responsible for 29 percent and Western Europe, 27 percent. India has contributed even less than China.

This is why both China and India feel the same deep sense of injustice over the fact that the West is trying to pass on to both a greater share of the economic burden in dealing with global warming. The only way to reduce greenhouse gas emissions is to put an economic price on them. China and India deeply resent any effort to make them pay an economic price for current "flows" of greenhouse gas emissions when the Western industrialized countries refused to pay any economic price for the "stock" of emissions.

Given this deep injustice over the historical record, the Western countries initially agreed to the Kyoto Protocol, which was adopted in December 1997. Both Bill Clinton and Al Gore supported the Kyoto Protocol, but they made no effort to put it before the US Senate for ratification because they knew it would not succeed. When George W. Bush became president in 2001, he withdrew the American signature from the Kyoto Protocol. Since then, the political climate in the US has turned even more decisively against the Kyoto Protocol. Why? The simple answer is that the Kyoto Protocol imposes a clear obligation upon all the rich countries to reduce greenhouse gas emissions while imposing no obligations on relatively poor developing countries like China and India.

The common interest that China and India had in retaining the Kyoto Protocol surfaced clearly at the infamous Copenhagen Conference in December 2009. Both wanted to retain the Kyoto Protocol as the defining international agreement to deal with global warming. President Obama, by contrast, could not support the Kyoto Protocol since the US Congress vociferously opposed it. Hence, Obama was desperate to secure in Copenhagen a new agreement that would override the Kyoto Protocol. He may have actually succeeded in this because in the final agreement in Copenhagen all the participants agreed in principle not to raise global temperatures beyond 2°C, but without agreeing on any specific measures to achieve this goal.

Obama's efforts to ignore China and India's concerns led to a famous shouting match between a Chinese official and Obama. This is what happened: without having received an invitation, President Obama barged into a room where the leaders of Brazil, China, India, and South Africa were meeting. Obama, in his desperation, even shouted at Premier Wen Jiabao. To everyone's surprise, President Hu Jintao's special representative on climate change and vice chairman of the National Development and Reform Commission of China, Xie Zhenhua, broke all protocol by shouting back at Obama.

And why did he shout? He knew exactly what Obama was trying to do. Obama had come to Copenhagen empty-handed. Despite America having been historically the largest emitter of greenhouse gases and despite continuing to be the largest per capita emitter of them, the American delegation had come to the conference with no concrete offers to reduce global warming. The American Congress did not authorize Obama to make any substantial concessions to *reduce* absolute greenhouse gas emissions. Instead, all that Obama could do was to get agreement to reduce the *pace of increase* of GHG emissions. Hence, Obama's sole mission was to persuade Brazil, China, India, and South Africa to agree (though not legally) that by 2020 the total increase in temperature should not be beyond 2°C. Equally significantly, with this new agreement Obama secured something much more important: he effectively buried the Kyoto Protocol because the Copenhagen Accord succeeded it. By burying the protocol, Obama essentially undermined the interests of China and India in preserving it. This was why the Chinese official was shouting at the last-minute huddle.

The Copenhagen conference was not the only global arena where China and India had common interests. The Cancun WTO conference in 2003 was another: China and India had a common interest in putting a greater burden on the richer industrial countries to make more concessions to secure an agreement to conclude the Doha Development Round. The concessions would not even be new. At the conclusion of the Uruguay round in Marrakesh in 1994, the Western developed countries had explicitly agreed that they would reduce and eliminate their wasteful and hugely damaging agricultural subsidies. This was the common understanding with which the Doha Development Round was launched in November 2001. Yet when the crunch came in Cancun, the West refused to compromise on the subsidies. The American delegation knew that it could not give up its cotton subsidies to secure the agreement of the cotton-producing West African states. Hence, to avoid being portrayed as the "bad guy," America engineered a collapse of the Cancun meeting.

In Cancun, China and India also shared a common interest in making sure that the richer developed states made bigger concessions. However, unlike Copenhagen, no Chinese official shouted or stole the limelight in opposing America. Instead, the Indian commerce minister, Kamal Nath, took the lead in condemning America and Western Europe for not compromising. In a joint ministerial statement with Bo Xilai, the Chinese commerce minister, he said, "Unless the outcome of the [trade] negotiations upholds the proposals of developing countries resulting in real and effective reduction of trade distorting domestic support coupled with meaningful disciplines, substantial improvement in market access by developed countries and eliminations of all form of export subsidies, the aspirations of the developing countries, as built in the mandate, will not be fulfilled."[42]

Both China and India feel very strongly the acute sense of injustice over the efforts by the richer Western countries to pass on a higher burden for resolving global climate change and trade negotiations to them. They feel very shortchanged. One of India's chief climate change negotiators, Shyam Saran, has expressed well this sense of injustice. He has emphasized that India will not sacrifice its development to deal with climate change: "Developing countries have the responsibility to engage in sustainable development but their emission reductions will be the result of sustainable development, not the other way round. In another speech Shyam Saran said that states' "ability to adapt to climate change is also linked to the level of development. Richer and more advanced states are better equipped to cope with climate change than are poorer countries. Therefore, development is the best form of adaptation, even if development in a developing country results, in the foreseeable future, to an increase in GHG emissions." The message is clear—development first.[43]

Yet there are signs that Chinese leaders are concerned about growing carbon emissions and have put in place ambitious plans to limit China's emissions. Indeed, Rob Elsworth of *The Guardian* has argued that "China may steal a march on Europe" in the fight against climate change. The article goes on to say that:

> China has realised that alongside command and control measures, attitudes need to be changed fundamentally to embrace innovation and sustainability. This has caused China, through the adoption of the 12th five-year plan [FYP], to pursue a more sustainable economic model, focusing on qualitative economic and social development. The newly adopted plan runs till 2015 and includes prominent energy efficiency and carbon intensity targets. Touted as the greenest FYP ever, it introduces emission trading as one of the innovative new policy tools to be tested. China has already announced pilot projects to be implemented in five municipal areas—Beijing, Chongqing, Shanghai, Shenzhen and Tianjin—and two provinces—Guangdong and Hubei—from 2013. . . . China is advancing rapidly. Many challenges remain but the speed of advancement and the ambition of its emissions trading plans are remarkable. Europe needs to realise that its position as the world leader in carbon pricing will not remain so for long particularly if it fails to act to revive its own ailing scheme.[44]

Common Long-Term Interests and Challenges

Moving ahead, however, both China and India will now have to deal with a new political reality in which the richer Western countries no longer feel confident about the future. Rich self-confident democracies may have allowed politicians to make compromises. But when populations become fearful for their future, they will punish any politicians who try to persuade them to accept any short-term political sacrifice for the greater global good. In an age of anxiety, Western politicians will not be able to make significant concessions to conclude negotiations on climate change and/or trade. A greater burden would then shift onto the shoulders of China, India, and other developing countries. So the time has come for both China and India to think about the clear long-term interests they have in collaborating with each other in many areas of common interest.

Both China and India can sustain their rapid economic growth only if the relatively open 1945 rules-based order is sustained and, indeed, strengthened. Both China and India are increasingly plugging their economies into the global economic grid. In so doing, they are demonstrating great common faith that this global economic grid will carry on. What happens if this grid falls apart? Who is going to rebuild it?

China and India have essentially been "free riders" exploiting the advantages of this global economic good without sustaining it. When I first made this point at a forum where both Chinese and Indian thinkers were present, both united and retorted angrily to me that both China and India have been playing by the rules of the 1945 order and not violating it. True! But the question remains: Who have been the custodians of this rules-based order? The answer, of course, is America and the EU. And why should America and the EU continue to be custodians of the multilateral order in which the primary beneficiaries have become China and India? Pure common sense dictates that both China and India should put in a stronger common effort to keep the global economic grid functioning. Sadly, Chinese and Indian policymakers have not yet accepted the reality that they have to do more to keep the current institutions of global governance going.

A second common challenge for both China and India is the need for open global access to natural resources. Both countries have been roaming actively around the world in search of critical natural resources such as oil and gas, iron and coal, bauxite and aluminum. As a report from Rice University's Baker Institute states, "In recent years, rising Chinese oil and natural gas demand has been a major feature influencing global energy markets. Chinese oil consumption has close to doubled over the last decade and now represents over 10 percent of global world demand, with oil imports topping 5 million b/d [barrels a day] last year. China's imports of liquefied natural gas have also soared from 1 bcm [billion cubic meters] in 2006 to 7.63 bcm in 2009, making China a major force in Asian energy markets."[45] The same story is true for India. Consumption of coal in India is increasing at 9 to 10 percent a year, while India's oil imports are expected to more than triple from 2005 levels by 2020.[46] In some cases, zero-sum competition is unavoidable. If both China and India want to buy oil from Saudi Arabia, the highest bidder will win. However, without China and India colluding (which would naturally be attacked), both sides can develop rules that will ensure that the competition takes place in a civilized fashion. Both share a common interest in ensuring that the rules encourage open and continuing access to key resources. Such collaboration is growing, notably between Indians and Chinese in Africa.

In January 2006, Beijing and New Delhi promised to exchange information when bidding for oil resources abroad. "Unbridled rivalry between Indian and Chinese companies is only to the advantage of the seller," China's official Xinhua News Agency quoted Indian petroleum and natural gas minister Mani Shankar Aiyar as saying.[47]

According to an article by Consultancy Africa Intelligence, a consulting firm specializing in African affairs;

> China and India have chosen not to compete, but to cooperate, in the oil industry in Sudan since 2004. Up until the 1990s, Western oil companies dominated, but the withdrawal of these companies following the conflict in Darfur provided opportunities for China and India to step in. Since the West left Sudan, China has played a dominant role in constructing an oil export sector.
>
> In the case of India, the 2003 withdrawal of the Canadian oil company, Talisman, from the Greater Nile Oil Project of Sudan following pressure from human rights groups, provided India's national oil company with the opportunity to take over. Talisman sold its shares to ONGC Videsh. Since 2004, both China and India bought shares and became partners in the Greater Nile Oil Project. Crude oil in South Sudan is currently pumped by the Chinese National Petroleum Corporation, India's ONGC Videsh, and Malaysia's Petroliam Nasional Berhad.
>
> During this process, it was noticeable that China and India started to strengthen their relations at a senior diplomatic level in order to spur further oil exploration. In April 2005, when Chinese Premier Wen Jiabao visited India, the two Governments issued a joint declaration. This became a watershed event for accelerating cooperation in the energy sector. Specifically, Article 9 of the declaration describes collaboration to explore and exploit natural resources in other countries. Recently, Article 17

of the Joint Communiqué of India and China of 2010 confirmed that China and India would enhance their cooperation in multilateral issues, including the energy sector.

Subsequently, Sudan experienced a significant transition; that is, South Sudan gained independence on 9 July 2011 as a result of the 2005 peace deal. China's foreign minister paid a visit to South Sudan immediately. Considering that China had close relations with Khartoum, this gesture is assessed as quick thinking. India was also one of the first countries to recognise the new nation. Nearly 90% of the oil resources are located in South Sudan. By establishing "new" diplomatic relationships with South Sudan, China and India made sure that they would keep their oil exploration rights.[48]

There are other geopolitical challenges in which there are incentives for the two countries to discover shared solutions. Maintaining rising nutrition levels (which are to be welcomed) requires both China and India to import more food. Food, however, is a politically sensitive commodity. When food prices rise, politicians, especially in developing countries, panic and begin immediately to ban exports. Such behavior is immensely destructive in the long run. As Raghuram Rajan says in his book *Fault Lines*:

> Whenever food prices rise, a number of countries start banning food exports. Although in the very short term such measures ensure that their citizens have access to cheap food, they deprive domestic farmers of higher prices and make them less eager to grow food. They also make other countries feel insecure and attempt to grow their own food, even if it is grossly inefficient for them to do so: the fields of grain that now appear in the middle of the Arabian desert are unlikely to be the best use of water in that location. The net outcome is that the myopic actions by governments to protect their citizenry in the short run result in global food insecurity and inefficient methods of production in the long run.[49]

Rajan recommends coordinated global action: "We need a global agreement to ensure that international food markets will not be disrupted by government action—but no government today will risk being accused by the opposition of signing away its ability to ensure that its citizens have food."[50] Despite this obvious common interest in developing a fair and equitable regime in food supplies, neither China nor India has even begun a dialogue in this area. Both sides also share a common interest in developing a common global assessment of the relatively predictable expected demand in the coming decades and the relatively unpredictable supply of food.

A third common challenge is secure sea-lanes. One of the biggest leaps in the global order in the post-1945 era has been the virtual elimination of piracy (with the possible exception of the Somali coast). In the past two decades, the enforcer of last resort in keeping vital sea-lanes open has been the US Navy. Even though it has been carrying out its global operations in response to a vital American national interest, the US Navy has also been delivering a global public good that both China and India have benefited from. But with enormous and unending budget deficits, the US will have difficulty justifying its levels of military expenditures. Indeed, with the diminution of interstate wars, why maintain a thirteen-carrier navy? Logically, there will be, in relative terms, a significant shrinking of the navy in the coming decades. Both China and India will be affected by this shrinkage. Hence, both should begin a dialogue on keeping sea-lanes secure. On March 1, 2012, at a meeting between Indian external affairs minister S M Krishna and visiting Chinese foreign minister Yang Jiechi, India and China agreed to establish and institutionalize a maritime dialogue. "Both India and China are major maritime nations, we have long coastlines, we have active navies. So, both of us felt that it would be useful to have a dialogue on maritime issues," the spokespersons said.[51]

In the maritime area, China and India also have a common interest in developing a viable long-term global regime for preserving fish stocks. There seems to be a growing global consensus that humanity's harvesting of fish stocks has become unviable. Indeed, *Newsweek* notes, "The oceans have changed more in the last 30 years than ever before. In most places, the seas have lost upwards of 75 percent of their megafauna.... By the end of the 20th century, almost nowhere shallower than 3,000 feet remained untouched by commercial fishing. Some places are now fished down to 10,000 feet."[52] Moreover, a World Bank report, "The Sunken Billions," calculates that the major fish stocks of the world would produce 40 percent more if they were fished less.[53] Since China and India will produce the world's largest new middle classes in the near future, they will suffer the most deprivation if future fish stocks diminish. The current generations of middle classes are benefiting at the expense of future generations of Chinese and Indian middle classes. What are China and India doing to protect this common future interest?

A fourth, and most obvious, common challenge that China and India face is global warming. If the forecasts of the consequences of global warming prove to be accurate, both China and India will emerge as big losers. As the Stern Review, a report on the economics of climate change commissioned by the British government, states, "Melting glaciers will initially increase flood risk and then strongly reduce water supplies, eventually threatening one-sixth of the world's population, predominantly in the Indian sub-continent and parts of China."[54] Yet while they share a common long-term interest in preventing global warming, they also share a common short-term interest in not paying too heavy an economic price for reducing current GHG emissions. Both share a vital common interest in apportioning a larger share of the economic burden on the richer developed countries that have been emitting greenhouse gasses for centuries without paying an economic price. This clear common interest led to both China and India cooperating closely at the Copenhagen conference in 2009.

Finally, a fifth common interest is the geography of neighbors: China and India will want to preserve stability on their common borders. To cite two obvious examples, if both Afghanistan and Pakistan fall apart and become havens for terrorist groups, both China and India will suffer as both have disgruntled domestic Islamic groups willing to collaborate with external terrorist groups. Indeed, if Pakistan collapses and its nuclear weapons are not secured, the consequences could be disastrous for the region.

Despite this clear common challenge, the dialogue between China and India is furthest apart on the issue of Pakistan. China perceives Pakistan as a reliable old-time ally that helped China consistently and that it will therefore not even contemplate abandoning. The Communist Party regime in China counts very few countries in the world as its natural friends. Pakistan is one of them. By contrast, India views Pakistan as the biggest thorn in its side. Even though New Delhi has overcome its obsession with Pakistan as its natural rival and competitor, it still believes that the Pakistan regimes have had a consistent long-term policy of undermining India's political order. There is, of course, no doubt that Pakistan has funded and masterminded terrorist operations in India, with the most tragic example being the attack on the Taj Mahal hotel and other parts of Mumbai in November 2008.

The common challenges and shared interests of China and India underscore that the relationship between the two countries will shift back and forth between competition and collaboration. Their geopolitics will, of necessity, have to be supple and not rigidly ideological. That way a win-win relationship is possible.

Islam and the West

The third most important geopolitical relationship is between Islam and the West. In some ways, it is the most obviously troubled. Most Western writings emphasize this aspect: there is a one-thousand-year history of distrust and conflict. Yet even here, there is room for careful optimism. In the great global convergence we are seeing, the Islamic world is also joining the march to modernity. Its aspirations are now similar to those in the rest of the world.

The Israel-Palestine Issue

The roots of the distrust between Islam and the West go back to the Crusades, but they have clearly been aggravated by the last two centuries of Western colonization and domination of large swaths of the Islamic world. There was a lot of humiliation. Even though direct Western colonization has receded, Western domination continues. Many Muslims continue to ask why only Muslim countries have been either attacked or bombed by the West over the past ten years.

While many of these historical issues matter, there is one cancerous tumor in the Islam-West relationship that provides the single biggest source of aggravation: the Israel-Palestine issue. It is the single biggest source of poison in the Islam-West relationship. However, it can be solved. Most thoughtful and reasonable analysts believe that the Taba Accords proposed by Bill Clinton in January 2001 still provides the best basis for resolving the issue. We have the theoretical solution if we can find the practical will to implement it.

After years of speaking and writing on the Middle East, I have found that the best way to kick this hornet's nest is to make some pronouncement or other on the Israel-Palestine issue, as happened when I wrote in the *Financial Times* on November 10, 2011, to say that time was no longer on Israel's side.[55] Israel has bet its long-term security by relying on American power to protect it from the global pressure it feels to return the Palestinian territories once and for all. However, American power in the global system has peaked. It can only decline. By contrast, the power of the Islamic world has troughed. It can only go up. Clearly, in the long term, Israel will have to deal with an adverse pincer movement.

I felt an enormous sense of psychological relief after I published the *Financial Times* column. I knew that it would be attacked. And it was. But I felt that I had done a duty to my Israeli friends by warning them not to keep walking relentlessly toward a cliff. When time is no longer on Israel's side, it should start working on compromise solutions as quickly as possible. I am aware of the complications: a fractured Israeli coalition government, the problem of Hamas, the weakness of the Palestinian Authority. But Israelis have only to ask a simple question: Will the situation be better or worse ten or twenty years from now? And if Israel wants to get a leading indicator of the troubled world that is coming, it should ask itself what happened to its relationship with Turkey, clearly the most moderate Islamic society in its neighborhood.

Fortunately, many prominent supporters of Israel have been calling on Israel to change course. In April 2012, four prominent Jewish individuals, Stephen Robert, Ami Ayalon, Orni Petruschka, and Gilead Sher, wrote articles in the *New York Times* calling for a review of Israeli policy and a two-state solution in the Middle East. Robert, an American former chancellor of Brown University, noted that the traditional Israeli feeling of victimhood, a legacy of World War II, was no longer supported by geopolitical evidence. He said:

> Israel has gone from a vulnerable little state, surrounded by tens of millions of hostile Arab neighbors, to the most powerful military force in the Middle East. Dangers will always exist, but the balance of military

power has inexorably shifted. Peace treaties with Egypt and Jordan render unlikely any hostile coalition of neighboring countries. Syria has overwhelming internal problems. Iraq isn't looking for another war. A nuclear-armed Iran could cause trouble in the whole region, certainly for Iraq and Saudi Arabia. My expectation is the major powers will not allow Iran to obtain nuclear weapons. And if military intervention is necessary, it is better led by the major powers. Of course, Israel itself is a nuclear power. It has brought the Jewish people from centuries of victimization to military power not imaginable half a century ago. But can the Jewish people segue from deeply ingrained victimhood to the moral and practical dictates of being a major power?[56]

Noting that "Israel is losing the moral high ground through much of the world," Robert further questioned, "How can a people persecuted for so long act so brutally when finally attaining power? Will we continuously see the world as 1938, or can we use the strength of our new power to forgive, while never forgetting the lessons of our past?"[57]

Similarly, Ayalon (a former head of the Israeli domestic security agency), Petruschka (an Israeli entrepreneur), and Sher (a former chief of staff for the Israeli prime minister) called on Israel to take back the initiative in forging a peaceful, two-state solution. Here is what they said: "Israel doesn't need to wait for a final-status deal with the Palestinians. What it needs is a radically new unilateral approach: It should set the conditions for a territorial compromise based on the principle of two states for two peoples, which is essential for Israel's future as both a Jewish and a democratic state."[58]

Since Israeli foreign policies are increasingly being called into question by Israelis themselves, it is ironic that Mitt Romney, a wealthy Mormon from Michigan, has made a public show of support for some of the policies of his former Boston Consulting Group colleague Benjamin Netanyahu. Indeed, according to the *New York Times*:

Mr. Romney has suggested that he would not make any significant policy decisions about Israel without consulting Mr. Netanyahu—a level of deference that could raise eyebrows given Mr. Netanyahu's polarizing reputation, even as it appeals to the neoconservatives and evangelical

Christians who are fiercely protective of Israel. In a telling exchange during a debate in December, Mr. Romney criticized Mr. Gingrich for making a disparaging remark about Palestinians, declaring: "Before I made a statement of that nature, I'd get on the phone to my friend Bibi Netanyahu and say: 'Would it help if I say this? What would you like me to do?'"[59]

Possible Resolutions

There are two positive new trends that Israel and the West can capitalize on in finding a solution to the Israel-Palestine problem. First, the distrust between Iran and its Arab neighbors, especially Saudi Arabia, has risen to an all-time high. There have been reports that Saudi Arabia is secretly egging on Israel to bomb Iran, although the Saudi government will have no choice but to condemn publicly such an Israeli airstrike. In a Forbes.com article, Peter Cohan notes that "Saudi Arabia's rage against the Shias exceeds its dislike of its Jewish neighbors" so much so that the Saudis were willing to provide Israel logistical support to attack Iran in June 2012.[60] In fact, American diplomatic cables exposed by WikiLeaks in November 2010 revealed that King Abdullah bin Abdul Aziz had told American officials to put a stop to Iran's nuclear program. Cables dating from 2008 documented the Saudi ambassador to the United States telling an American diplomat about King Abdullah's "frequent exhortations to the US to attack Iran and so put an end to its nuclear weapons program." The ambassador also asked the Americans to "cut off the head of the snake."[61] Despite this, the Saudis cannot openly support Israeli plans to strike Iran. Why? The simple answer is that it is politically toxic for any Islamic government to be seen defending or working with Israel as long as the Palestine issue is not resolved.

Most Arab governments now want to resolve the Israel-Palestine issue because they recognize that its perpetuation provides Iran with a potent political weapon to be used against Arab rulers. Iran can justifiably accuse them of pusillanimity in the face of Israeli intransigence. One reason Iran makes bellicose statements on Israel is to embarrass its Arab neighbors. However, it would be a mistake to take these bellicose statements literally. The Iranians are reasonably sophisticated in their own way. They have no national interest in fighting Israel. And Israel can best disarm Iran of this potent political weapon by reaching a deal on the Israel-Palestine issue.

The question of Iran's ostensible search for nuclear weapons is another issue. I belong to the school that says an Israeli airstrike would be futile. It would reunite the Iranian people and strengthen the government in power. An American strike on Iran would provide China with a major geopolitical gift just as America's invasion of Iraq did in 2003. I also believe that diplomatic solutions are possible.

The people of Iran want to join the march to modernity that is sweeping across the world. Hence, the best way to produce change in Iran is not through more sanctions and isolation. These methods never work. America has imposed economic sanctions on Cuba since 1960. More than fifty years have passed. Did sanctions either remove Fidel Castro or change the nature of Cuban society? The answer is obviously no. Indeed, if America had opened its doors to Cuba, the regime would have changed much faster. This is why America should give up its flawed approach of trying to isolate Iran and instead encourage more and more Iranians to travel abroad, especially to East Asia, to see how far behind Iran is falling. This will begin a slower but more effective transformation of Iran. To understand why engagement works, the West should do a case study on Myanmar, a regime that absolutely refused to change for decades. But the persistent engagement by ASEAN transformed the mind-set of the Myanmar leaders. The "drip, drip, drip" of sustained engagement and outreach will more effectively transform Iran than the "drop, drop, drop" of bombs that the West has utilized with great abandon in the Islamic world.

Second, rising interest in modernizing and opening up Islamic societies could work in the long-term interest of Israel and the West. Like middle classes everywhere in the world, the middle classes in the Islamic world have no interest in prolonging conflict. Their first priority is to improve their own living standards. The big lesson that all Arab and non-Arab rulers have learned from the events of the Arab Spring is that ruling classes that do not take care of their people no longer stay in power. In the past, Arab governments could distract attention from the lack of development by focusing on the Israeli bogeyman. But the most developed state in the Middle East is Israel. It will benefit a lot from this new focus on development if it removes the Palestinian obstacle. A geopolitical nightmare for Iran would be an Israeli-Arab front to check its westward influence.

All this seems beyond the scope of possibility, but in this rapidly changing world of ours, ostensible geopolitical miracles can happen. The emergence of Islamist parties in Turkey and the Arab world could easily be seen as an adverse development for Israel and the West, but it is not. These Islamist parties show no desire to emulate nineteenth-century caliphates but instead want to move forward into the twenty-first century. Modernization will require them to join the larger global mainstream of development. Their role model is the AKP party in Turkey. It has promoted economic development. Turkish GDP has increased from US $232 billion in 2002, the year the AKP came to power, to US $734 billion in 2010. Turkish per capita GDP has tripled to about US $10,000 dollars over the same period of time. Equally importantly, the AKP has protected its Islamic identity. Several commentators have noted the positive role model effects of the AKP. "Erdogan succeeded in establishing a viable model for political Islamism," said political scientist and Turkey specialist Dorothée Schmid of the French Institute for International Relations. Ami Lourai, a senior official from Tunisian Islamist party Ennahdha, told the French daily *Libération* in January 2011: "Turks showed the way: you can be religious and open to modernity and democracy at the same time." During a global economic downturn, Turkish unemployment was reduced. The Turkish economy grew at a staggering 9 percent in 2011. The AKP supervised this economic upturn while making Turkey more democratic and influential internationally.[62]

An Islamic world full of modernizing Islamist parties would have a completely different, even functional, relationship with the West. The dysfunctional era could end. We might even see positive changes in the countries that now seem to bring nothing but despair to the West. In his book *Zero-Sum World*, Gideon Rachman correctly identifies Pakistan as the one Muslim country that could become a "failed state." He notes, "Shortly before he took office, Obama received a four-hour intelligence briefing devoted entirely to Pakistan. He emerged shaken and convinced that Pakistan was the most dangerous international problem facing the United States."[63]

Yet even in Pakistan, there are positive trends. Many voices are speaking out bravely to say that Pakistan should change course and join the global mainstream. In a February 20, 2012, column on Project Syndicate, well-known Indian MP Shashi Tharoor praised the courage of a growing number of Pakistani politicians and members of the public who are advocating new approaches to India. He said:

> On a recent visit to Islamabad and Lahore, I sensed in private conversations a widespread desire to put the Kashmir dispute on the back burner and explore avenues of mutually beneficial cooperation with India. Pakistanis are saying it publicly, too. In a recent interview, the politician and religious leader Maulana Fazal-ur-Rehman spoke frankly about Kashmir: "Obviously, we are in favor of a political solution. . . . Things have changed so much. Now the concept of winning Kashmir has taken a back seat to the urgency of saving Pakistan."[64]

Younger Pakistanis are going even further. Columnist Yaqoob Khan Bangash, for example, openly derides the hallowed Pakistani argument that, as Muslims, Indian Kashmiris would want to join Pakistan. "Despite being practically a war zone since 1989, Indian Kashmir has managed higher literacy, economic growth, and per capita income rates than most of Pakistan," he wrote recently. "Why would the Kashmiris want to join Pakistan now? What do we have to offer them?" Quoting Bangash, Tharoor, who is a former Indian minister of state for foreign affairs and UN under-secretary-general, comments, "If such episodes reflect an incipient new national mood in Pakistan, it could well be time for India to seize the moment to build a lasting peace."[65]

A further sign of the thawing Indo-Pakistan relationship was provided when the CII organized a trade show for the first time ever in Lahore in February 2012. The Indian commerce minister, Anand Sharma, visited for the first time. Two weeks after his trip, Pakistan announced a change in rules to allow more Indian imports. Pankaj Mishra, an Indian novelist and essayist, wrote in Bloomberg on April 8, 2012:

> Recently in Karachi, I dropped in on a talk by the Pakistani journalist and TV anchor Kamran Khan at a Rotary Club meeting. Describing relations between India and Pakistan at a "crossroads," Khan exhorted his audience to feel shame about Pakistani involvement in the terrorist

attacks on Mumbai in 2008 that killed 164 people and have frozen India-Pakistan relations ever since. Khan lamented the many missed opportunities for a comprehensive agreement between India and Pakistan. Finally, he expressed great optimism about a trade deal announced in November—in the making for almost 16 years, and recently expanded—that would open up Pakistani markets for many more Indian products.[66]

No other Muslim country has as talented and as successful a diaspora as Pakistan does. Pakistanis have risen to senior positions in the leading multinational corporations and banks of the world. Their enormous success in the modern world provides real hope that Pakistan itself can thrive in modernity. With the right conditions, thousands could return to Pakistan just as thousands have returned to China and India.

The bottom line is that the Islamic world of 1.2 billion people is not immune from the larger global trends of convergence. Modern technology and frequent travel have opened Pakistani eyes to this new consensual cluster of norms sweeping across most of the developing world. As a result, Islamic populations are putting enormous political pressure on their governments to focus on economic development and not get distracted. Fortunately, there are enough success stories in the Islamic world to demonstrate that modernization and Islam can go hand in hand. Turkey, Indonesia, and Malaysia provide the best examples. Even more remarkably, Bangladesh, once almost a metaphor for despair in the Western mind, saw its economy grow by 6 percent on average in the first decade of the twenty-first century.

The Geopolitical Miracle of Southeast Asia

The grounds for optimism, despite all the potential problems that this chapter has outlined, lie in the geopolitical miracle that has occurred in Southeast Asia. For decades after World War II, it was one of the most troubled spots in the world. More lives were lost in the wars fought in Southeast Asia than in the entire Middle East. In the 1950s and 1960s, Communist insurgencies were raging all across the region. Then Cambodia, Laos, and Vietnam fell to Communist regimes in 1975. Every Western commentator, without exception, said that the non-Communist societies in Southeast

Asia, which had formed ASEAN in 1967, were doomed. They would fall like "dominoes." More wars followed. Vietnam invaded Cambodia in January 1979. China retaliated by attacking Vietnam. Hundreds of thousands of Chinese soldiers fought hundreds of thousands of Vietnamese soldiers. Nearly a million soldiers and civilians died in the Indochina War, and 2.4 million died in the Cambodian genocide. Few regions in the world were as ruined in the post–World War II era.

So how did this region emerge as the most stable and promising of the entire developing world today? First, the roots of the miracle are in ASEAN's prevention of wars among its member states. It has not yet achieved "zero prospect" of war as the EU has, but it is clearly moving in that direction. Second, it has promoted economic and many other forms of cooperation. Each year, about one thousand ASEAN meetings are held. And the organization has taken many bold steps, such as creating an "open-skies" agreement among ASEAN capitals. Air traffic in Southeast Asia has exploded as a result. A study by *The Nation* notes, "Air-travel growth in Southeast Asia over the next 20 years is expected to be 6.9 per cent, while the region's economy is projected to grow 4.3 per cent. The Asia-Pacific region will account for 44 per cent of travel in 20 years' time, up from about 34 per cent today."[67]

Third, ASEAN has consistently engaged all the great powers. It realized that trying to keep them out would have been futile. A sensible policy of engaging all great powers produced great dividends. When China proposed a free trade agreement with ASEAN, it spurred Japan and India to do the same. ASEAN has shared the fruits of its geopolitical acumen with other regions. Just north of Southeast Asia, in Northeast Asia, are three powerful states: China, Japan, and Korea. Logically, there should be an Association of Northeast Asian Nations to match ASEAN. None has been formed yet. While China, Japan, and Korea have held trilateral meetings, all the early meetings of these three powers were stimulated by their participation in various ASEAN-plus meetings. Indeed, relations plummeted in 1996 when Prime Minister Ryutaro Hashimoto visited the Yasukuni Shrine, which also enshrines the souls of Japanese war criminals from World War II. Quite naturally, these visits angered Chinese leaders and Sino-Japanese relations plummeted. After this happened, the only way for the leaders of China and Japan to break the ice was to meet each other on the fringes of an ASEAN summit in Manila. A Japanese professor and former ambassador to the Netherlands, Kazuhiko Togo, describes what happened:

> At the 1999 ASEAN plus Three Leaders Meeting in Manila, Japan surprised everyone by inviting leaders from China and Korea for a breakfast meeting. Given the complexity of the relations with these two countries, . . . for many Japanese, the harmonious images which were televised from Manila, at the heart of ASEAN, on the morning of 28 November 1999 evoked a great sigh of relief. The ingenuity evoked in holding the breakfast meeting at a triangular table was also warmly received by the Japanese television audience. The gathering of three Northeast Asian leaders immediately became a regular event at the fringe of ASEAN plus Three meetings. Tripartite cooperation started at government level. 2002 became the year of tripartite exchanges and many cultural events took place in each of the three countries. At the Bali Meeting in October 2003 a joint declaration of Tripartite Cooperation among the three countries was adopted.[68]

In short, ASEAN saved the day by facilitating face-saving meetings among the Northeast Asian leaders.

Fourth, ASEAN has now deepened its cooperation by going beyond government-to-government exchanges toward more and more people-to-people exchanges. University exchanges between ASEAN member states have multiplied. The ASEAN University Network currently comprises twenty-six participating universities. Singapore also offers the ASEAN Scholarship to promising students of the nine other member states for secondary school, junior college, and university education.[69] Even more encouraging, there exist a few online portals in which ASEAN youth can interact and share ideas, such as ASEANYouth.org and the ASEAN Youth Movement Facebook page.[70]

According to a March 2012 article in *The Diplomat*:

> A smartphone app called ASEAN One, which translates popular business phrases into 11 languages of the Southeast Asian region, was launched last week in Bangkok. Aside from ASEAN One, there are big-

ger projects that seek to foster unity in the region. There has been talk of sending a single regional team to the Olympics. Meanwhile, some economists are in favor of a single regional currency and even the establishment of a Southeast Asian bank network. In addition, tourism officials are currently studying the feasibility of adopting a single travel visa for the whole region.[71]

So the big question that the rest of the world needs to ask is, if one of the most unpromising geopolitical regions of the world can in a generation produce a geopolitical miracle, can the Middle East and other regions do the same? I firmly believe they can. The power of convergence makes possible miracles like those among the ASEAN countries. Equally importantly, ASEAN's experience also demonstrates how the realist and liberal-internationalist streams of geopolitics are at constant play with each other. While competition swirls among ASEAN countries and between ASEAN's neighbors, all the regional participants also realize how interdependent they have become. Trade has exploded in the ASEAN region, growing from $302 billion in 1990 to $2 trillion in 2010. In short, ASEAN provides a powerful microcosm of the great convergence that the world is experiencing.

CHAPTER
6

A Barrier to Convergence

THE BIGGEST PIECE OF GOOD NEWS THAT THIS BOOK HAS TO OFFER
is that the 88 percent of the world's population who live outside the West
want to converge toward Western living standards and have the same kind
of peaceful and prosperous lives that most Western citizens have enjoyed
over the past few decades. This is why the brightest young people outside the
West aspire to study in leading Western universities and return home with
the same set of aspirations and norms as their young Western counterparts.

All this should, in theory, facilitate the acceptance by the West of the
rest of the earth's inhabitants as equal citizens. Ironically, there remains a
deep psychological reluctance by many in the West to accept the simple
proposition that "we are all equal." This reluctance in turn stems from a
deeply held unconscious assumption that the West remains, in one way or
another, a morally superior civilization. This assumption has to be addressed squarely if we are to persuade the West to get off the proverbial
moral "high horse" and notice that it's walking on the same moral ground
as the rest of the world.

Tragically, the idea that the West is inherently a benevolent force on the
world stage is a deeply embedded myth. But the West is neither inherently
benevolent nor inherently malevolent. It is, in fact, no different in its behavior from the majority of states in the world. In short, the Western states
behave "normally," not "benignly," on the world stage.

Somehow, the suggestion that the West acts normally is seen as an anti-Western statement, at least as far as many influential Western journals and pundits are concerned. *The Economist* described my previous book on Asia as "an anti-Western polemic, designed to wake up Americans and Europeans by making them angry."[1] In its review of my book on America and the world, the *Financial Times* said that it belonged to the usual "denunciations" of "wicked US power."[2] Yet the truth is the exact opposite: I have always been and I will always remain a great admirer and friend of the West. I majored in Western philosophy in both my undergraduate and postgraduate education. In one of my earliest essays, entitled "Can Asians Think?," I described the European miracle as follows:

> It was Europe that leapt ahead. Something almost magical happened to European minds, and this was followed by wave after wave of progress and advance of civilisations, from the Renaissance to the Enlightenment, from the scientific revolution to the industrial revolution. While Asian societies degenerated into backwardness and ossification, European societies, propelled forward by new forms of economic organisation, military-technical dynamism, political pluralism within the continent as a whole (if not within all individual countries), and the uneven beginnings of intellectual liberty, notably in Italy, Britain, and Holland, produced what would have been called at the time the "European miracle"—had there been an observing, superior civilisation to mark the event. Because that mix of critical ingredients did not exist in any of the Asian societies, they appeared to stand still while Europe advanced to the centre of the world stage. Colonisation, which began in the 16th century, and the industrial revolution in the 19th century, augmented and entrenched Europe's dominant position.[3]

I am ready to acknowledge that the West has done a lot of good for the world. I would not have been where I am today if I had not had the benefits of a Western education in Singapore and Canada.

Yet the West has done a lot of harm too. Two centuries of colonial exploitation have left deep scars all around the world. Western domination damaged the psychological self-confidence of several civilizations, especially in Asia, Africa, and the Islamic world, damage from which these societies are only now beginning to recover. Many contemporary Western minds dismiss colonial exploitation as errors of the past. Yet these same Western minds gloss over the fact that the US and the UK launched an illegal war in Iraq, NATO forces kill innocent civilians with drone attacks in Afghanistan and Pakistan, and the biggest defender of democracy and human rights, the United States of America, reintroduced torture in the twenty-first century. All this happened in the last decade or so. This is why very few of the people who live outside the West believe that the West is inherently benevolent. Most of them believe that the West is just like the Rest.

So why, then, does this myth persist? One of the biggest sources is the belief that the West is inherently benevolent because of the foreign aid it gives to the world. Yet most development economists have known, for example, that America is among the least generous of all Western countries in the amount of foreign aid that it gives out. Among the OECD countries, it is ranked number nineteen out of twenty-three because it only gives out 0.21 percent in foreign aid,[4] even though the OECD countries have pledged to give out 0.7 percent of their GNP in foreign aid. Despite this abysmal American record being well known, the American population continues to believe that America is very generous and doles out massive amounts in foreign aid. A 2010 Quaire survey showed that Americans believe that foreign aid as a percentage of the federal budget is 25–27 percent.[5] Based on these statistics, Ezra Klein created a chart in the *Washington Post* that vividly shows the contrast between American beliefs and reality when it comes to foreign aid (see Figure 6.1).

It is not surprising that the American people believe that America is a generous country in foreign aid. They hear it all the time in the writing and speeches of American leaders in all spheres.

Given this deeply and widely held belief in America and in other Western countries that the West demonstrates its inherent generosity through its generous foreign aid programs, this chapter will spend some time dissecting the real nature and impact of Western aid programs. In doing so, let me acknowledge that there is already a trove of writing about Western foreign aid. Much of it has documented some of the big failures. *The White Man's Burden: Why the West's Efforts to Aid the Rest Have Done So Much Ill and So Little Good* by William Easterly argues that development aid since

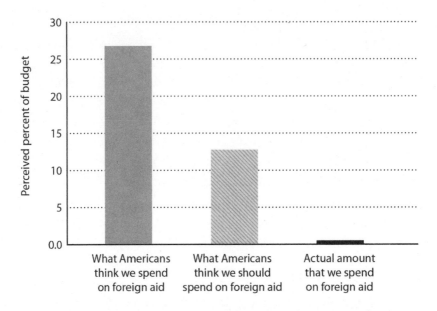

FIGURE 6.1 American Misperceptions of US Foreign Aid. *Source:* Data from
http://www.worldpublicopinion.org/pipa/pdf/nov10/ForeignAid_Nov10_quaire.pdf.

the establishment of mammoth international aid agencies, such as the
UNDP, the World Bank, and the WFP, has not worked partly because aid
agencies have been too ambitious. They have often proposed solutions important to the donors rather than to the recipients. Moreover, the lack of
accountability to aid recipients and the absence of feedback mechanisms
have aggravated inefficiency in development aid. To Easterly, foreign aid
is "the other tragedy of the world's poor . . . the tragedy in which the West
spent $2.3 trillion on foreign aid over the last five decades and still had not
managed to get twelve-cent medicines to children to prevent half of all
malaria deaths. The West spent $2.3 trillion and still had not managed to
get three dollars to each new mother to prevent five million child deaths. . . .
It's a tragedy that so much well-meaning compassion did not bring these
results for needy people."[6]

Dambisa Moyo's best-selling book *Dead Aid* has documented how
Western aid has crippled Africa's development by taking away incentives
for self-development. African countries have become addicted to aid and
hooked on a cycle of repaying the interest on their loans. Instead of solving

Africa's problems, aid has exacerbated them. Equally importantly, Chapter 5 of the book *Fixing Failed States: A Framework for Rebuilding a Fractured World* by Ashraf Ghani and Clare Lockhart documents in graphic detail how the aid complex has become fundamentally dysfunctional.

I want to add one more level of criticism of Western aid programs. I challenge the widely held assumption that the intention behind Western aid is to do good to the recipients. Instead, I believe that if a large-scale objective study were done of Western foreign aid, it would demonstrate that the primary intention is to enhance the national interests of the donors and not to help the interest of the recipients. Even more sadly, few Western taxpayers are aware that the aid money designated to promote their national interests has actually been hijacked by a few firms. Clare Lockhart has told me, "The aid complex now benefits a very narrow group of commercial firms who act as a cartel and have captured taxpayers' money. It is not to the benefit of the public or governments of donors that these firms capture windfalls and perform poorly—a very narrow group are benefiting."[7]

Where is the evidence for this allegation that aid is never intended to help the beneficiary? There is a massive amount. In this chapter, I will highlight several examples to make my case: the failure of the OECD; the corruption of US aid to Afghanistan; how IMF aid is tied to voting patterns of UN Security Council members; the slow, often ineffective, expensive, and self-serving food aid; and the duplication of efforts by donors and the increasing amount of aid going to corrupt countries.

The Failure of the OECD

The Western countries have disbursed a lot of foreign aid (according to their official figures). The OECD, for example, claims that annual Western aid disbursements have increased significantly from $53 billion in 2000 to $133 billion in 2011. However, there is also no doubt that the aid has not benefited most of the intended beneficiaries. The gap between the amount of aid dispensed and the few good results ought to lead us to look for a systemic design flaw in Western aid. The flaw is not difficult to figure out: much of the aid was designed to further the interests of the donors. Indeed, Ghani and Lockhart note that "donors prepare their own, often conflicting, priorities on investment, and after years of OECD declarations, have never been able to agree on coordination arrangements between themselves. Because donors differ in their degree of emphasis on gender, human rights or social protection, the ground reality becomes a quilt of confusing practices and strategies."[8]

Many knowledgeable and reasonably well-informed people in the West are aware of the paltry good results that have come from foreign aid, and yet they are not troubled by this poor performance. Privately they think, "We in the West were generous and tried to help. However, those Africans and Asians were incompetent and wasted our aid. What can we do? We cannot make them as competent as the West." When aid fails, the recipients are blamed, but never the donors. Academics have a name for this— the Samaritan's Dilemma—the idea that donors are good Samaritans but aid recipients cannot be trusted to do good for themselves and will abuse the Samaritan's goodwill.

One person who experienced directly the condescension that Western aid officials feel toward their recipients was Chinua Achebe, the legendary Nigerian novelist. He was invited to attend an OECD meeting in early 1989. Unsure why a novelist from Nigeria had been invited to speak at a meeting of European, American, Canadian, and Australian bankers and economists, he walked into the meeting with some trepidation: "As I listened to them . . . I was left in no doubt, by the assurance they displayed, that these were the masters of our world, savoring the benefits of their success." Yet it soon dawned on Achebe that what he was part of was no less than "a fiction workshop" in which these Western bankers would prescribe theories ostensibly to help the developing world. Here is what he said: "Here you are, spinning your fine theories, to be tried out in your imaginary laboratories. You are developing new drugs and feeding them to a bunch of laboratory guinea pigs and hoping for the best. I have news for you. Africa is not fiction. Africa is people, real people. . . . Have you thought, *really* thought, of Africa as people?"[9] His essay is worth reading in full to understand how poorly Western aid donors understand the recipients they are trying to help.

The reason that many knowledgeable and reasonably well-informed people have come to believe that failures in development are due to recipients and not donors is because very large and credible international development institutions, like the OECD and the World Bank, monitor Western aid flows. Surely, if the OECD and the World Bank are monitoring and reporting on Western aid flows, they can confirm objectively that the West has tried its best. But the fact is that both the OECD and the World Bank are tightly controlled by Western donor countries, so tightly that they cannot possibly be objective and independent in their evaluations.

The OECD ought to carry out a root-and-branch analysis of its role and place in the world. In theory, its mission (according to its name) is to promote economic cooperation and development. In reality, it has served as a rich man's club. Indeed, I recall the time when the OECD was proud to be called that. Of course, no OECD official would have admitted that his or her work was to defend the rich. But during three decades of interaction with OECD representatives, I constantly sensed that they viewed with condescension all the views expressed by Third World representatives. They were confident that they were the real custodians of the "holy grail" of economic development.

This arrogance and condescension would have been understandable if the OECD had developed a sterling record of promoting either economic cooperation or development. Sadly, the OECD has never fulfilled the mission suggested by its name. Its predecessor, the Organisation for European Economic Cooperation (OEEC) may have fulfilled its role of managing and implementing the Marshall Plan for Europe. As Ghani and Lockhart emphasize, "The Marshall Plan still stands as a unique act of visionary statesmanship—and an illuminating example of a strategic instrument for state-building."[10] Why hasn't the OECD asked itself this obvious question: Why has it failed when the OEEC succeeded? Indeed, the OECD has no real success story to speak of.[11]

In an article entitled "From 'Club of the Rich' to 'Globalisation à la Carte'? Evaluating Reform at the OECD," published in *Global Policy*, Judith Clifton and Daniel Díaz-Fuentes document what the organization has and has not achieved. They describe well the historical context in which the role of the OECD evolved: "Contemporary scholars understood that the purpose of the OECD was to help consolidate the transatlantic military and economic alliance between North America and Europe in a context of the Cold War and of increased interdependence."[12] But the Cold War ended more than twenty years ago. The OECD should have reinvented itself to stay relevant. It failed to do so and thereby confirmed that it was destined to become a "sunset organization."[13]

The tragedy here is that the OECD could have played a valuable role globally. Each year, the OECD countries dispense billions of dollars in aid. If these billions of dollars had been well spent, billions of people could have been rescued from poverty. Instead, most official development assistance was wasted. Countries like Tanzania and Zambia, which received more aid per capita than most countries, had little to show for it. What happened? Why did billions of dollars fail to foster economic cooperation and development? Institutionally, there was no better global organization than the OECD to solve this mystery. But it failed.[14]

Clifton and Diaz-Fuentes explain the institutional factors that prevented the OECD from providing independent and objective analysis. It was funded by donor countries. It was also staffed by donor countries. Indeed, as the article documents, for a long time three countries, France, the US, and the UK, provided most of the staff. No organization bites the hand that feeds it. Hence, instead of reviewing objectively the failures of the donor countries, OECD officials assumed that all the flaws were the fault of the aid recipients. The following telling line from Clifton and Diaz-Fuentes captures well the attitudes of the OECD analysts: "OECD reports on non-members took the form of 'unidirectional' recommendations, since it was assumed that its members and staff enjoyed superior policy 'know-how' based on the assumption of the superior functioning of their economies."[15]

In short, despite its name and ostensible mission, the role of the OECD was not to serve the interests of aid recipient countries. This is why they kept their deliberations as secret as possible. As Clifton and Diaz-Fuentes write, "The tradition of holding 'secretive' meetings dates back to the OEEC's organization of meetings to discuss the sensitive topic of Marshall Plan aid allocation. But their opaque nature has aroused suspicion and criticism from observers, who have claimed that they served as places where the richest member countries could forge common postures with their allies before taking their agenda on to other international organizations or back home."[16]

Equally and importantly, the authors point out that the OECD was not completely honest about what the "developed" countries had done at earlier stages of their development: "Economists such as Chang and Grabel

(2004) and Rodrik (2008) have argued how western countries' insistence on 'best practice' policy such as free trade for the developing world amounts to denying their own use of trade instruments in the past."[17] When the United States was developing its economy in the nineteenth century, it raised tariff barriers to keep out cheap British imports. Now it refuses to let developing countries do the same.

The existential question that the OECD faces is what its future role will be in a world where "economic cooperation and development" are going on well and especially well without any major OECD contribution. The one region in the world that is now excelling in economic cooperation and development is Asia. Trade is growing much faster in East Asia than in Europe or North America. No Asian policymaker I have met (and I have met several) has ever said to me that the OECD has made any kind of contribution to the greatest success story in economic cooperation and development.[18]

Clifton and Díaz-Fuentes end their article with a pointed question: "If the OECD does not reform substantially, it faces a decisive challenge: the organization needs the emerging economies, but do they need the OECD?"[19] The truly sad answer to this question is that the OECD may be beyond repair. The best thing that the OECD countries can do is to shutter the OECD and use all the money saved to set up think tanks and schools of public policy in the developing world. When I served as ambassador to the UN, Western officials complained frequently that many UN bodies were set up without any sunset provisions. Since the OECD is clearly a sunset organization, the West should lead by example and shut it down.[20] The simple and hard truth is that the OECD has become a narrow and self-serving club that has lost its mission and purpose and serves neither the interests of its own societies nor those it states it intends to benefit.

There are all too many examples of how Western aid was never designed with the primary purpose of helping the ostensible recipients. In case after case, donor interest came first. But it is important to separate the nature of the policies from many of the people who worked on their implementation. Many individuals who dispense foreign aid do so with the intention of doing good. Indeed, many believe that without foreign aid, poverty cannot be eradicated. One such extremely generous soul whom I knew personally was the American official and academic Harlan Cleveland (now deceased).

He was a very good man. He believed foreign aid was indispensable. This is what he wrote in his book *Birth of a New World*:

> No matter how well each developing country manages to mix public and private enterprise and how skillfully it uses initiatives, subsidies, and incentives to maximize both economic growth and social fairness, it is clear that the developing world will need major inputs of public grants and loans and private investment from Europe, Japan, and North America to achieve the kinds and rates of growth that will make fairness an acceptable goal. A strategy of "doing something about poverty" will require an assured source of incentive funds for development. Those funds should be raised by an international development tax.[21]

There are many good souls like Harlan in the Western development industry. Yet I also know that many of these good souls were overridden by others in their governments. When Richard Holbrooke (who died in 2010), one of the toughest American officials I knew, was assistant secretary of state for the Asia-Pacific, he told me that one of his key responsibilities was to educate US Agency for International Development (USAID) officials and remind them that the primary purpose of American foreign aid was to enhance American national interests, not to do good for the world.

Some Western aid has unquestionably done good. Not all has gone to waste. In Bhutan I saw a beautiful Japanese bridge traversing a deep gorge, no doubt helping to connect communities and save travel time. (Japan is a member of the OECD.) In Pakistan, I was truly impressed by the good work done by the Lahore University of Management Sciences, a business school started with USAID funds. Even Singapore, which had succeeded primarily through self-reliance, not foreign aid, had benefited enormously from the wise advice dispensed by two UNDP development experts sent to Singapore, namely, Dr. Albert Winsemius and I. F. Tang. Yet despite the many good examples we can find of success, the big question remains: Why did most of Western foreign aid fail so miserably?

My rough estimate is that for every $1 given out in foreign aid, particularly bilateral aid, technical assistance, conditional aid, economic aid, food aid, and military aid, 20¢ gets spent on administrative expenses of the donor country (paying for salaries of their own officials); 20¢ goes to consultants employed by the donor country (and the consultants are often their own citizens); 30 to 40¢ goes to procuring equipment or services provided by the donor country (to help the industries of the donor country); and if the recipient country is lucky, it will actually receive 20 to 30¢ out of every foreign aid dollar that was ostensibly given to it. I would like to challenge the development experts in the OECD and the World Bank to provide an alternative estimate if they believe that mine is wrong.

The Corruption of Aid to Afghanistan

My claim that the recipient country would be lucky to get 20 to 30¢ out of any $1 given to it may seem excessively harsh. Yet it is also clear that in some cases, the recipient countries have received much less. One extreme study of waste is provided by Clare Lockhart. A villager in Afghanistan told her, "We would like to tell you the story of $150 million going up in smoke. We heard on the radio that there was going to be a reconstruction programme in our region to help us rebuild our houses after coming back from exile, and we were very pleased."[22]

This was the summer of 2002. The village was in a remote part of Bamiyan Province, in Afghanistan's central highlands, and several hours' drive from the provincial capital—utterly cut off from the world. UN agencies and NGOs were rushing to provide "quick impact" projects to help Afghan citizens in the aftermath of war. That $150 million could have transformed the lives of the inhabitants of villages like this one.

But it was not to be, the young man explained:

After many months, very little had happened. We may be illiterate, but we are not stupid. So we went to find out what was going on. And this is what we discovered: the money was received by an agency in Geneva, who took 20 per cent and subcontracted the job to another agency in Washington DC, who also took 20 per cent. Again it was subcontracted and another 20 per cent was taken; and this happened again when the money arrived in Kabul. By this time there was very little money left; but enough for someone to buy wood in western Iran and have it shipped by a shipping cartel owned by a provincial governor at five times the cost of regular transportation. Eventually some wooden beams reached our villages. But the beams were too large and heavy for the mud walls that we can build. So all we could do was chop them up and use them for firewood.[23]

Under the officially audited figures of the OECD, this $150 million would have been Western "aid" to Afghanistan. In reality, several Western interests and corporations, and one corrupt local governor, were the real beneficiaries. The Afghans got firewood. So is this Afghan case a wild aberration or an indication of what "normally" goes wrong?

Indeed, an estimated 70 percent of all aid to Afghanistan between 2002 and 2004 was spent on the internal costs of the UN agency presence. Sadly, these failures of Western aid in Afghanistan did not stop there. Ghani and Lockhart, both former UN advisers to Afghanistan, point to USAID's 2005 school building program in Afghanistan as an example. Although USAID had promised the government of Afghanistan that it would build 1,100 schools within two years, it ended up building only eight within this time— of which six had already collapsed. Citizens interviewed in 2007 in Afghanistan expressed a sense of betrayal by the international community given the waste, inefficiency, and corruption.[24] Stories like these illustrate Ghani and Lockhart's statement that "instead of opening countries up to legitimate entrepreneurial activity, the aid system epitomizes the side of capitalism that is fundamentally exploitative, comprised of extractive industries and technical assistance brigades."[25] I have no doubt that most Western leaders would dismiss these Afghan cases as aberrations, but I don't think so. They are just more extreme examples of the norm.

The Actual Nature of IMF Aid

In "Rhetoric Versus Reality: The Best and Worst of Aid Agency Practices," a carefully documented study on foreign aid, William Easterly and Claudia R. Williamson found that in much of the 1980s to the mid-1990s, between 50 and 80 percent of aid was tied to recipients spending aid money on goods and services from the donor country, voting in line with it in international forums such as the United Nations, or following policy prescriptions like opening up markets to goods from donor countries. After the Cold War, tied aid dropped significantly, suggesting that Western donors no longer saw the ne-

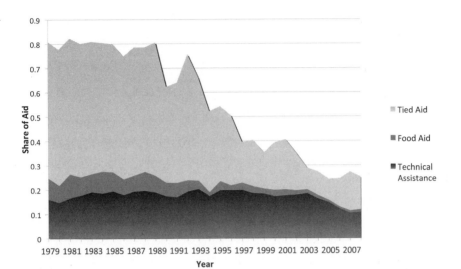

FIGURE 6.2 Share of Tied Aid to Total Aid, 1979–2007. *Source:* Based on William Easterly and Claudia R. Williamson, "Rhetoric Versus Reality: The Best and Worst of Aid Agency Practices," *World Development* 39, no. 11 (2011): 1930–1949.

cessity of buying loyalty. Figure 6.2 clearly shows that Western aid was designed to be a mechanism for bribing developing countries to support Western interests; the interests of the recipient countries were peripheral, at best. This is why Ghani and Lockhart note that "in this global context, aid quickly became a means of rewarding rulers on the basis of whether their foreign policies were with or against one of the superpowers—rather than whether they were pursuing any particular developmental agenda."[26]

Every time a developing country joins the UN Security Council, it suddenly finds that the amount of foreign aid increases during the two years that it serves on the UNSC. Why? The vote of the developing country is suddenly useful to the interests of the donor country, and so it gets more foreign aid. Foreign aid follows "interests." And if the developing country dares to vote against the interests of the donor country in the UNSC, it is either threatened with or actually dealt a blow of reduced foreign aid. In short, the foreign aid that is in theory meant to help the "poor" is actually used as an instrument of blackmail in international relations.

Three scholars from Yale University and ETH Zurich, Axel Dreher, Jan-Egbert Sturm, and James Raymond Vreeland, have investigated whether temporary members of the UN Security Council receive favorable treatment from the International Monetary Fund. Looking at data for 191 countries over the period 1951–2004, they found a "robust positive relationship between temporary UN Security Council membership and participation in IMF programs, even after accounting for economic and political factors."[27] Another study found that average US aid increases by 54 percent and average UN development aid by 7 percent when a country is elected to the Security Council.[28] Dreher and colleagues cite the case of Tanzania as indicative:

> Following independence in 1961, the government did not enter into an IMF arrangement for a decade and a half. Then Tanzania ran for election to the UNSC in the fall of 1974. That year it received an IMF loan of 6.3 million special drawing rights (SDR) with no policy conditions attached. The government received another unconditional IMF loan for 3.15 million SDR in 1975. Tanzania then entered into a one year Standby Arrangement for 10.5 million SDR on 21 August 1975. The policy conditions associated with this arrangement were notably weak. The IMF merely requested that domestic credit usage by the public sector be constrained. Tanzanian President Julius Nyerere used his high international profile and his country's first seat on the UNSC to negotiate for IMF loans and soft conditionality, and by the end of 1975, Tanzania appeared to have very positive relations with the IMF.
>
> What is particularly interesting about this case is that Tanzania voted along with the United States, Japan, the United Kingdom and France—the members of the UNSC who had the most influence at the IMF—on every UNSC resolution passed in 1975. Early in 1976, however, after already having received nearly 10 million special drawing rights in loans from the IMF, the Tanzanian government decided to vote for some resolutions that were not supported by all of the powerful members of the IMF. In March, Tanzania voted for a resolution condemning US Cold War ally South Africa's aggression against Angola. The US, Japan, the United Kingdom, France, and Italy abstained from this resolution. In April, Tanzania voted for a resolution calling for Indonesia to withdraw from East Timor; the US and Japan abstained. And in July, Tanzania voted for a resolution condemning South Africa's attack on Zambia; the US abstained. Interestingly, the IMF never disbursed the Stand-by Arrangement loan that had been signed in August 1975.

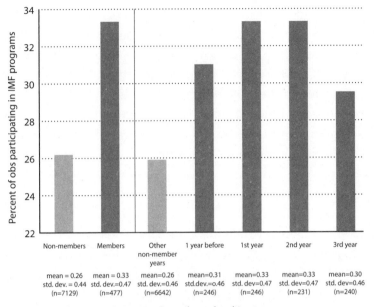

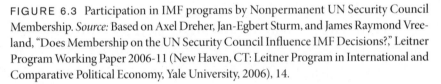

UN Security Council membership status

FIGURE 6.3 Participation in IMF programs by Nonpermanent UN Security Council Membership. *Source:* Based on Axel Dreher, Jan-Egbert Sturm, and James Raymond Vreeland, "Does Membership on the UN Security Council Influence IMF Decisions?," Leitner Program Working Paper 2006-11 (New Haven, CT: Leitner Program in International and Comparative Political Economy, Yale University, 2006), 14.

Further anecdotes abound: Gabon achieved independence in 1960 and never entered into an IMF arrangement until 31 May 1978, about 5 months after joining the UNSC for the first time. During its tenure as a UNSC member, it voted on several important resolutions, siding with the US, France, Germany, and Canada—and against the Soviet Union—on issues such as a UN Interim Force set up in Lebanon and Namibian independence. Gabon did support some resolutions condemning South Africa where the US, UK, France, Germany, and Canada abstained. The IMF disbursed exactly half of the agreed upon 15 million SDR loan to Gabon.[29]

The authors note the following:

As [Figure 6.3] illustrates, governments not serving on the UN Security Council participate in IMF programs only 26.2 percent of the time, while governments serving on the UNSC participate 33.3 percent of the time. This increase by over 25 percent (or of more than 7 percentage points) of the baseline probability is highly significant. . . . Restricting our attention to only those observations of countries that actually serve on the UNSC, we see that participation in IMF programs is lower the years before and after service on the UNSC than it is during service. Comparing these with all remaining observations reveals that already the year after membership is no longer statistically different, in contrast to especially the years during membership. In other words, the increase in IMF program participation rates does appear to be driven by UNSC membership.[30]

This indisputable correlation between IMF assistance and Western interests in the UNSC should help to remove any doubts that, while in theory the IMF and the World Bank are independent international organizations, they have in practice served as instruments of Western geopolitical power. Indeed, even relatively strong and independent heads of these two institutions have found that they could not stand up to direct pressures from the American government. In his memoirs, former World Bank chief James Wolfensohn tells an extremely revealing story of how crucial decisions are made by the World Bank:

In late August [1998], I took a call from Deputy Secretary Lawrence Summers at the US Treasury. It was 11:00PM, and without any preamble, he said that he had been talking to the IMF and to the Russians, and they needed cash immediately. He explained that the IMF was putting a rescue package together and said bluntly that the Bank needed to commit $6 billion immediately as part of the financing. If we did not agree, he continued, we would break the whole deal and he was certain that the World Bank would be blamed for the collapse.

I was appalled. Financial bailouts were a job for the IMF and not, I believed, for us. I had not been consulted about any of this; nor had I attended any of the crisis meetings. I had no details beyond what I had seen in the press and what Larry had just told me. Neither I nor my colleagues had been involved in a single negotiation with the Russians. "We're not fire-fighters, Larry," I said. "This isn't how the system was set up." I was angry. Such a demand was a direct affront to the integrity of our work at the Bank. Worse than that, we had no executive mechanism to put together such funds at short notice. I certainly did not see our role as jumping to salute at the US Treasury's order. . . . But I realised that Summers would not be calling without President Clinton's support. . . .

At the emergency board meeting I called the next morning, the ground had been prepared. The executive directors from the wealthy countries were very simply instructed on how to vote. The poorer, developing countries were shocked by the amount of money requested and were resistant to the idea, but the rich member countries that were the dominant shareholders voted to say yes.[31]

One justification that could be offered for the US Treasury's arm-twisting of the World Bank to provide loans to Russia is that it was intended for a good cause. Russia had devalued the ruble, defaulted on all its debts, and declared a moratorium on paying foreign creditors, resulting in massive inflation and placing severe stress on Russian state social services. Indeed, there was a real danger of the Russian economy collapsing. Given the urgent and perilous situation, it was perfectly understandable for the US Treasury to call on the World Bank to help put out a dangerous fire. Russia was in trouble. Russia needed help. The World Bank could help. This may seem reasonable. This is why it is important to stress here that the World Bank and IMF have allowed themselves to be arm-twisted to engage in some completely unreasonable and even immoral activities.

One particularly shocking story was told by the Nobel laureate Joseph Stiglitz about the IMF and Ethiopia. "In 1996 Ethiopia repaid a U.S. bank loan early, using some of its reserves. The transaction made perfect sense. In spite of the solid nature of its collateral (an airplane), Ethiopia was paying a far higher interest rate on its loan than it was receiving on reserves. But the United States and the IMF objected."[32] And what was the consequence of this objection? The IMF suspended its programs to Ethiopia. In short, because an American bank was deprived of a high interest, secure-collateral loan, the US Treasury used the IMF to punish Ethiopia. US policy and IMF policy were driven by the commercial interests of one bank. (Note: by the way, if this story is untrue, the IMF should open its books to reveal the truth. Sadly, when the IMF does so, we will discover a torrent of such sad tales.)

I do not mean to be unfair to the IMF and World Bank. I have no doubt that they can point to countless instances in which they have done a lot of good for poor developing countries. Their record is not a record of total failure. Indeed, by and large, both institutions have received more positive than negative coverage in the Western media. Most Western books on these institutions tend to highlight the positive dimensions.

However, even when the Western media have criticized the IMF and the World Bank for their ostensible failures, they have rarely criticized them for serving primarily as instruments of Western power to further Western interests. Indeed, it may be useful for the Western media to reflect on why they couldn't see what the rest of the world could see clearly about the IMF and the World Bank. Both institutions have bent to Western wishes and interests in their analytical work of understanding the world and in their substantive work of dispensing assistance.

The IMF has come in for a lot of criticism for having failed to anticipate the 2008–2009 Western financial crisis. To try to understand why the IMF had failed so miserably, the IMF's Independent Evaluation Office produced a fifty-one-page report. It is worth reading. The report highlights that the then–chief economist of the IMF, Professor Raghuram Rajan, did warn about the dangers of the complex financial products created by American institutions. The report says, "Despite the importance of the economic counsellor's position, there was no follow-up on Prof Rajan's analysis and concerns—his views did not influence the IMF's work programme." In contrast, says the report, the IMF "often seemed to champion the US financial sector and the authorities' policies, as its views typically paralleled those of the US Federal Reserve."[33] Let me emphasize one point here: US citizen interests and the US economy would have been best served had the IMF's warnings been heeded. Indeed, the fact that Rajan's correct and dire warnings about financial instruments were not heeded speaks perhaps not so much to the IMF serving larger American interests but to US policy on the IMF having been captured by one stream within the economics profession. This neoliberal school, epitomized by Alan Greenspan, believed that markets could do no wrong. Hence, they resisted any suggestion that the state should intervene to curb or restrain the financial sector.

The Independent Evaluation Office's findings on the IMF's grave mishandling of the 2008 financial crisis was reinforced by a scathing resignation letter from Peter Doyle, then a senior economist in the IMF's European Department:

> After twenty years of service, I am ashamed to have had any association with the Fund at all.
>
> This is not solely because of the incompetence that was partly chronicled by the [Office of Internal Audit and Inspection] report into the global crisis, and the [Triennial Surveillance Review] report on the surveillance ahead of the Euro Area crisis. Moreso, it is because the substantive difficulties in these crises, as with others, were identified well in advance but were suppressed here. Given long gestation periods and protracted international decision-making processes to head off both these global challenges, timely sustained warnings were of the essence. So the failure of the Fund to issue them is a failing of the first order, even if such warnings may not have been heeded.[34]

This revelation by the IMF Independent Evaluation Office that the IMF adhered more closely to American financial sector interests than to its own chief economist will not come as a shock to any senior policymaker anywhere in the world. It is well known. But why was the public kept ignorant about this reality? Why has the world's press not written about this? The IMF is physically located in Washington, DC, the home of the freest press in the world. Why did this free press not reveal that an institution designed to serve the interests of 7 billion people was serving only the interests of 300 million people? The simple answer is that the American media, while doing a great job of challenging American domestic policies, have generally become the cheerleader for American interests abroad. Even though the *Washington Post* is physically located a few blocks away from the IMF and has a reputation for Watergate-style exposures, it did not expose this intellectual corruption of the IMF, the world's most powerful international financial body.

To make matters worse, the American media even contributed to an equally dangerous myth. Since UN-bashing has become a political sport in Washington, the American media were never short of stories on the bureaucratic and political shortcomings of the UN. An implicit contrast was always made between the shabby performance of the UN in New York and the modern and efficient performance of the IMF and the World Bank. I experienced this myth well as, during my ambassadorships, IMF officials walked into the UN with the arrogant posture of "masters of the universe" and viewed with contempt and condescension the discussions in UN committees about creating a more just and equitable world economic order. Their body language expressed this view: "While you guys are busy talking, we are busy saving the world." This is how Joseph Stiglitz describes the attitudes of IMF officials:

> It's not fair to say that IMF economists don't care about the citizens of developing nations. But the older men who staff the fund—and they are overwhelmingly older men—act as if they are shouldering Rudyard Kipling's white man's burden. IMF experts believe they are brighter, more educated, and less politically motivated than the economists in the countries they visit. In fact, the economic leaders from those countries are pretty good—in many cases brighter or better-educated than the IMF staff, which frequently consists of third-rank students from first-rate universities. (Trust me: I've taught at Oxford University, MIT, Stanford University, Yale University, and Princeton University, and the IMF almost never succeeded in recruiting any of the best students.)[35]

In a convergent age, the time has come to be honest about why the gap between the positive reputation of the IMF and World Bank in the West and the poor substantive record of both institutions is so great. A complex ecosystem generated by Western governments, Western media, and, indeed, some Western NGOs has propagated the myth that the West is essentially a benevolent force on the world stage. If we can begin to understand better the actual track record of both these institutions, we will begin to comprehend clearly the actual role and contribution of the West to the rest of the world. The IMF and World Bank are bellwether institutions. If they have done a spectacular job of helping the world, the West deserves to brag about its benevolence. If they have performed miserably, the West needs to engage in deep introspection to understand why two institutions that it has dominated for decades have not lived up to their promise.

Some of the strongest criticisms of these two institutions have come from credible Western scholars. Stiglitz has documented well the failures of the IMF. In March 2012, when the world began discussing the issue of who should succeed Robert Zoellick as the president of the World Bank, two former senior officials of the World Bank wrote critically of how the performance of the World Bank had deteriorated over time. Ian Goldin, a former World Bank vice president, wrote a column in the *Financial Times* in which he said, "The World Bank is flirting with irrelevance." "With emerging markets now accounting for more than half the global economy, there is no excuse for delaying a global search for the best-qualified candidate to head the World Bank. The Bank is in danger of becoming irrelevant because the development of global capital markets and a network of national and regional development institutions, as well as a vibrant global scholarly and policy community to give expert advice, is rendering it marginal to all but the poorest countries."[36] In response, Danny Leipziger, another former vice president of the Bank, said that Goldin's article "[failed] to deal with the root causes of the declining relevance of the World Bank. Its potential irrelevance is not due to increased competition in the markets for money and ideas, but rather to neglect of long-simmering management problems and singular lack of vision in its leadership." He concluded, "The key to revitalising the World Bank rests with new leadership."[37] Ghani and Lockhart also note that, although "completed projects by the World Bank are rated 72% satisfactory, less than 50% of them are sustainable."[38]

Self-Serving Food Aid

The poor record of the World Bank and the IMF in helping to enhance global interests as opposed to Western interests should not be seen as exceptions to an otherwise benevolent record of the West on the world stage. Instead, they serve as good illustrations of how the West performs badly in its declared mission of helping the rest of the world. An example from an area where many lay Westerners believe that the West is playing an extremely benevolent role drives home the point. It would be no exaggeration to say that many in the West believe that if not for Western food aid, millions would be worse off. This is why it may come as a shock to many in the West to discover that millions in the Third World are actually worse off because of Western food aid.

Frederic Mousseau, a senior fellow at the Oakland Institute and an internationally renowned food security consultant, has identified the following as the main problems associated with food aid: (1) it is a donor-driven system; (2) it promotes the domestic interests of donor countries, (3) it is a foreign policy tool, (4) international institutions that distribute food aid are driven by exporters, and (5) development is not necessarily the objective.[39] Mousseau is not alone in his criticisms of food aid. Christopher B. Barrett, an economist at Cornell University, shows that American governmental food aid—which feeds 70 million people a year at a cost of up to $2 billion—is slow, often ineffective, and expensive. He notes in particular that US food aid is really intended to support domestic farm prices, promote commercial agricultural exports, and advance America's geostrategic aims: "American food aid was started to try to promote trade, to dump surpluses and to help the maritime industry. All of these objectives are caught up in food aid; it's not just about feeding the hungry. It's not even primarily about feeding the hungry. That is just the way it's sold." Barrett claims about 50¢ of every $1 the government spends on food aid isn't spent on food. Instead, the money is spent on shipping, processing, and other costs. "Although food aid has been invaluable over the last 50 years it has literally saved or helped hundreds of millions of lives, it underperforms its potential by a great deal. And it does so largely because it's trying to serve too many different objectives, objectives which are largely outdated."[40]

Duplication and Aid to Corrupt Countries

To make matters worse, the obvious unnecessary duplication of multilateral institutions in the area of food aid has created a mess. Instead of a single institution, we see unnecessary competition among these global institutions: the Food and Agriculture Organization, the WFP, and the International Fund for Agricultural Development. According to a report by Oxfam International, Ethiopia gets 70 percent of its food aid from the US, but this help comes at a cost. US food aid money must be spent on food grown in the US, at least half must be packed in the US, and most of it must be transported in US ships. For roughly $1 spent on aid, the US taxpayer spends $2 on transportation.[41]

Again, Western interests, not the interests of poor recipients, predominate. Indeed, when it comes to dispensing Western aid, Western interests were more important than Western values. In theory, the mission of the West during the Cold War was to support the promotion of democracy. In practice, the West did the exact opposite. From 1960 to 1990, autocratic regimes supporting the US had their share of aid increase from 45 percent of total in 1960 to around 70 percent by 1990. In defiance of recipients' needs, and donor countries' declared values, aid was demonstrably being allocated in order to produce foreign policy outcomes beneficial to the donors.

Before any Western reader begins to get tired of the "anti-Western rhetoric" of this chapter, let me emphasize one point: the biggest beneficiary of any objective audit of the real impact and value of Western foreign aid will be the Western taxpayer, the ordinary Western citizen, and, most of all, those citizens of the West who for more than sixty years have believed in the principle of giving to poorer countries around the world and have done so in the belief that their generosity will not be abused. As Western societies wrestle with an era of austerity, most Western governments, including the American government, will have to make serious budgetary cuts. Since many ordinary Western citizens believe that the West should continue to "aid the poor," there will be a temptation by many good souls to protect the Western aid budgets. Under the present system, any such protection would be misplaced. It wouldn't help the West. Nor would it help the Rest.

If this chapter is right in its bold claim that Western aid was never designed to help the recipients, all parties will benefit from an open audit of Western aid programs. There could be benefits for both donors and recipients if, for example, a lot of duplication is removed. Interestingly, many Western governments are aware that such duplication is taking place. The OECD-organized Paris High Level Forum on Aid Effectiveness took place from February 28 to March 2, 2005. It brought together representatives from the international development community, including senior representatives from partner countries, and bilateral and multilateral donors. More than one hundred signatories endorsed the Paris Declaration on Aid Effectiveness, which called for a more effective dispensing of aid. One of the key declarations, labeled "Harmonization," called on "donor countries [to] coordinate, simplify procedures and share information to avoid duplication."[42] Ghani and Lockhart also note that the parallel funding of projects has rendered aid more ineffective: "The largest impact of the aid system has been to undermine the use of the country's budget as the central instrument of policy."[43]

Four years later, progress on the 2005 goals remained uncertain. In its Development Co-operation Report (DCR) for 2009, the OECD's Development Assistance Committee concluded:

> The ever-growing number of donors and aid agencies and mechanisms across the world is making "aid increasingly fragmented and reducing its effectiveness." As a result, "the international development effort now adds up to less than the sum of its parts." ... The DCR defined fragmentation of international development cooperation as aid "that comes in too many small slices from too many donors, creating high transaction costs and making it difficult for partner countries to effectively manage their own development." It noted that "African countries with between 24 and 30 active donors are the following: the Democratic Republic of Congo, Angola, Kenya, Tanzania, Uganda, Rwanda, Burundi, Ethiopia, Sudan, Egypt, Cameroon, Ghana, Mali, Niger, Burkina Faso, Zambia, Lesotho and South Africa. Countries where between 15 and 23 donors account for less than 10 percent of the country's aid are: South Africa, Nigeria, Kenya, Tanzania, Rwanda, the DRC, Cameroon, Egypt, Tunisia and Senegal."[44]

According to Barbara Unmuessig, a former counselor at the UN Conference on Environment and Development, between 2007 and 2009 more than fourteen new bilateral and multilateral international mechanisms for the financing of environmental development policy were created, "making coherence and complementarity of international cooperation even more difficult. For developing countries, it is extremely difficult to cope with this endless flow of new agencies and mechanisms." Unmuessig claims, "This growing fragmentation of aid demands more competent personnel and institutions in developing countries, represents an insurmountable challenge, and erodes the effectiveness of cooperation."[45]

Duplication is not the only area where Western taxpayers will discover "savings" from foreign aid. Any objective audit will also show that there is vast corruption going on at both the donor and recipient ends.

At the recipient end, many Western citizens will undoubtedly be surprised to discover that Western aid to "corrupt" countries has gone up, not

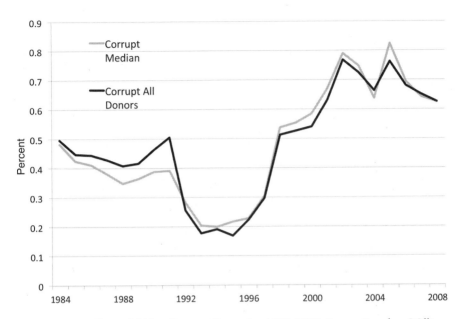

FIGURE 6.4 Share of Aid to Corrupt Countries, 1984–2008. *Source:* Based on William Easterly and Claudia R. Williamson, "Rhetoric Versus Reality: The Best and Worst of Aid Agency Practices," *World Development* 39, no. 11 (2011): 1930–1949. Data is from the *International Country Risk Guide*'s corruption index.

down, despite constant claims to the contrary. According to Easterly and Williamson, from 1994 to 2008—at the height of the good governance rhetoric—the share of aid to corrupt countries went from around 20 percent to about 80 percent, clearly a mismatch between donor rhetoric and reality (see Figure 6.4).

All the Western aid saga shows is that there is no moral deficit in the rest of the world in need of Western compensation; at the same time, the West has never attempted to compensate for that supposed deficit. Instead, the West should begin to work practically and pragmatically with the rest of the world in fashioning a better world order.

One of the most moral persons I have met is Stephen Green, a lay preacher who, quite amazingly, went on to become the group executive chairman of HSBC plc and subsequently a minister of state for trade and investment in the government of Prime Minister David Cameron. Green wrote a wonderful book on the good that men and women can do in this world called *Good Value: Reflections on Money, Morality, and an Uncertain World*. In it, he describes the noble efforts of two young men from

Australia and the UK who rescued orphans in Kenya and India. Surprisingly, I felt very troubled on reading this account. After some reflection, I decided to share my concerns with him. I told him, quite frankly, that the remarkable stories of two young men who rescued orphans from Kenya and India, though heartwarming, also had a downside as they perpetuated the myth that the world could be saved only by brave white men who were prepared to go to distant corners to save the world. I added that Asia's experience conveyed a different perspective. It was only when Asians began to believe that they could improve their situation themselves that their societies began to take off.

In short, it is critical for the former colonized societies to develop the psychological self-confidence to succeed. Since I had grown up in a British colony, I had experienced firsthand the mental colonization that led me to believe that I was a second-class citizen. My generation worked hard at expelling this myth from our minds. We succeeded. Consequently, our societies have succeeded. Today, few in Asia think that they are inferior in any way.

In this new global environment, the rest of the world will feel much less aggravated if the West takes a few steps off the top of the moral high ground that it has claimed for so long, or at least agrees to share the space. As Harvard professor Stephen Walt argues, "Americans (in particular) take too much credit for global progress and accept too little blame for the areas where US policy has in fact been counterproductive." He also points out:

> Most statements of "American exceptionalism" presume that America's values, political system, and history are unique and worthy of universal admiration. They also imply that the United States is both destined and entitled to play a distinct and positive role on the world stage. The only thing wrong with this self-congratulatory portrait of America's global role is that it isn't true for non-Americans—which is to say, most of us. Although the United States possesses certain unique qualities—from high levels of religiosity to a political culture that privileges individual freedom—the conduct of U.S. foreign policy has been determined primarily by its relative power and by the inherently competitive nature of international politics. By focusing on their supposedly exceptional qualities, Americans blind themselves to the ways that they are a lot like everyone

else. This unchallenged faith in American exceptionalism makes it harder for Americans to understand why others are less enthusiastic about U.S. dominance, often alarmed by U.S. policies, and frequently irritated by what they see as U.S. hypocrisy, whether the subject is possession of nuclear weapons, conformity with international law, or America's tendency to condemn the conduct of others while ignoring its own failings. Ironically, U.S. foreign policy would probably be more effective if Americans were less convinced of their own unique virtues and less eager to proclaim them.[46]

And in an era of convergence—and that is happening quite independently of any US contribution—American exceptionalism is an idea that has not only had its day, it has also become a destabilizing anachronism. We can and will come together, but not on solely American terms.

CHAPTER

7

Converging on Global Governance

A DIRTY LITTLE SECRET IS THAT INSTITUTIONS OF GLOBAL GOVERNANCE are weak today by design, rather than by default. I know how well kept this secret is after having lived in New York City, the home of the UN, for more than ten years. I would regularly encounter many senior members of the American establishment who would lament to me the poor state the UN was in. They assumed that it was a result of either the UN being dominated by the poor and weak states of Africa and Asia or by the weak quality of its bureaucrats. They would assure me that they wished that the UN could perform as well as Western organizations did.

To the best of my knowledge, not one senior New York figure seemed to be aware that there had been a long-standing Western strategy, led primarily by Washington, to keep the UN weak. Even during the Cold War, when Moscow and Washington disagreed on everything, both nations actively conspired together to keep the UN weak. They did so through a variety of instruments: selecting pliable secretaries-general, such as Kurt Waldheim; bullying the UN secretary-general into dismissing or sidelining competent or conscientious UN civil servants who showed any backbone; squeezing UN budgets; and, of course, planting CIA and KGB spies in all corners of the UN system. All this was well known to anyone who worked within the UN system.

As we move into the era of the great convergence, when the world clearly needs stronger global village councils, the time has come for the West to begin a fundamental rethink of its long-held policy that it serves long-term Western interests to keep institutions of global governance weak. Let me acknowledge quickly that Western strategy has been more nuanced. While it has kept the UN system at large weak, it has kept the UN Security Council relatively strong and effective because it has been able, by and large, to control and dominate the UNSC. Similarly, the West has allowed both the IMF and World Bank to function better than the UN because through the system of "weighted voting," the West has been able to retain control of both those institutions. Since the IMF and World Bank were established, the head of the IMF has always been a European and the head of the World Bank has always been an American. In short, the West has adopted an intelligent long-term strategy. If it can control an international institution, it allows that institution to become strong and occasionally effective. If it cannot control an international institution, it deliberately debilitates that institution.

This once-intelligent long-term strategy is no longer intelligent as the West progressively loses relative power within the international system. With only 12 percent of the population of the global village and an inevitably declining share of economic and military power, the West's hard-core long-term geopolitical interests will quite naturally switch from trying to preserve Western "dominance" to trying to put in long-term safeguards to protect the West's "minority" position in a new global configuration of power. Having lived as a member of an ethnic minority (Sindhi) within an ethnic minority (Indian) in an ethnic majority (Chinese) state, I know well from personal experience that the best way to protect minority rights is through strengthening the rule of law and strengthening the institutions that promote it. This is what most institutions of global governance are designed to do. The time has come for the West to work on strengthening, rather than weakening, these institutions. I hope that this book will help to stimulate a major debate in Western capitals on the wisdom of keeping to old policies.

It has also been a constant Western strategy to bypass established institutions of global governance by reporting to either ad hoc groups (like the G-8) or to selected multilateral organizations dominated by the West (like the OECD or NATO). The blunt truth is that all these Western-dominated institutions are going to become sunset organizations. Resorting to them would be an act of futility. Even George W. Bush, a unilateralist at heart, had to abandon the G-8 at the height of the 2008–2009 Western financial crisis and resort to the G-20 in an effort to save the global economy. This was discussed earlier in the Introduction of this book.

The G-20 is clearly more globally representative than the G-8. The website of the G-20 proudly proclaims that it is "the premier forum for international cooperation on the most important aspects of the international economic and financial agenda. It brings together the world's major advanced and emerging economies. The G20 includes 19 country members and the European Union, which together represent around 90% of global GDP, 80% of global trade and two-thirds of the world's population."[1] The G-20 can do a lot of good. The London meeting of April 2009 led by Prime Minister Gordon Brown probably saved the world economy. Subsequent G-20 meetings in Pittsburgh, Toronto, Seoul, Cannes, and Los Cabos have achieved little or nothing.

This is not surprising. When the crisis was over, the G-20 nations went back into their bad old habits of focusing on short-term national interests, which trumped long-term global interests. Even Brown has expressed his disappointment with the G-20: "At G8 and G20 summits, world leaders have tended to be mere spectators as Europe has gone from one failed intervention to another."[2]

Despite the failures and shortcomings of the G-20 process, many G-20 members would still like the G-20 to evolve and become a major institution of global governance. Sadly, it can never become one for a simple reason: it lacks the legitimacy to speak on behalf of the world as a whole. Even though it is broadly representative, it lacks any kind of constitutional mandate or any kind of standing under contemporary international law. It cannot replace the universalist global institutions belonging to the UN family. If we are going to get global convergence on norms and institutions to manage our global village, we have to focus on the established and legitimate global institutions. In trying to improve or reform them, we will have to confront a paradox: there is a near-universal consensus that all our major global institutions need to be reformed significantly and soon, but there is virtually no consensus on how. All efforts to reform them so far have failed and failed spectacularly. Just look at what has happened with three of the most powerful global institutions: the UN Security Council, the IMF, and the World Bank.

The UN set up the Open-ended Working Group on Security Council Reform in 1993. Twenty years have gone by. Nothing has changed. Similarly, nothing has changed with the IMF or World Bank. When Dominique Strauss-Kahn became the head of the IMF in 2007, European leaders acknowledged that the "gentlemen's agreement" according to which the IMF would always be led by a European and the World Bank by an American was an anachronism. They suggested that Strauss-Kahn would be the last European to head the organization.[3] When the G-20 leaders met in London in April 2009, they announced that future leaders of the IMF and World Bank would be selected on the basis of merit and not on the basis of geography.[4] Yet in blatant violation of their own declaration, European leaders reclaimed their "hereditary" right to the headship of the IMF in May 2011, and the US government flatly announced that Robert Zoellick would be succeeded by another American after he stepped down in June 2012.[5] No non-American need apply to become the head of the World Bank.

> On Capitol Hill, lawmakers said the World Bank job should stay in US hands. "I think it ought to be (an American) given the balance between that and the IMF and the interests that we have right now," said Senate Foreign Relations Committee Chairman John Kerry, a Democrat from Massachusetts. Senator Richard Lugar of Indiana, the committee's top Republican, echoed that sentiment: "Ideally I would like to see an American replace him. . . . That would be my preference." Nancy Birdsall, who heads the Center for Global Development in Washington, said that while the United States was committed to an open process on paper, domestic politics necessitated an American successor.[6]

Hence, Jim Yong Kim was chosen not because he was the best candidate but because it would have been politically suicidal for any American politician to concede America's hereditary claim to the World Bank presidency.

So why is it so inherently difficult to reform global institutions? This subject has been much debated. Scholars have produced reams of technical reasons. And there is no unanimity among scholars either. Yet I believe that there is a simple reason that all the efforts at reform have failed: the major countries of the world have tried to reform their institutions in an ad hoc fashion, without first getting agreement on the principles that should guide reform. In so doing, all the major countries have been putting the cart before the horse.

Many of the key principles that should underpin global governance are similar to the principles that underpin national governance, with one key exception that this chapter will spell out. I believe that these same principles can be used to guide reform of the other major global institutions.

So what are they? They are the key principles of democracy, the recognition of power imbalances, and the rule of law. The first and third principles are easy to understand: they also apply to national governance. Nonetheless, it is useful to elucidate how the key principles of democracy can apply to global governance. For example, one key principle of democracy is that every citizen has equal moral worth. This is the philosophical justification for the practice of one person, one vote in every democracy in the world. Although obvious today, this principle was not considered obvious in America just two hundred years ago; then a black slave was deemed to have "two-thirds" the worth of a white citizen. And black slaves had no votes or say in the governance of their societies. To drive home this provocative comparison even more, many Western approaches to global governance are more akin to pre–Civil War America, as many human beings in our world do not have voices or views or interests represented in key institutions of global governance. This goes against a key principle of democracy. Hence, there is an urgent need to reform global governance.

The key principles of democracy should, in theory, be welcomed by the Western countries since they worship democracy at home. In practice, however, Western governments have vehemently opposed the democratization of global institutions as the Western populations are increasingly becoming a smaller and smaller minority of the global population. This effectively means that if we apply the practice of one person, one vote in global governance, the Western population would provide only 12 percent of the votes of the global population. This would lead quite naturally to a dramatic reduction of Western power in the global system. At the same time, the second principle—the recognition of power imbalances—is not explicitly accepted in national governance, but it is absolutely critical for global governance because failure to consider it will kill all efforts for reform.

The problem with our present global order is not that we have failed to acknowledge the second principle. Indeed, the problem is the exact opposite. Realpolitik considerations of power have overwhelmed the principles of democracy. However, this has, in turn, created a major problem for all major global institutions: they are slowly but steadily losing their legitimacy in the eyes of the majority of the world's population. If these global institutions are not perceived to represent the views of the people, loss of legitimacy will come naturally.

We all know that we live in an era in which the majority of the world's population has gone from being passive and disempowered to becoming active and empowered. They have become more outspoken in demanding that their views be taken into consideration. Technology is enabling the voices of the majority to be heard clearly and loudly. Hence, while all the major global institutions could safely ignore the views of the majority of the world's population in the twentieth century, they will do so at great peril to themselves now. The principles of democracy need to be injected with greater vigor into global institutions.

In theory, the ideal solution for global governance is to inject the practice of "one person, one vote" into selecting the leaders and managers of global institutions. Few scholars have dared to suggest this as a solution, but at least one, Jan-Aart Scholte, has advocated a global democracy. He argues, "Shortfalls of accountability (especially democratic accountability) in respect of global governance agencies constitute a major challenge to the delivery of effective and legitimate public policy."[7] In practice, however, the global system will not accept "one person, one vote" as it would give China (1.3 billion people), India (1.2 billion people) and Africa (1 billion people) a simple majority in global decisionmaking since together they would represent just over half of the world's population.

All this exposes the existential dilemma that global institutions face. On the one hand, the majority of the world's population must *perceive* these global institutions to be legitimate and representative of their point of view. On the other hand, since the *international* system is based on cooperation not among the peoples of the world but among the nations of the world (where there is great inequality of power), it is also essential that global institutions are effectively supported by the world's most powerful nations. Much as we would like to, we cannot ignore the power dimensions in international affairs. As Hans Morgenthau said, "International politics, like all politics, is a struggle for power."[8]

No reform of the global system will work if power is not factored in. That is why the League of Nations failed and why the UN has survived. In the League of Nations the United States was allocated the same voting rights as, say, Belgium. There was no built-in incentive for the US to join, and it never did, despite Woodrow Wilson having made the Fourteen Points speech that established the League (for which he was awarded the Nobel Prize in October 1919).

The Issue of the Veto

By contrast, the United States had a powerful vested interest to stay on in the UN system: its veto power in the Security Council. Inis Claude put it well in his classic work, *Swords into Plowshares*, where he explained:

> When we deplore the veto as an impediment to the functioning of the United Nations, we might recall that it was essential to the formation of that organization. The great powers not only asserted an irresistible demand for special privilege, but also put forward a cogent claim for special status in recognition of the special role they were expected to play, and the special responsibilities that they were expected to bear, in the United Nations. . . . In their acceptance of the veto, the statesmen of the rank and file at San Francisco were acknowledging, however reluctantly, the reality of inequality and the realism of the proposition that the creation and operation of an international organization genuinely relevant to world politics would require significant concessions to that reality.[9]

When I served as the Singapore ambassador to the UN, it was fashionable to criticize the veto as being wrong in principle. In theory, this is a legitimate point of view. If the vast majority of the world's population, for example, wants to see a two-state solution, with Israel and Palestine being given equal rights, it is surely wrong in principle for one state, America, to veto it. Yet the veto serves a useful purpose of delivering a warning that if the world tries to impose a solution on Israel, American military power will protect it. And a direct clash between the UN and America would mean a disaster for the UN. Similarly, in theory, it would be legitimate for the UN to send peacekeepers to protect the territorial integrity of Georgia. But it would be equally fatal for UN forces to confront Russian forces. The Russian veto therefore serves a useful signaling function.

The veto is also functional in other respects. During periods of UN-bashing in the US, one reason that America never quit the UN was because it knew how valuable the veto power was and how much control it gave over the UN system. Equally importantly, the daily interaction among the veto-wielding great powers in the UNSC has prevented the serious deterioration of great-power relations and has often led to the betterment of relations among the great powers.[10]

Now, against the background of the danger of a new round of geopolitical competition and misunderstanding between America and China, their daily interaction in the UNSC has helped to improve their relations. David Bosco quotes a German ambassador, Gunther Pleuger, whom I got to know well in the UN, saying, "The [permanent members] do not get as confrontational with each other as they do with the 'tourists,' as they call the nonpermanent members."[11] America and China have often "conspired" together to move their agendas through the UNSC. I observed this with my own eyes, and one of my colleagues actually overhead a Chinese diplomat telling an American diplomat, "Let us keep it among ourselves in the P5." This is why David Bosco could comfortably conclude from his analysis of P5 behavior that "the council members, particularly the Five, did not hesitate to champion their own companies in ways that skirted standard UN procurement rules."[12] In short, despite all the P5's geopolitical rivalries, the daily interaction in the UNSC also encouraged cooperation and even collusion. It may not be noble in principle, but it eases the working of the world.

Entrenching the great powers in the UN system and encouraging them to cooperate have demonstrated that the veto can be functional. Yet it also can be dysfunctional in many respects. It has, for instance, led to manifest corruption. Anyone who wants proof of such corruption should read Paul Volcker's Oil-for-Food report. Volcker, a man of unquestionable integrity, painfully documented how the P5 had abused their veto powers (and therefore direct control over the UN Secretariat) to channel lucrative commercial contracts in Iraq to their own companies. "In essence, the responsibility for the failures must be broadly shared, starting, we believe, with member states and the Security Council itself," Volcker said in his presentation of the Oil-for-Food report to the UNSC.[13]

The UNSC started the Oil-for-Food Program in 1996 to allow Iraq to sell enough to pay for food and other necessities for its population, which was suffering from strict UN sanctions imposed after the first Gulf War. These sanctions did not hurt Saddam Hussein or his regime. Instead, they hurt innocent people. Babies starved. In response to a massive public outcry, the UNSC relented and agreed to allow Saddam Hussein to import some food to feed his people by selling some oil, which led inevitably to corruption.

Hussein managed to pocket $1.8 billion. So how did this happen? Volcker's report was very critical of the UN Secretariat for failing to spot and stop the corruption. In this regard, the report may have been unfair. The UN Secretariat could have prevented corruption only if it were an independent agency. My two years in the UN Security Council, however, removed any illusion I had that the UN Secretariat possessed any such independence. It was tightly controlled by the P5 and served only as an execution agency of their needs and interests. I was therefore truly outraged when the American and British media went to town attacking the UN Secretariat once again without asking the obvious question: Who controlled and who made the decisions for the UN Secretariat on the *actual contracts* that Hussein was allowed to sign? The simple answer is that each and every contract that Hussein benefited from was authorized by the P5, each of whom had many ministries scrutinizing the contracts.

The signature corruption that took place in the Oil-for-Food contracts was not that some UN Secretariat officials benefited from kickbacks but that the P5 benefited from the many trade-offs engendered by the program. The understanding among them was that if one approved a contract for a company from another P5 country, the other would grant reciprocal approval. The P5 countries engaged in trade-offs at that level of detail. This is why the vast majority of companies that benefited from the Oil-for-Food Program were companies from the P5 countries, including American companies such as Exxon Mobil Corp, Chevron Texas Corp, and El Paso Corp. The P5 knew well that any major discussion of Volcker's report would inevitably indict them. Hence, even though it was a major report, it was only discussed in a short single formal sitting of the UNSC. The Costa Rican delegation then suggested that the report be discussed in the UNGA and had a new item included in the UNGA agenda. That was in 2005. To date, no session has been set aside in the UNGA for such a discussion. The reason is simple: the P5 made it clear to the Secretariat that they did not want such a debate in the UNGA. Since the P5 essentially control the UN Secretariat, their wishes were heeded.

Both the P5 and the other 188 member states of the UN need a sharp wake-up call to move away from some of the more dysfunctional aspects of the veto. I am the first to concede that the veto has done well to entrench the great powers in the UN system and encourage their cooperation and collaboration. But the unchecked powers of the veto have also led to corruption and abuse. In our transparent world, the absolute dictatorial powers of the veto must be balanced with accountability and responsibility if it is not to be destroyed completely in due course.

P5 Distortions

It is clear that the P5 has distorted the UN system to serve the interests of five countries, often at the expense of the interests of the vast majority of the world's population. Their domination of the UNSC and their pursuit of national over global interests have led to significant failures. Moreover, the P5 are allowed to use their veto *implicitly* in many closed-door consultations. Thus, Security Council rules of procedure remain "provisional" after nearly six decades because the P5 do not want to be bound by any rules in their behavior. Total control is what they seek. When I was permanent representative of Singapore on the council, my delegation made several suggestions to improve the working methods of the council. We ran into a lot of resistance, best encapsulated by the comments of a P5 permanent representative who expressed surprise that the "tourists" were trying to change the arrangements of the council. The P5 then, and now, believe that they "own" the Security Council. Representatives elected by the other 191 member states should not make any claim of co-ownership.[14]

The institutional cowardice of the UN Secretariat in facing down the P5 is shared by the IMF and the World Bank. One reason the IMF did not see the Western financial crisis of 2008–2009 coming is that as an institution it had developed a culture of never criticizing the Western states.

Raghuram Rajan, the chief economist of the IMF from October 2003 to December 2006, documented some of his experiences with the IMF. He noted, "Historically, the world's great powers have been reluctant to see independent, strong multilateral organisations emerge. When strong, multilateral organisations have not been independent; and when independent, they have been largely irrelevant. The growing power of developing countries like China and India is unlikely to change this situation because they too have little desire for their policies to be scrutinised."[15] Rajan observes ruefully that "it is not just undemocratic countries that repress free speech; democratic countries that preach in public about the need for transparency and honest appraisals are often the ones that lean most heavily on international organizations in private to alter their message."[16]

Some readers may shrug off these tales of the institutional cowardice of leading global institutions as a small inconvenience that does little damage to the world. But it is no small matter: lives can be lost when global institutions fail to perform their designated duties. The job of the UN Security Council on the world stage is like any city fire department. When the New York City Fire Department receives a call that a fire has broken out, it responds immediately without checking the address of where the fire has broken out. It responds equally quickly and effectively regardless of whether it has broken out on Park Avenue or in Harlem. By contrast, the UNSC responds quickly and effectively only when the residents of Park Avenue (i.e., the P5 members) are affected and either does not respond or responds ineffectively when the residents of Harlem (read Africa in this case) are affected. No modern city would accept a fire department that discriminates against its poor majority population. Similarly, our modern world can no longer accept a UNSC that does not act when poorer or weaker countries are threatened. This is why the UNSC needs to engage in deep reflection to assess whether it is steadily losing its legitimacy in the eyes of the majority of the world's population.

Many American liberals are convinced that after the horrific failure to respond to the crisis in Rwanda, the UNSC and the international community learned their lesson and will never allow a genocide like Rwanda to happen again. This belief is completely misguided and unfounded, as

I discovered when I served on the UNSC in 2001 and 2002. In April 2001 (seven years after the genocide in Rwanda), I joined a UNSC mission that visited several countries in Africa, including Rwanda and Burundi. The visit to Burundi was unforgettable. Burundi has the same ethnic tensions between Hutus and Tutsis as Rwanda. When our plane landed in the capital city, Bujumbura, we received a vivid firsthand reminder of how dangerous the situation was. The pilot told us to rush into the city and complete our business before sunset. He warned us that after sunset, the rebels would penetrate closer into the city and occasionally shell the airport too. Fortunately, we completed our business in Bujumbura in time and flew out of Bujumbura just as the sun was setting. I felt an incredible sense of personal relief when the plane took off safely.

A few weeks after our return to New York, several UNSC ambassadors, including me, were invited to lunch with Gareth Evans, a former Australian foreign minister who was then head of the International Crisis Group (ICG). The ICG had been doing excellent work in monitoring and reporting on crisis situations. At the lunch, Evans asked us a simple question. He said, "You have been to Burundi. You have seen how dangerous the situation is. This time, if genocide breaks out in Burundi, will the UNSC act to stop it or will it once again remain inactive, as it did in Rwanda?" After a few awkward moments of silence, one P5 ambassador bravely and honestly said, "My country has no national interests in Burundi. We will not intervene." Soon the other P5 ambassadors agreed with him. The non-P5 ambassadors said, as a matter of fact, that if the P5 countries did not lead any intervention, they would not have the resources to prevent genocide in Burundi. Evans was understandably and suitably shocked to learn that, despite the universal statements in the West that the world would never allow another Rwanda genocide again, it could allow one next door in Burundi if the P5 put their national interests ahead of global interests in deciding how the UNSC should react to global challenges.

The P5 and Judicial Review

This chapter has discussed so far the tensions between the first two principles of reforming global governance. But the Rwandan genocide (one of the most horrifying failures of the UNSC) also reveals a built-in tension between the second principle of recognition of power imbalances and the third principle of rule of law. In theory, the whole world agrees on the principle of rule of law. As recently as the UN World Summit in 2005, all the UN member states unanimously recognized the need for "universal adherence to and implementation of the rule of law at both the national and international levels" and reaffirmed their commitment to "an international order based on the rule of law and international law."[17]

In an article entitled "An International Rule of Law?," the dean of the NUS Law Faculty, Simon Chesterman, observes that the rule of law has been embraced "across the political spectrum," on the right by Friedrich Hayek and on the left by Marxist historian E. P. Thomson, who said, "But the rule of law itself, the imposing of effective inhibitions upon power and the defense of the citizen from power's all-intrusive claims, seems to me to be an unqualified human good."[18] Nevertheless, Chesterman is right in saying that, even while there is universal agreement that we should promote the rule of law domestically and internationally, the major powers, led especially by the US in recent decades, do not want any of their actions to be subjected to any kind of judicial process. Domestically, if a country's police force *knowingly* allowed genocide to take place, there would be a huge public clamor for judicial review of the actions of the police force and the members who failed in their duties would be charged with criminal negligence. However, at the international level, when the UNSC fails to carry out its duties to prevent genocide, the UNSC, especially the P5, never tolerates any kind of judicial review.

Chesterman describes well how this lack of judicial review of UN institutions came about:

> The United Nations lacks a formal process to establish the *vires* of its organs as the question of interpreting the Charter powers of each was quite consciously left to the organs themselves. The I.C.J. does not exercise the functions of a constitutional court, though an organ may choose to submit a relevant question to it for an advisory opinion. In the Lockerbie case, a direct clash loomed between the Security Council and the Court when both were seized of issues arising from the bombing of Pan Am Flight 103 on December 21, 1988 over Lockerbie, in Scotland. The Court declined to rule on the merits in provisional measures and preliminary

objections proceedings in 1992 and 1998, but even as it affirmed the discretion of the Security Council the Court implicitly asserted its own
power to determine the limits of that discretion.[19]

The last sentence of this quote is very significant because it suggests that
some judicial authorities can review UNSC discussion. This would clearly
alarm all P5 members, including America.

I know from my own experience how alarmed the American government was by any potential judicial review of the UNSC. When I presided
over the council in May 2002, I received a request from the ICJ to give a
briefing on the work of the ICJ and the UNSC to the UNSC. I thought that
this was an excellent idea, and I supported it. However, when this ICJ proposal was discussed in the UNSC, the US delegation opposed a public
briefing. I cannot recall why. I do recall responding to the US delegation
that the question of whether or not we should have a public briefing was a
"procedural" issue. Hence, a simple majority vote could establish whether
the UNSC members wished to have a public or private briefing.

The response of the American delegation was ingenious. It said that
whether or not the discussion on the public briefing was a "procedural" or
"substantive" issue was in itself a substantive issue. This is not a trivial point.
The UN founders intended the veto to be used for substantive matters, not
procedural matters. In practice, the P5 have extended it to procedural questions, leading to what is called the "double veto." David Bosco has told me
that there was quite a bit of research and writing on this double veto in the
1950s and early 1960s. He cites one notable article—"The Double Veto and
the Four-Power Statement on Voting in the Security Council"—and notes
that the legality and propriety of the tactic have never been fully resolved.[20]

By framing the issue in this way, the American delegation signaled that
it was ready to exercise its veto powers in the UNSC to prevent a "public
briefing" by the ICJ. As a result of this American threat, the other UNSC
members caved in and agreed to a closed-door private briefing, in which, as
expected, the ICJ gave a completely innocuous briefing on its recent work.

To this day, I still do not understand how it would have undermined
any American national interests to allow the ICJ to give the briefing in public. I can only attribute this American discomfort with the ICJ in general
because the ICJ serves the global interest and not necessarily American in-

terests. Sean D. Murphy, of the George Washington University School of Law, notes:

> Since 1946, the United States has had an uneasy relationship with the International Court of Justice (I.C.J. or Court). On the one hand, the United States embraces the rule of law within its own society and, in principle, within the international system of states. The United States has been and remains an active participant in cases before the Court, orally appearing before the court several times even in recent years. On the other hand, the United States has never been willing to submit itself to the plenary authority of the Court, and has typically reacted negatively to decisions by the Court that are adverse to U.S. interests. As is well known, in reaction to decisions that were reached by the Court, the United States refused to participate in the proceedings on the merits of the case brought by Nicaragua in 1984, withdrew from the Court's compulsory jurisdiction in 1986, and recently terminated its acceptance of the Court's jurisdiction over disputes arising under the Vienna Convention on Consular Relations.[21]

This refusal by the American delegation to allow a public briefing by the ICJ to the UNSC may seem to be a trivial procedural tussle. But often such issues can bring out the hard realities of the international system. One of these is that the US and most other major powers are reluctant to accept any international rule of law imposed on themselves. This is why the US refused to sign the Law of the Sea Treaty in 1982 and withdrew from the ICJ in 1985 during the Reagan administration. The US did allow the establishment of the very expensive International Criminal Tribunal for Rwanda (ICTR) in 1994 and for the former Yugoslavia (ICTY) in 1993. The ICTR and ICTY were given a free hand to investigate the criminal deeds of war criminals in these territories. However, when the chief prosecutor of the ICTY, Louise Arbour, said that the ICTY might begin an investigation on the legality of the NATO bombings in Kosovo, enormous political pressure was put on her to cease and desist. Here again, domestically no such double standards would have been allowed to protect the mighty and powerful from the rule of law. Internationally, however, such double standards are par for the course.

The big question that our global order therefore faces is how we square the universal drive to promote the greater rule of law among ordinary people in all corners of the world with the powerful resistance of the great powers to any kind of rule of law imposed on them. The first and third principles of the reform of global institutions would push for greater rule of law globally. The second principle would resist it. The tensions between these three principles are real and cannot be breezily dismissed.

However, they are subject to pragmatic resolution. Chesterman provides wise advice on how we should work to promote greater adherence to international rule of law: "At the international level anything resembling even this limited idea of the rule of law remains an aspiration. Yet seeing the rule of law as a means rather than an end, as serving a function rather than defining a status, more accurately reflects how the rule of law developed and has been imported or imposed around the world. And for international law, this understanding appropriately highlights the political work that must be done if power is to be channeled through law."[22]

In short, we should refrain from promoting the international rule of law as an abstract ideal requiring our conformity. This ideal may well take a century or more for us to realize. Instead, we should move forward pragmatically step by step and try to secure small wins in promoting greater adherence to the rule of law. The P5 will, for example, resist fiercely any efforts to improve judicial review on the decisions and actions of the UNSC. However, the P5 should also take note that there is a rising tide of judicial cases questioning on the validity and legitimacy of UNSC measures against individuals, as evidenced in the Watson Institute's report "Strengthening Targeted Sanctions Through Fair and Clear Procedures":

> Five recent cases before the European Court of Justice, along with legal challenges in national courts in Europe, North America, and elsewhere (including two lawsuits in Turkey and one in Pakistan), have raised important questions about Security Council measures passed under Chapter VII of the UN Charter that target individuals and entities. These legal actions represent a potentially significant challenge to the efficacy of targeted sanctions. This is of particular concern, given the increasing importance of targeted sanctions in the global effort against international terrorism.[23]

Proposals for Reform

In view of this rising questioning of both the antiquated structure and the arbitrary practices of the UNSC, the P5 should now become aware that they face a Hobson's choice. If they resolutely refuse to change the structure, they will retain their permanent seats, but the UNSC will slowly and steadily lose its legitimacy. This trend may be irreversible. And as Chapter 3 has documented, political storms can sweep out absolute dictators like the P5 in a completely unanticipated fashion. The recommendation that I am putting forward in this chapter for the reform of the UNSC will therefore serve the interests of the P5 in the long run. They should consider them seriously rather than dismiss them out of hand as they are likely to do.

We should not underestimate the difficulties of persuading all the major powers of the world to agree to some concrete proposals for reform. Any such proposal will inevitably have winners and losers. Yet plain common sense can tell us a lot about how to reform global institutions, particularly that it would be manifestly absurd to have the five victors of World War II in 1945 remain as the five permanent members of the UNSC in 2015, seventy years after the end of the war. Plain common sense also tells us that in a world where Europe's share of the global population has shrunk to 8 percent, it would be unjustifiable for Europe to retain 40 percent of the permanent seats of the UNSC, in the form of two individual seats out of five for the UK and France. Europe will have to make way for Asia, Africa, and Latin America to be better represented.

To show that some kind of reform formula could open the way for the reform of global institutions, the best place to start is with reforming the hardest—the Security Council. We will never be able to work out a formula that will satisfy either 100 percent of the world's population or 100 percent of the world's countries. However, if we can persuade 80 percent of the world's population or 80 percent of the world's countries to accept such a formula, we would have taken a major step forward in trying to achieve a global consensus in reforming global institutions.

Any such formula should give equal consideration to the three principles for reform spelled out in this chapter. And we have to balance these principles with some elements of common sense, including that the regions currently not represented at all as permanent members of the UNSC, such as Africa and Latin America, will have to be represented. Common sense also dictates that it would be sheer folly to try to evict the world's largest nuclear power, Russia, from permanent membership, even if it does not meet the criteria of population or share of global power rankings. Equally importantly, if we want to have a functional rather than a dysfunctional UNSC, we will have to strictly control the number of veto-wielding permanent seats.

On the basis of these criteria, we can suggest a new Security Council with seven permanent members. The US, China, and Russia would retain their historical claims. The UK and France would logically give up their seats to a single European seat representing Europe's common security and foreign policy. The three remaining seats would then be allocated to Africa, Asia, and Latin America. It would be fair for Asia to get two out of seven seats since Asia provides 55 percent of the world's population. Because China and India each have more than one-seventh of the world's population, it would make logical sense for both to get one seat each out of seven permanent seats. Securing agreement on how to allocate the seven permanent seats would not be difficult to work out. The logical seven candidates would be the EU, US, China, India, Russia, Brazil, and Nigeria.

Since the "permanent" members of the UNSC enjoy enormous privileges, this quite naturally leads to enormous resentment from those countries that feel they are equally deserving. A simple way to reduce the resentment is to attach significant responsibilities to these enormous privileges. Two such responsibilities are easy to mention. First, while all the permanent members should continue to pay their UN dues on the well-established principles of "capacity to pay," each permanent member should pay a minimum additional sum to reflect their privileged status. As Franklin Delano Roosevelt once said, "Great power involves great responsibility."[24] Hence, each permanent member should pay a minimum of 5–8 percent of the UN budget. If any of them claim that they are unable to make such a minimum payment (which in real terms would be an inconsequential sum of $206 million a year), they should automatically disqualify themselves for taking on the global responsibilities that a permanent member should take on. Second, the permanent members should also agree to serve as the ultimate "police departments" and "fire departments" of the world in the field of international peace and security. Hence, if genocide were about to break out in Rwanda or Burundi, Sudan or Syria, the new permanent members should see it as their constitutional responsibility to prevent such genocides. The natural resentment of their privileged status will dissipate when it is made clear that permanent members also bear heavy burdens.

The other key reason that the UN has not been able to secure agreement on UNSC reform is that for every potential winner in a new formula of allocating new permanent seats, there will be losers. To put it simply, if India gets in, Pakistan will be aggrieved; if Brazil gets in, Argentina and Mexico will be aggrieved; and if Nigeria gets in, South Africa and Egypt will be aggrieved. To solve this problem of "near-losers," we can create a new category of seven "semipermanent" seats that are open to competition only among a limited number of member states that again qualify on the basis of their relative weight in the three principles already spelled out. This new category would then make all the near-losers winners in the new formula as they would thus have to compete for seats among a limited pool rather than having to compete among the 188 nonpermanent member states.

If we give equal weight to both share of global population and share of global power, then we could pick out, say, twenty-eight states that might compete for these seven seats. Since each semipermanent member would serve a two-year term, this would give these states a chance to return to the council every eight years instead of having to wait several decades. The current formula of competition among all 188 states has meant that even a relatively heavyweight country like India was kept out of the UNSC for two decades from 1992 to 2011 between its term in 1991–1992 and its term in 2011–2012. The seven semipermanent seats would help to win over the near-losers. At the same time, since the UN works on the basis of regional groupings, the twenty-eight seats could be allocated on this basis: nine seats for Asia-Pacific, seven seats for Africa and Western Europe, four for Latin America, and one for Eastern Europe to reflect their relative weights in the new political order. I have no doubt that there will be some disagreement about how to allocate these semipermanent seats among the regional groups. However, if we use the average of a country's share of global population and of GDP, we can work out the list of the twenty-eight deserving countries. Table 7.1 lists the countries that could be selected.

TABLE 7.1 Selected Semipermanent Members of the UN Security Council

Country	GDP 2010	% of Global GDP 2010	Population 2010	% of Global Population 2010	Share of 2010 Global GDP and Population	UN Regional Group	Global Ranking
JAPAN	$5,488,416,495,785	8.69%	127,450,459	1.85%	5.27%	Asia-Pacific	4
GERMANY	$3,258,947,368,421	5.16%	81,776,930	1.19%	3.17%	Western European and Others	5
FRANCE	$2,549,027,263,158	4.04%	65,075,569	0.94%	2.49%	Western European and Others	7
INDONESIA	$708,026,840,495	1.12%	239,870,937	3.48%	2.30%	Asia-Pacific	8
UNITED KINGDOM	$2,251,898,461,538	3.57%	62,231,336	0.90%	2.23%	Western European and Others	9
ITALY	$2,043,639,726,121	3.24%	60,483,385	0.88%	2.06%	Western European and Others	11
MEXICO	$1,035,870,880,242	1.64%	113,423,047	1.65%	1.64%	Latin American and Caribbean	12
CANADA	$1,577,040,082,218	2.50%	34,126,181	0.49%	1.50%	Western European and Others	13
SPAIN	$1,383,344,736,842	2.19%	46,070,971	0.67%	1.43%	Western European and Others	14
PAKISTAN	$176,869,569,654	0.28%	173,593,383	2.52%	1.40%	Asia-Pacific	15
KOREA, SOUTH	$1,014,890,141,871	1.61%	49,410,000	0.72%	1.16%	Asia-Pacific	17
BANGLADESH	$100,357,022,444	0.16%	148,692,131	2.16%	1.16%	Asia-Pacific	18
TURKEY	$731,144,392,556	1.16%	72,752,325	1.06%	1.11%	Western European and Others	19
PHILIPPINES	$199,589,447,424	0.32%	93,260,798	1.35%	0.83%	Asia-Pacific	21
IRAN[1]	$331,014,973,186	0.54%	72,289,291	1.07%	0.81%	Asia-Pacific	22
EGYPT	$218,894,280,920	0.35%	81,121,077	1.18%	0.76%	African	23
THAILAND	$318,907,879,752	0.51%	69,122,234	1.00%	0.75%	Asia-Pacific	24
VIETNAM	$106,426,845,157	0.17%	86,927,700	1.26%	0.71%	Asia-Pacific	26
SOUTH AFRICA	$363,523,195,188	0.58%	49,991,300	0.73%	0.65%	African	27
POLAND	$469,781,791,045	0.74%	38,183,683	0.55%	0.65%	Eastern European	28
ETHIOPIA	$29,684,016,194	0.05%	82,949,541	1.20%	0.63%	African	29
ARGENTINA	$368,710,961,381	0.58%	40,412,376	0.59%	0.59%	Latin American and Caribbean	30
COLOMBIA	$288,764,794,424	0.46%	46,294,841	0.67%	0.56%	Latin American and Caribbean	31
VENEZUELA	$393,807,511,437	0.62%	28,834,000	0.42%	0.52%	Latin American and Caribbean	33
DR CONGO	$13,109,525,211	0.02%	65,965,795	0.96%	0.49%	African	34
ALGERIA	$161,979,441,019	0.26%	35,468,208	0.51%	0.39%	African	40
TANZANIA	$22,915,004,297	0.04%	44,841,226	0.65%	0.34%	African	43
KENYA	$32,198,151,217	0.05%	40,512,682	0.59%	0.32%	African	45

[1]2010 data unavailable, figures from 2008.
Source: Data from World Bank 2010, http://databank.worldbank.org.

Any formula for reform of the UNSC must also win the support of the majority of the UN member states, which mostly comprises relatively small states. They command the largest share of votes in the UN General Assembly. If they do not support a formula for reform, there will be no reform. Hence, all these small states should also get seven elected seats in the revised UNSC. In theory, the 160 remaining states that will have to compete for these seven seats will be seen as "losers." Currently, they can, in theory, compete for ten nonpermanent seats in the UNSC. But in practice, they will be winners. Why? There has never been a level playing field in the competition among all the UN member states. Many of the middle powers, such as Brazil (ten times), Egypt (five times), and Japan (nine times), have served frequently in the Security Council. But small states, such as Singapore (one time), the United Arab Emirates (one time), and Guyana (two times), serve very rarely. The creation of semipermanent seats for the middle powers may, paradoxically, create more political space for representation by the small states in a new twenty-one-member UNSC.

This twenty-one-member council would be superior to the current fifteen-member council in many ways. It would enjoy greater "representational" legitimacy since a much larger percentage of the world's population would be represented in its deliberations. Hence, it would respect the first principle of democracy in its new composition. Also, since geopolitics is also about geography, it would be an obvious improvement to have a permanent member from each of the regional groups. Each region has its own geopolitical dynamics. The permanent member from each region would be under pressure to represent that region's interests. All this could help to promote greater geopolitical stability. Equally importantly, the middle powers of the world, which have hitherto resented their exclusion from the Security Council and which resent the enormous effort they have to put into getting reelected once a decade or so, would feel happier at the prospect of automatically rejoining the council every eight years. The middle powers would also be winners. The smaller states should also benefit from this new formula since they would not have to compete with the middle powers for the scarce number of elected seats in the council.

Much of the media commentary on UNSC reform has been relatively ill informed. It has focused on the "overt" struggles for government membership by states like Japan and Germany, Brazil and India. It has failed to acknowledge what all well-informed UN ambassadors know to be a hard political fact: the main obstacle to UN reform lies in Washington. America sees enormous benefits from retaining the present composition. Zalmay Khalilzad, the US ambassador to the UN from 2007 to 2009, acknowledged this in a December 2007 diplomatic cable leaked by WikiLeaks. "We believe expansion of the Council, along the lines of the models currently discussed, will dilute U.S. influence in the body. . . . Addition of new permanent members with veto rights would increase the risk to U.S. interests from Council expansion exponentially."[25] Even more cynically, in an effort to block the addition of more veto-wielding permanent members, Khalilzad suggested, "We should quietly allow discontent with P-5 veto prerogatives to ensure the veto is not extended to new members while joining Russia and China in stoutly defending existing P-5 vetoes."[26] In so doing, Khalilzad was acknowledging a widely known political reality: there is growing anger and dissatisfaction with the veto.

For the record, I should add here that the US government has also supported the claims to permanent membership of Japan and India. In so doing, America has acknowledged that more vetoes can be added to the UNSC. Hence, a net addition of two new vetoes should not be viewed as a major setback by Washington.

The Advantages of the 7-7-7 Formula

In conclusion, let me emphasize one point. The failure of the Open-ended Working Group on Security Council Reform to make any progress after twenty years of meeting was not an accident. Several forces worked to ensure its failure. The P5, quite naturally, wanted their privileged status to carry on in perpetuity. Hence, while they paid lip service—and in some cases eloquent lip service—to the need for change, they were privately ecstatic that no change had come. They would be quite happy to see another twenty years of gridlock. Similarly, a whole range of middle powers that saw themselves only as potential losers worked very hard to perpetuate this gridlock. This is why Pakistan and Argentina, Italy and South Korea (to name a few) worked hard to block any kind of change, including (as indicated in Chapter 3) changes in the working methods of the UNSC that could benefit the world as a whole. This was obviously an act of massive irresponsibility. These middle powers were essentially saying, "I don't care if the world burns. I only care about blocking my bigger neighbor from succeeding." Such narrow definitions of national interest are one reason that reform of our global order is so difficult.

This is why my proposed formula of seven permanent seats, seven semipermanent seats, and seven elected seats is superior to all previous formulas put forward for UNSC reform. It creates winners at all levels, including middle powers that have blocked all UNSC reform ruthlessly. The only real losers will be the UK and France. But they will be compensated in other ways. First, they will give up their permanent seats in favor of a common European seat that they can also participate in (and they can reach a private agreement with their European partners to have a "permanent" presence in a permanent European seat). Second, they will not have to worry about trying to defend the legitimacy of a UNSC that is "frozen" in the old order. France and the UK would gain little by being permanent members of an organization that is progressively losing its legitimacy.

The other big advantage of the 7-7-7 formula is that it is dynamic. It can and should be reviewed every ten years. Hence, if the economy of any middle power does exceptionally well and it is qualified to join the group of twenty-eight on the basis of the stipulated criteria, it could well claim a semipermanent seat. This principle of creating mechanisms for constant review and change in major international organizations would represent a major leap forward in human history because all major international organizations, including the UNSC, the IMF, and the World Bank, have hitherto stoutly resisted mechanisms for constant review. Yet as we move into a world of even more rapid changes and major shifts of power, it would be fatal for any international organization not to have mechanisms for constant review. Indeed, provisions for change should be an essential requirement for all international organizations.

Over time, if this new group of twenty-one were established in the UNSC, it would also demonstrate its inherent supremacy to the G-20 group set up by Bush in response to the 2008–2009 financial crisis. The main defect of the G-20 is that its composition was the result of an arbitrary selection process. In April 1999, the finance minister of Canada, Paul Martin, had a visionary idea of expanding the discussion on financial issues beyond the traditional G-8 economies. Thirteen years have passed. The world has changed significantly. But the list of the G-20 once again remains frozen.

In private, many G-20 members admit that the composition of the G-20 is flawed. Europe is over-represented. Even though the EU has only 8 percent of the world's population and 25 percent of the total world GDP, it has seven out of twenty seats in the G-20.[27] In addition, the EU is represented by two leaders, European Commission president Jose Manuel Barroso and European Council president Herman Van Rompuy. To make matters worse, Spain is always "invited" as a guest. Such over-representation by Europe clearly indicates that the G-20 exemplifies a picture of the past, not the future. In addition, there are no provisions for change and reform. New emerging economies that are outperforming the old developed economies cannot get an invitation to join the G-20.

At the end of the day, it does not take a rocket scientist to work out the principles of reform for all the major international organizations. The three points of respecting the principles of democracy, recognizing the power imbalances in the world, and emphasizing the rule of law should guide all reform of international organizations. Clearly the 7-7-7 composition of the UNSC would see a greater "democratic" representation in the council, an inclusion of all established emerging powers, and an inclusion of small states, which then will have a vested interest in promoting greater adherence to the rule of law.

Conclusion:
Because Everything That Rises
Must Converge

THE GREAT CONVERGENCE THAT OUR WORLD IS EXPERIENCING IS now irreversible. Too many forces have been unleashed to shrink the world. They will only gain momentum in the coming decades. And if we look at our lives carefully, no matter where we live, we can clearly begin to see that our lives are being affected daily by events or decisions made all across the planet.

The great minds of our planet will therefore have no choice but to focus on how we manage the small, dense, and deeply interconnected global village we have created. The traditional units of old global social and political order, including the veritable nation-state, are proving to be less and less useful in managing these great changes. We have to keep searching for new approaches and new solutions.

Yes, there will be crises and catastrophic events. Wise geopolitical thinking is always needed. This book has suggested that solutions can be found to even some of the most intractable geopolitical challenges. The larger positive global trajectory is too strong to be derailed. The living conditions and aspirations of billions will continue to improve. The world will get smaller and smaller and more and more densely interconnected and interdependent. Much of this will be driven by a force that is irresistible and irreversible: technology. There will continue to be major improvements in science and technology. The iPad 2 has as much computing power as a Cray 2 supercomputer of 1985. This pace of development will continue, supported by millions of new engineers and scientists emerging in all corners of the world. And the world will keep rolling forward faster and faster.

Our global challenge is to take advantage of this positive momentum and adapt both our own societies and global institutions to keep pace. Fortunately, no revolutions are needed. Small evolutionary steps can make a huge difference. There is plenty of "low-hanging fruit" we can pick if we want to make adjustments to our global order. We do not need, for example, a major retooling. We can make use of the existing international institutions and reform them or use them more wisely. So this book will conclude with three specific suggestions for improving the global order: stimulate increasing amounts of global conversation, bring an end to anachronistic policies, and engage in the development of a global ethic.

Global Conversation

The first suggestion is to encourage more and more global conversations that bring together all the world's countries. Put simply, we need to finally create a global parliament. Alfred, Lord Tennyson wisely anticipated such a development in 1835 with his poem "Locksley Hall":

> *Till the war-drum throbb'd no longer, and the battle-flags were furl'd*
> *In the Parliament of man, the Federation of the world.*
> *There the common sense of most shall hold a fretful realm in awe,*
> *And the kindly earth shall slumber, lapped in universal law.*[1]

Today, the world has become so integrated that the need for a global meeting place has become truly urgent. If we had to create a global assembly point from scratch, it would be quite a challenge. We would argue over location, format, rules of procedure, and so on. Fortunately, we do not have to start from scratch. We have a global assembly that meets every year and often draws in all the world's leaders, including Barack Obama and Mahmoud Ahmadinejad, Angela Merkel and Xi Jinping. That assembly is called the United Nations General Assembly. Every country in the world, except Palestine, is represented there.

The UNGA has grown barren and sterile over the years; this notional "Parliament of man" has become marginalized. The West, especially America, did not like to feel isolated in many of the UNGA debates, from the Middle East question to questions of economic equity. Hence, in a shrewd assessment of its short-term interest, America decided that the best thing to do was to marginalize the UNGA. The American media have helped by demonizing the UN in recent decades.

But now that we are reaching the end of the era of Western domination of world history,[2] it may not be so wise to continue policies that belonged to a different era. The West may find that the UNGA provides a simple "one-step shopping center" where ideas can be exchanged and traded in a setting whose rules of procedure are inherently Western. Here, 12 percent of the world population can engage the other 88 percent in an environment that the West should be comfortable with.

One of the oldest truths about the human condition is that direct conversation always helps. There is no substitute for face-to-face dialogue. The UNGA provides a perfect venue for just such conversation. Sadly, instead of being used this way, the UNGA has become a virtual echo chamber. Delegates read out their national country positions without attempting to have a real dialogue. This was not always the case. The records of 1950s and 1960s show that then it was a vigorous debating chamber, especially between the Soviet Union and America; this was also the case in the 1980s, when the Soviet invasion of Afghanistan and the Vietnamese invasion of Cambodia were robustly challenged. Thanks to the UNGA, global opinion moved decisively against these invasions.

Marshaling global opinion and understanding it should be one of the primary roles of the UNGA. It has an intrinsic ability to do so. The halls are ready, the rules of procedure are accepted, and the UN chamber, most importantly, enjoys global legitimacy. All we need to do is to change the present-day attitude that it is pointless to debate global issues in this global chamber. As more and more global issues come our way, we need to find out quickly and in one venue what the 7 billion inhabitants of the planet want. It was wise of the Obama administration to convene the UNGA on February 17, 2012, to vote on the UNSC resolution on Syria that earlier had been vetoed by China and Russia. This was a quick way of assessing global opinion on an urgent and vexed issue. Having initiated this practice, the UNGA should now be *automatically* convened to assess any UNSC resolution as soon as it is vetoed. Nothing could be easier.

One of the inherent civilizational strengths of the West is that it leads the world in debates and discussions. Given these enormous inherent skills, the West should not be afraid to engage in a genuine debate with the rest of the world. It should take the lead in changing the prevailing culture and ethos of the UNGA debates. Instead of formal statements prepared in capitals far away from the debating chamber, the Western delegates should listen carefully to the views expressed and respond directly to them.

I know that this can be done as I have done it myself. When debating the Soviet chorus in the UNGA, I would often respond extemporaneously, trying to refute each point. Extemporaneous speeches were listened to more carefully. The cut and thrust of a real debate get more attention than a formal recitation. Sadly, the American delegate was often the most constrained as he or she had to read from a text that had resulted from a lengthy negotiation process among several powerful agencies in Washington. No word could be changed without offending someone, even if the American speech was clearly out of tune with what had been said and did not respond to all the views expressed in the chamber. From time to time, there have been brilliant American ambassadors who have engaged the rest of the UN. But they have more often been the exception rather than the rule. America and the West are not short of good debaters. The debating chamber is there. Let us try to use it well.

The UNGA does not provide the only global assembly, although it debates and discusses the most competitive range of issues. Each year, many other global assemblies meet on a variety of subjects—health and labor, education and weather. All these institutions were created in a rush of enthusiasm after the end of World War II when there was a real sense of urgency about fixing the world. Many of these institutions have been allowed to languish. A comprehensive global effort to revive them would help sustain a whole range of effective new global institutions. It was truly foolish of the West to weaken institutions like the WHO and IAEA when challenges such as global pandemics and nuclear proliferation are becoming more real by the day. The simple truth is that many of the other members of the UN family have done a lot of good work that has gone unnoticed. But at key moments they have made the world safer and more secure.

The global environment poses another major challenge. The fragile atmosphere of the earth covers 100 percent of our planet. In many ways it is even more precious territory for sustaining human life. Without oxygen we are doomed. Hence, we should be making an even bigger effort to create a global treaty or convention covering the atmosphere. The vital point to emphasize here is that we have no Plan B. If we destroy the atmosphere, we have no other planet to evacuate to. Hence, for example, even though it will be very difficult to find an equitable formula to reduce greenhouse gas emissions that are polluting the fragile atmosphere of our earth, we cannot afford to give up. We have to step up the global conversation within the UNGA and other UN bodies and eventually find a formula that is fair and equitable to all. This can be done. And it will be helped by the continual improvements in green technology that are coming our way. An open and honest discussion in a new global parliament may actually show a surprising level of agreement on the need to find global solutions to global challenges.

An End to Anachronistic Policies

My second suggestion is an equally easy one to implement: destroy the clearly anachronistic policies of the Western world toward both the UN and the larger processes of multilateralism. This will be easy to implement for two reasons. First, by ending the current Western policies of weakening multilateralism and multilateral institutions, we will now be serving the long-term interests of the Western world and the global community. Bill Clinton was foresighted when he said in 2003 that it would be in the long-term interest of America and the West to strengthen, rather than undermine, a global rules–based order as it would help to check the behavior and ambitions of emerging powers, such as China and India. It is always easier to persuade the West to implement policies that would serve its long-term interests. Until recently, most, if not all, Western policymakers have worked on the old assumption that weaker multilateralism would serve Western interests. Now, and for the foreseeable future, stronger multilateralism will serve long-term Western interests better.

There will be short-term inconveniences. Tony Blair hinted at these: "What's the obstacle? It is that in creating more effective multilateral institutions, individual nations yield up some of their own independence. This is a hard thing to swallow. Let me be blunt. Powerful nations want more effective multilateral institutions—when they think those institutions will do their will. What they fear is effective multilateral institutions that do their own will. But the danger of leaving things as they are, is ad hoc coalitions for action that stir massive controversy about legitimacy; or paralysis in the face of crisis."[3] The new constraints on Western power, especially American power, will be uncomfortable, but anyone chafing against these new constraints should bear in mind that all the emerging powers will also be subject to the same constraints.

Second, it will be easy to destroy anachronistic Western policies on multilateralism because the financial costs of doing so will be minimal. As a result of the "zero-growth" budget policies of the Western world toward the UN family of institutions over the past few decades, the actual financial cost of running all our multilateral institutions is truly minimal. In 2010, global GDP stood at $63 trillion.[4] Global defense spending amounted to $1.63 trillion in 2010.[5] The UN regular budget stood at $2.58 billion per year for the year 2010–2011, or 0.16 percent of global defense spending.[6] If humanity as a whole cannot find the wisdom to transfer 0.16 percent from increasingly unnecessary global defense expenditures to increasingly necessary multilateral expenditures, then it has stepped off "the escalator of reason" that Steven Pinker wrote about. This is not inconceivable: humanity is capable of enormous stupidity.

Humanity is also capable of changing course if it can be persuaded of the wisdom of such a move. Now that it is clear that stronger multilateral processes and institutions would serve long-term Western interests and also be very cheap, we should embrace them. Once Western policies are changed and we begin to channel more resources to strengthen multilateral institutions, we can also begin to adapt some other simple and sensible policies to strengthen multilateral institutions.

We should introduce the concept of meritocracy in the selection of the heads of all multilateral institutions by picking the strongest possible candidate to run these organizations. This may seem to be an obvious requirement—and it is. So it is truly astonishing that so few in the world are aware that is has been the policy of the P5 to pick the "weakest" possible candidate to run, for example, the UN. No Western power will admit this. However, there are occasional slips that reveal the truth. John Bolton does this in his book *Surrender Is Not an Option: Defending America at the United Nations and Abroad* when he quotes Condi Rice saying, "I'm not sure we want a strong secretary general."[7] Paul Kennedy, a Yale professor of international history who has written extensively on the UN, says that the selection system for a UN secretary-general is in large part designed to pick a "blank sheet." "It is one of the golden rules that the UN doesn't want someone who is controversial and who, in carrying through policies, has offended or got the back up of other countries. People may snort in indignation about faceless bureaucrats, but it was almost certain that the process would throw up someone who was not a household name."[8] America practices meritocracy at home. It must now share this virtue with the global village of which it is a part.

The IMF and the World Bank suffer from a different problem. Here too the principle of meritocracy does not apply. Candidates are picked on the basis of their geographic origins: America for the World Bank and Europe for the IMF. In theory, this is wrong. And in theory, all the major governments in the world, including the Western governments, have admitted that this must change. This is why the G-20 statement issued in London stated that "we agree that the heads and senior leadership of the international financial institutions should be appointed through an open, transparent, and merit-based selection process."[9] In theory, Western policies have changed. In practice, they have not.

But it can be done. When the Western governments make a shrewd and careful recalculation of their long-term interests and realize that those interests are best served by stronger multilateral institutions, they will see many benefits flowing from applying meritocracy to selecting the heads of these institutions. Stronger and more dynamic heads will in turn attract other talent to join these organizations, especially if more financial resources will in turn enable better terms and conditions for the staff. More talented staff will then mean better-performing organizations. Better-performing organizations will then mean greater public standing and esteem. A virtuous cycle is possible. Strong, respected, and capable multilateral institutions will in turn mean a more stable world order. And a more stable world order will serve both Western and non-Western interests.

As a natural consequence, there will also be a rebalancing of the power equilibrium between national governments and multilateral institutions.

Right now, the governments of the major powers enjoy more political clout and influence than the multilateral institutions. If the latter become more effective and raise their standing, the national governments will have to treat them with greater respect. This will create some discomfort in the short term. But it will at the same time constrain arbitrary and capricious behavior on the part of individual governments.

We should welcome any small steps toward creating a world where individual national actions are subject to more and more review by representative and responsible international bodies. The fact of international scrutiny will change the behavior of nation-states significantly. Nation-states are ever more subject to peer pressure. International scrutiny by multilateral bodies, especially more effective and more respected multilateral bodies, has the power to change the behavior of nation-states. This isn't utopianism. All the progressive improvements we have seen in the world order in the past few decades, exemplified best by steadily diminishing interstate wars, have confirmed that we are actually well on the way to creating a better world. All we have to do is to identify the processes that have brought this about and strengthen them. Multilateralism is one of the most critical.

Multilateralism, especially the thousands of multilateral agreements produced each year as a result of more and more multilateral meetings, has in turn produced a new "worldwide web" that has gone unnoticed. Unlike the World Wide Web of the Internet, which has provided a platform for greater global connectivity, the worldwide web of multilateral agreements has served to both constrain and guide the behavior of nation-states. One steady secular trend can clearly be observed as we watch the behavior of nation-states. Since the end of World War II, all nation-states have begun to behave more "decently" toward their own citizens and toward their neighboring states. This slow and steady improvement is no accident. The trend is driven by other forces emerging on the global stage. And I have no doubt that the worldwide web of new multilateral agreements has steadily changed the behavioral pattern of nation-states.

The Development of a Global Ethic

The third suggestion for creating a better global order is to continue applying a little more water and more fertilizer to a new budding plant in our global environment: the emergence of a "global ethic." Over time, as human communities grew in size and complexity, our sense of moral obligation to other men and women extended from family to larger clans, from clans to tribes, from tribes to fiefdoms, and from fiefdoms and principalities to budding nation-states. This evolution did not, of course, progress in a straight line and varied from region to region. Yet there is also no doubt that over time our sense of the moral community that we belong to has grown steadily in size.

Today, more and more philosophers are noting that our sense of moral community is now slowly but steadily extending to every other member of the human race. In Chapter 1, I quoted Peter Singer, who says that the communications revolution has spawned a "global audience" that creates the basis for a "global ethics."[10] And how did this global ethic emerge? Another philosopher who is paying close attention to this phenomenon is David Rodin of Oxford. Rodin answers that "we are 'pushed' toward a global ethic by the need to address urgent issues that are increasingly global in nature, and we are 'pulled' toward a global ethic by a universal core implicit in the very idea of ethics—a core articulated most powerfully by the idea of human rights."[11]

I agree with Rodin that several forces are generating this global ethic. One paradoxical point to note is that technology can create compassion. Technology, of course, is a material force and has no soul. Yet when technology destroys distances, it extends our sense of moral compassion and our sense of moral obligation to other human beings. One recent dramatic example of the moral impact of technology was provided by a video produced by a charity group in California on Uganda's notorious war criminal Joseph Kony. In the first three days after its release on March 5, 2012, *Kony 2012* was watched by 40 million people all over the world, and by the end of the month the number had grown to almost 90 million.[12] Suddenly, people everywhere became aware that a Ugandan war criminal was on the loose. Anyone who doubts the need for a theory of one world should look at how the film generated a reaction in all corners of our world.

We have known for more than a decade that Kony and the Lord's Resistance Army (LRA) have been raping and looting, maiming and killing children and innocent civilians. When I served on the UN Security Council in 2001–2002, we used to receive reports about his activities. The P5 had also known about his blatantly immoral activities for a long time, but they did nothing and felt no obligation to do anything in response because they reckoned that no one in the world really cared. One night, people all over the world went from moral indifference to moral outrage. On March 21, less than a month after the international debut of *Kony 2012*, Senator Chris Coons (D-DE) introduced in the US Senate a nonbinding resolution "condemning Joseph Kony and the Lord's Resistance Army for committing crimes against humanity and mass atrocities, and supporting ongoing efforts by the United States Government and governments in central Africa to remove Joseph Kony and Lord's Resistance Army commanders from the battlefield" (S. Res. 402). The resolution received bipartisan cosponsorship from forty-six other senators owing to the immense popularity of the video. Senator Lindsay Graham (R-SC), a cosponsor of the resolution, said, "When you get 100 million Americans looking at something, you will get our attention. This YouTube sensation is gonna help the Congress be more aggressive and will do more to lead to his demise than all other action combined."[13]

On March 23, the African Union unveiled its plan to dispatch 5,000 soldiers to apprehend and "neutralize" Kony. The international task force includes troops from Uganda, South Sudan, the Central African Republic, and the Democratic Republic of Congo, the countries most adversely affected by the LRA, and is supported by 100 US troops deployed to capture Kony prior to the release of *Kony 2012*.[14] As of August 2012, Kony still has not been apprehended and is believed to be in the Central African Republic commanding between 200 and 700 troops.[15]

Another force generating this global ethic is logic, especially moral logic. All theories of morality rest on one single assumption: all human beings in the world enjoy the same rights, regardless of whether they are white or black, African or Alaskan, Asian or Latin American. In practice, for most of human history, human beings were not treated equally.

We crossed a significant threshold in human history when we adopted the Universal Declaration of Human Rights (UDHR) in December 1948. Yet while lip service was paid to the UDHR by societies all around the world for several decades after that, the general assumption was that each society had a right to determine how it treated its own citizens. Over time, as technology has made all societies (with the exception of North Korea) more transparent, it is hard for any society anywhere to get away with massive violations of human rights. And we crossed another significant threshold in human history in December 2005 when the UN General Assembly announced that the global community had a "responsibility to protect" citizens oppressed by their own governments. The 2005 World Summit Outcome Document stated, "The international community, through the United Nations, also has the responsibility to use appropriate diplomatic, humanitarian and other peaceful means, in accordance with Chapters VI and VIII of the Charter, to help protect populations from genocide, war crimes, ethnic cleansing and crimes against humanity."[16]

Much of this concern for protecting people in all corners of the world has come from Western societies. It is mobilized by technology that makes people aware of suffering across the globe and by the moral logic that all human beings deserve protection. Logic has, however, always been a double-edged sword. Many Western commentators have, for example, highlighted the harm done to poor African citizens by incompetent or even malevolent African governments. Curiously, when the same Africans suffer the consequences of harmful actions by benign and competent Western governments, Western commentators are slower to express moral outrage. Often there is a deafening silence. Expensive cotton subsidies given by the US Congress to rich American farmers or expensive agricultural subsidies given by the European Union to rich European farmers have hurt and impoverished African farmers. Why is there no moral compassion, or outrage, shown about this?

The emergence of a global ethic will, of course, make it more and more difficult to have double standards like these. Indeed, the force of moral logic will insist that the impact of all harmful actions should be treated with the same moral attention. And as the world gets smaller and smaller, we will find that a lot of our domestic actions will have global consequences and could hurt other people. Here again Rodin describes the process well:

> It should be obvious that as the world globalizes, more and more issues that were once local or regional come within the domain of global ethics. Today many of our most urgent policy issues are global in this way: climate change and environmental degradation; management of the trade and financial systems; management of the food, water, agricultural and

forestry systems; preventing and treating infectious diseases including pandemics; preventing the proliferation and use of weapons of mass destruction; preventing armed conflict and genocide; eliminating poverty; management of the oceans; and ensuring the security of cyber space. This overwhelming (yet incomplete) catalogue of devilish problems vividly demonstrates why the development of effective principles of global ethics is among the most important intellectual tasks of our time.[17]

I agree. The development of effective principles of global ethics is one of our most important intellectual tasks. The good news is that it can be done. Most of the key principles of human ethics are found in all human societies. The principle of "we must treat others as we wish others to treat us" can be found everywhere. This means that, for example, if Americans are concerned that the increased level of greenhouse gas emissions from China could damage their environments and livelihoods and they want the Chinese to exercise restraint, they need to first ask how their own greenhouse gas emissions have hurt Africans and others and what they have done to restrain themselves. The whole world would be better off if the 7 billion citizens of planet earth become more and more aware of the global impact of their activities. As Martin Luther King wisely noted, "An individual has not begun to live until he can rise above the narrow horizons of his particular individualistic concerns to the broader concerns of all humanity."[18]

This is where a theory of one world would help us a lot. It would provide a bedrock upon which we could rest a moral theory of one world. There will, of course, be disputes for many decades to come on what this new global ethic will encompass. It may be safer to begin with a narrower definition of this coverage as most of us will feel for a long time a greater sense of moral obligation to those who live in our immediate neighborhood.

But we should not be surprised if we rapidly move away from this minimalist approach. It is clear, for example, that the status and role of women vary from society to society. We can and should insist that all women in the world enjoy the same fundamental rights. We should all condemn ferociously the way the Taliban treated Afghan women when it ruled Afghanistan. Yet at the same time, the role and place of women in Islamic societies will be different for a long time from the role and place of women in conservative Christian societies and in liberal Western societies. These differences will remain for a long time. A hundred years ago, there was little outrage in the West about the practice of female circumcision—it was hardly known in the West. Today, there is enormous moral outrage. What happened? Our sense of moral compassion has expanded.

And our sense of moral compassion toward all the other 7 billion global inhabitants of this planet will continue to expand. The world will continue to shrink and shrink. Technology will eliminate distance. When we used to live in small villages, we would inevitably develop a sense of moral community in the village, a sense of moral compassion in the village, and a sense of moral compassion toward all the other villagers. In the next few decades, we will increasingly realize that our village is a world and not that our world is a village.

APPENDIXES

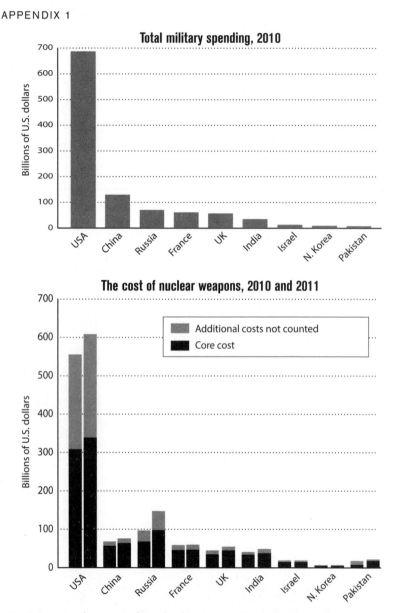

Note: *Core* costs refer to researching, developing, procuring, testing, operating, maintaining, and upgrading the nuclear arsenal (weapons and their delivery vehicles) and its key nuclear command-control-communications and early warning infrastructure. *Full* costs add unpaid/deferred environmental and health costs, missile defenses assigned to defend against nuclear weapons, nuclear threat reduction, and incident management. Not included are air defenses, antisubmarine warfare, and nuclear-weapons-related intelligence and surveillance expenses.

Source: Based on Arms Control Association with primary sources SIPRI Military Expenditure Database, IISS Military Balance, and CIA World Factbook.

APPENDIX 2 All UN Member States

Country	GDP 2010	% of Global GDP 2010	Population 2010	% of Global Population 2010	Share of 2010 Global GDP and Population	UN Regional Group	Global Ranking
EU	$16,149,366,578,224	25.58%	502,302,566	7.29%	16.43%	N.A.	N.A.
CHINA	$5,930,529,470,799	9.39%	1,337,825,000	19.40%	14.40%	Asia-Pacific	1
UNITED STATES	$14,447,100,000,000	22.88%	309,349,689	4.49%	13.68%	Western European and Others	2
INDIA	$1,684,323,716,503	2.67%	1,224,614,327	17.76%	10.22%	Asia-Pacific	3
JAPAN	$5,488,416,495,785	8.69%	127,450,459	1.85%	5.27%	Asia-Pacific	4
GERMANY	$3,258,947,368,421	5.16%	81,776,930	1.19%	3.17%	Western European and Others	5
BRAZIL	$2,143,035,333,258	3.39%	194,946,470	2.83%	3.11%	Latin American and Caribbean	6
FRANCE	$2,549,027,263,158	4.04%	65,075,569	0.94%	2.49%	Western European and Others	7
INDONESIA	$708,026,840,495	1.12%	239,870,937	3.48%	2.30%	Asia-Pacific	8
UNITED KINGDOM	$2,251,898,461,538	3.57%	62,231,336	0.90%	2.23%	Western European and Others	9
RUSSIA	$1,487,515,608,183	2.36%	141,920,000	2.06%	2.21%	Eastern European	10
ITALY	$2,043,639,726,121	3.24%	60,483,385	0.88%	2.06%	Western European and Others	11
MEXICO	$1,035,870,880,242	1.64%	113,423,047	1.65%	1.64%	Latin American and Caribbean	12
CANADA	$1,577,040,082,218	2.50%	34,126,181	0.49%	1.50%	Western European and Others	13
SPAIN	$1,383,344,736,842	2.19%	46,070,971	0.67%	1.43%	Western European and Others	14
PAKISTAN	$176,869,569,654	0.28%	173,593,383	2.52%	1.40%	Asia-Pacific	15
NIGERIA	$196,837,602,740	0.31%	158,423,182	2.30%	1.30%	African	16
KOREA, SOUTH	$1,014,890,141,871	1.61%	49,410,000	0.72%	1.16%	Asia-Pacific	17
BANGLADESH	$100,357,022,444	0.16%	148,692,131	2.16%	1.16%	Asia-Pacific	18
TURKEY	$731,144,392,556	1.16%	72,752,325	1.06%	1.11%	Western European and Others	19
AUSTRALIA	$1,131,623,072,708	1.79%	22,299,800	0.32%	1.06%	Western European and Others	20
PHILIPPINES	$199,589,447,424	0.32%	93,260,798	1.35%	0.83%	Asia-Pacific	21
IRAN[1]	$331,014,973,186	0.54%	72,289,291	1.07%	0.81%	Asia-Pacific	22
EGYPT	$218,894,280,920	0.35%	81,121,077	1.18%	0.76%	African	23
THAILAND	$318,907,879,752	0.51%	69,122,234	1.00%	0.75%	Asia-Pacific	24
NETHERLANDS	$774,228,947,368	1.23%	16,615,394	0.24%	0.73%	Western European and Others	25
VIETNAM	$106,426,845,157	0.17%	86,927,700	1.26%	0.71%	Asia-Pacific	26
SOUTH AFRICA	$363,523,195,188	0.58%	49,991,300	0.73%	0.65%	African	27
POLAND	$469,781,791,045	0.74%	38,183,683	0.55%	0.65%	Eastern European	28
ETHIOPIA	$29,684,016,194	0.05%	82,949,541	1.20%	0.63%	African	29
ARGENTINA	$368,710,961,381	0.58%	40,412,376	0.59%	0.59%	Latin American and Caribbean	30
COLOMBIA	$288,764,794,424	0.46%	46,294,841	0.67%	0.56%	Latin American and Caribbean	31
SAUDI ARABIA	$450,792,000,000	0.71%	27,448,086	0.40%	0.56%	Asia-Pacific	32
VENEZUELA	$393,807,511,437	0.62%	28,834,000	0.42%	0.52%	Latin American and Caribbean	33
DR CONGO	$13,109,525,211	0.02%	65,965,795	0.96%	0.49%	African	34
SWITZERLAND	$529,394,883,630	0.84%	7,826,153	0.11%	0.48%	Western European and Others	35
BELGIUM	$466,694,736,842	0.74%	10,895,785	0.16%	0.45%	Western European and Others	36
UKRAINE	$136,418,622,767	0.22%	45,870,700	0.67%	0.44%	Eastern European	37
SWEDEN	$461,939,112,344	0.73%	9,378,126	0.14%	0.43%	Western European and Others	38
MALAYSIA	$237,796,914,597	0.38%	28,401,017	0.41%	0.39%	Asia-Pacific	39
ALGERIA	$161,979,441,019	0.26%	35,468,208	0.51%	0.39%	African	40
NORWAY	$417,752,649,007	0.66%	4,889,252	0.07%	0.37%	Western European and Others	41
AUSTRIA	$376,575,381,579	0.60%	8,389,771	0.12%	0.36%	Western European and Others	42
TANZANIA	$22,915,004,297	0.04%	44,841,226	0.65%	0.34%	African	43
PERU	$153,882,824,181	0.24%	29,076,512	0.42%	0.33%	Latin American and Caribbean	44
KENYA	$32,198,151,217	0.05%	40,512,682	0.59%	0.32%	African	45
GREECE	$299,102,434,666	0.47%	11,315,508	0.16%	0.32%	Western European and Others	46

(continues)

APPENDIX 2 (*continued*)

Country	GDP 2010	% of Global GDP 2010	Population 2010	% of Global Population 2010	Share of 2010 Global GDP and Population	UN Regional Group	Global Ranking
MOROCCO	$90,802,867,575	0.14%	31,951,412	0.46%	0.30%	African	47
SUDAN	$66,996,504,056	0.11%	33,603,637	0.49%	0.30%	African	48
IRAQ	$81,112,411,282	0.13%	32,030,823	0.46%	0.30%	Asia-Pacific	49
CHILE	$216,308,875,370	0.34%	17,113,688	0.25%	0.30%	Latin American and Caribbean	50
UNITED ARAB EMIRATES	$297,648,476,848	0.47%	7,511,690	0.11%	0.29%	Asia-Pacific	51
DENMARK	$312,214,946,619	0.49%	5,547,683	0.08%	0.29%	Western European and Others	52
ROMANIA	$161,628,748,545	0.26%	21,438,001	0.31%	0.28%	Eastern European	53
AFGHANISTAN	$17,243,112,604	0.03%	34,385,068	0.50%	0.26%	Asia-Pacific	54
PORTUGAL	$227,196,842,105	0.36%	10,637,346	0.15%	0.26%	Western European and Others	55
UGANDA	$17,197,398,887	0.03%	33,424,683	0.48%	0.26%	African	56
UZBEKISTAN	$39,332,771,014	0.06%	28,562,400	0.41%	0.24%	Asia-Pacific	57
KAZAKHSTAN	$148,047,348,241	0.23%	16,323,287	0.24%	0.24%	Asia-Pacific	58
CZECH REPUBLIC	$197,656,387,435	0.31%	10,519,792	0.15%	0.23%	Eastern European	59
NEPAL	$16,013,938,825	0.03%	29,959,364	0.43%	0.23%	Asia-Pacific	60
ISRAEL	$217,443,434,073	0.34%	7,623,600	0.11%	0.23%	Western European and Others	61
FINLAND	$236,475,000,000	0.37%	5,363,352	0.08%	0.23%	Western European and Others	62
SINGAPORE	$213,154,518,683	0.34%	5,076,700	0.07%	0.21%	Asia-Pacific	63
ANGOLA	$82,470,894,868	0.13%	19,081,912	0.28%	0.20%	African	64
GHANA	$32,174,576,820	0.05%	24,391,823	0.35%	0.20%	African	65
YEMEN	$31,042,729,623	0.05%	24,052,514	0.35%	0.20%	Asia-Pacific	66
SYRIA	$59,147,033,452	0.09%	20,820,311	0.30%	0.20%	Asia-Pacific	67
IRELAND	$205,252,607,859	0.33%	4,474,356	0.06%	0.20%	Western European and Others	68
SRI LANKA	$49,567,521,670	0.08%	20,653,000	0.30%	0.19%	Asia-Pacific	69
MOZAMBIQUE	$9,209,366,611	0.01%	23,390,765	0.34%	0.18%	African	70
HUNGARY	$128,631,634,125	0.20%	10,000,023	0.15%	0.17%	Eastern European	71
COTE D'IVOIRE	$22,920,506,112	0.04%	19,737,800	0.29%	0.16%	African	72
CAMEROON	$22,480,348,401	0.04%	19,598,889	0.28%	0.16%	African	73
MADAGASCAR	$8,720,543,554	0.01%	20,713,819	0.30%	0.16%	African	74
ECUADOR	$57,978,116,000	0.09%	14,464,739	0.21%	0.15%	Latin American and Caribbean	75
NEW ZEALAND	$142,476,978,417	0.23%	4,405,200	0.06%	0.14%	Western European and Others	76
GUATEMALA	$41,340,507,361	0.07%	14,388,929	0.21%	0.14%	Latin American and Caribbean	77
CUBA[1]	$60,806,200,000	0.10%	11,253,665	0.17%	0.13%	Latin American and Caribbean	78
BURKINA FASO	$8,825,364,008	0.01%	16,468,714	0.24%	0.13%	African	79
MALI	$9,422,377,319	0.01%	15,369,809	0.22%	0.12%	African	80
KUWAIT	$124,348,317,665	0.20%	2,736,732	0.04%	0.12%	Asia-Pacific	81
NIGER	$5,410,507,420	0.01%	15,511,953	0.22%	0.12%	African	82
QATAR	$127,332,413,913	0.20%	1,758,793	0.03%	0.11%	Asia-Pacific	83
DOMINICAN REPUBLIC	$51,576,212,063	0.08%	9,927,320	0.14%	0.11%	Latin American and Caribbean	84
BELARUS	$55,220,932,614	0.09%	9,490,000	0.14%	0.11%	Eastern European	85
MALAWI	$5,054,150,506	0.01%	14,900,841	0.22%	0.11%	African	86
TUNISIA	$44,238,228,308	0.07%	10,549,100	0.15%	0.11%	African	87
CAMBODIA	$11,242,266,334	0.02%	14,138,255	0.21%	0.11%	Asia-Pacific	88
SLOVAKIA	$87,077,443,709	0.14%	5,430,099	0.08%	0.11%	Eastern European	89
AZERBAIJAN	$52,905,998,879	0.08%	9,054,332	0.13%	0.11%	Eastern European	90
ZAMBIA	$16,192,867,758	0.03%	12,926,409	0.19%	0.11%	African	91

(*continues*)

APPENDIX 2 (*continued*)

Country	GDP 2010	% of Global GDP 2010	Population 2010	% of Global Population 2010	Share of 2010 Global GDP and Population	UN Regional Group	Global Ranking
SENEGAL	$12,855,297,513	0.02%	12,433,728	0.18%	0.10%	African	92
LIBYA[2]	$62,360,446,571	0.11%	6,262,667	0.09%	0.10%	African	93
ZIMBABWE	$7,475,995,911	0.01%	12,571,454	0.18%	0.10%	African	94
BULGARIA	$47,726,844,946	0.08%	7,534,289	0.11%	0.09%	Eastern European	95
CHAD	$8,540,674,846	0.01%	11,227,208	0.16%	0.09%	African	96
BOLIVIA	$19,649,724,656	0.03%	9,929,849	0.14%	0.09%	Latin American and Caribbean	97
SERBIA	$38,444,296,921	0.06%	7,291,436	0.11%	0.08%	Eastern European	98
RWANDA	$5,624,294,585	0.01%	10,624,005	0.15%	0.08%	African	99
CROATIA	$60,851,743,541	0.10%	4,418,000	0.06%	0.08%	Eastern European	100
HAITI	$6,634,579,143	0.01%	9,993,247	0.14%	0.08%	Latin American and Caribbean	101
GUINEA	$4,735,882,580	0.01%	9,981,590	0.14%	0.08%	African	102
BENIN	$6,558,349,890	0.01%	8,849,892	0.13%	0.07%	African	103
HONDURAS	$15,343,558,028	0.02%	7,600,524	0.11%	0.07%	Latin American and Caribbean	104
OMAN	$57,849,155,213	0.09%	2,782,435	0.04%	0.07%	Asia-Pacific	105
JORDAN	$26,425,379,367	0.04%	6,047,000	0.09%	0.06%	Asia-Pacific	106
COSTA RICA	$36,217,527,244	0.06%	4,658,887	0.07%	0.06%	Latin American and Caribbean	107
BURUNDI	$2,026,862,708	0.00%	8,382,849	0.12%	0.06%	African	108
EL SALVADOR	$21,427,900,000	0.03%	6,192,993	0.09%	0.06%	Latin American and Caribbean	109
LEBANON	$39,006,223,284	0.06%	4,227,597	0.06%	0.06%	Asia-Pacific	110
PARAGUAY	$18,331,385,476	0.03%	6,454,548	0.09%	0.06%	Latin American and Caribbean	111
PAPUA NEW GUINEA	$9,480,047,959	0.02%	6,858,266	0.10%	0.06%	Asia-Pacific	112
URUGUAY	$39,411,996,710	0.06%	3,356,584	0.05%	0.06%	Latin American and Caribbean	113
TAJIKISTAN	$5,641,741,963	0.01%	6,878,637	0.10%	0.05%	Asia-Pacific	114
LITHUANIA	$36,306,384,146	0.06%	3,286,820	0.05%	0.05%	Eastern European	115
TURKMENISTAN	$20,000,701,754	0.03%	5,041,995	0.07%	0.05%	Asia-Pacific	116
SLOVENIA	$46,908,328,071	0.07%	2,048,583	0.03%	0.05%	Eastern European	117
LAOS	$7,181,441,152	0.01%	6,200,894	0.09%	0.05%	Asia-Pacific	118
NICARAGUA	$6,590,593,827	0.01%	5,788,163	0.08%	0.05%	Latin American and Caribbean	119
PANAMA	$26,777,100,000	0.04%	3,516,820	0.05%	0.05%	Latin American and Caribbean	120
TOGO	$3,176,118,222	0.01%	6,027,798	0.09%	0.05%	African	121
LUXEMBOURG	$52,982,763,158	0.08%	506,953	0.01%	0.05%	Western European and Others	122
SIERRA LEONE	$1,909,761,902	0.00%	5,867,536	0.09%	0.04%	African	123
KYRGYZSTAN	$4,794,361,821	0.01%	5,447,900	0.08%	0.04%	Asia-Pacific	124
GEORGIA	$11,638,264,782	0.02%	4,452,800	0.06%	0.04%	Eastern European	125
BOSNIA-HERZEGOVINA	$16,647,485,125	0.03%	3,760,149	0.05%	0.04%	Eastern European	126
ERITREA	$2,117,008,130	0.00%	5,253,676	0.08%	0.04%	African	127
REPUBLIC OF CONGO	$12,007,880,067	0.02%	4,042,899	0.06%	0.04%	African	128
LATVIA	$24,009,680,460	0.04%	2,239,008	0.03%	0.04%	Eastern European	129
CENTRAL	$1,984,747,842	0.00%	4,401,051	0.06%	0.03%	African	130
AFRICAN		0.02%	3,204,284	0.05%	0.03%	Eastern European	131
REPUBLIC	$11,858,216,877						
ALBANIA	$13,872,093,023	0.02%	2,702,300	0.04%	0.03%	Latin American and Caribbean	132
JAMAICA	$5,811,584,073	0.01%	3,562,062	0.05%	0.03%	Eastern European	133
MOLDOVA	$9,371,175,470	0.01%	3,092,072	0.04%	0.03%	Eastern European	134

(*continues*)

APPENDIX 2 *(continued)*

Country	GDP 2010	% of Global GDP 2010	Population 2010	% of Global Population 2010	Share of 2010 Global GDP and Population	UN Regional Group	Global Ranking
ARMENIA	$9,371,175,470	0.00%	3,092,072	0.04%	0.03%	Eastern European	134
LIBERIA	$987,900,000	0.00%	3,994,122	0.06%	0.03%	African	135
MAURITANIA	$3,613,898,829	0.00%	3,459,773	0.05%	0.03%	African	136
BAHRAIN	$22,945,456,867	0.00%	1,261,835	0.02%	0.03%	Asia-Pacific	137
BOTSWANA	$14,904,834,649	0.00%	2,006,945	0.03%	0.03%	African	138
CYPRUS	$23,132,450,331	0.00%	1,103,647	0.02%	0.03%	Asia-Pacific	139
TRINIDAD AND TOBAGO	$20,945,274,102	0.01%	1,341,465	0.02%	0.03%	Latin American and Caribbean	140
NAMIBIA	$11,133,250,765	0.00%	2,283,289	0.03%	0.03%	African	141
MONGOLIA	$6,200,357,070	0.01%	2,756,001	0.04%	0.02%	Asia-Pacific	142
ESTONIA	$18,822,715,730	0.00%	1,340,161	0.02%	0.02%	Eastern European	143
MACEDONIA	$9,137,543,773	0.00%	2,060,563	0.03%	0.02%	Eastern European	144
GABON	$13,199,637,410	0.01%	1,505,463	0.02%	0.02%	African	145
LESOTHO	$2,179,350,967	0.01%	2,171,318	0.03%	0.02%	African	146
MAURITIUS	$9,714,391,397	0.00%	1,280,924	0.02%	0.02%	African	147
EQUATORIAL GUINEA	$14,500,472,162	0.00%	700,401	0.01%	0.02%	African	148
GAMBIA	$1,050,158,837	0.01%	1,728,394	0.03%	0.01%	African	149
BRUNEI	$12,369,689,792	0.00%	398,920	0.01%	0.01%	Asia-Pacific	150
ICELAND	$12,550,944,497	0.00%	318,041	0.00%	0.01%	Western European and Others	151
GUINEA-BISSAU	$835,390,893	0.01%	1,515,224	0.02%	0.01%	African	152
SWAZILAND	$3,697,606,785	0.01%	1,055,506	0.02%	0.01%	African	153
MALTA	$8,163,841,060	0.01%	415,995	0.01%	0.01%	Western European and Others	154
TIMOR-LESTE	$875,100,000	0.00%	1,142,502	0.02%	0.01%	Asia-Pacific	155
FIJI	$3,173,108,251	0.01%	860,623	0.01%	0.01%	Asia-Pacific	156
BAHAMAS	$7,771,258,000	0.01%	342,877	0.00%	0.01%	Latin American and Caribbean	157
MONTENEGRO	$4,110,821,471	0.00%	631,490	0.01%	0.01%	Eastern European	158
DJIBOUTI[2]	$1,049,054,417	0.02%	872,090	0.01%	0.01%	African	159
GUYANA	$2,259,288,026	0.02%	754,493	0.01%	0.01%	Latin American and Caribbean	160
SURINAME	$4,350,523,600	0.02%	524,636	0.01%	0.01%	Latin American and Caribbean	161
BHUTAN	$1,516,117,590	0.02%	725,940	0.01%	0.01%	Asia-Pacific	162
COMOROS	$541,097,579	0.02%	734,750	0.01%	0.01%	African	163
MONACO[2]	$6,108,770,906	0.00%	35,377	0.00%	0.01%	Western European and Others	164
BARBADOS	$4,109,500,000	0.02%	273,331	0.00%	0.01%	Latin American and Caribbean	165
CAPE.VERDE	$1,659,053,271	0.01%	495,999	0.01%	0.00%	African	166
SOLOMON ISLANDS	$678,625,482	0.03%	538,148	0.01%	0.00%	Asia-Pacific	167
LIECHTENSTEIN[2]	$4,826,167,676	0.01%	35,772	0.00%	0.00%	Western European and Others	168
MALDIVES	$2,075,500,000	0.02%	315,885	0.00%	0.00%	Asia-Pacific	169
ANDORRA[1]	$3,712,034,267	0.03%	82,577	0.00%	0.00%	Western European and Others	170
BELIZE	$1,401,000,000	0.04%	344,700	0.00%	0.00%	Latin American and Caribbean	171
SAMOA[1]	$1,899,809,580	0.02%	181,809	0.00%	0.00%	Asia-Pacific	172
VANUATU	$688,904,851	0.04%	239,651	0.00%	0.00%	Asia-Pacific	173
ST. LUCIA	$1,198,907,909	0.01%	174,000	0.00%	0.00%	Latin American and Caribbean	174
SAN MARINO[1]	$1,899,809,580	0.00%	31,198	0.00%	0.00%	Western European and Others	175
ANTIGUA AND BARBUDA	$1,153,788,955	0.01%	88,710	0.00%	0.00%	Latin American and Caribbean	176

(continues)

APPENDIX 2 *(continued)*

Country	GDP 2010	% of Global GDP 2010	Population 2010	% of Global Population 2010	Share of 2010 Global GDP and Population	UN Regional Group	Global Ranking
SEYCHELLES	$963,006,565	0.00%	86,525	0.00%	0.00%	African	177
GRENADA	$783,602,099	0.00%	104,487	0.00%	0.00%	Latin American and Caribbean	178
SAO TOME AND PRINCIPE	$201,037,917	0.00%	165,397	0.00%	0.00%	African	179
ST. VINCENT AND THE GRENADINES	$674,770,633	0.00%	109,333	0.00%	0.00%	Latin American and Caribbean	180
MICRONESIA	$297,451,433	0.00%	111,064	0.00%	0.00%	Asia-Pacific	181
TONGA	$357,482,868	0.00%	104,058	0.00%	0.00%	Asia-Pacific	182
ST. KITTS AND NEVIS	$673,200,093	0.00%	52,402	0.00%	0.00%	Latin American and Caribbean	183
DOMINICA	$471,851,098	0.00%	67,757	0.00%	0.00%	Latin American and Caribbean	184
KIRIBATI	$151,175,994	0.00%	99,546	0.00%	0.00%	N/A	185
MARSHALL ISLANDS	$162,935,850	0.00%	54,038	0.00%	0.00%	Asia-Pacific	186
PALAU	$171,345,539	0.00%	20,472	0.00%	0.00%	Asia-Pacific	187
TUVALU	$31,351,969	0.00%	9,827	0.00%	0.00%	Asia-Pacific	188
MYANMAR	data unavailable		data unavail.				
KOREA, NORTH	data unavailable		data unavail.				
SOUTH SUDAN	data unavailable		data unavail.				
SOMALIA	data unavailable		data unavail.				
NAURU	data unavailable		data unavail.				

[1]2010 data unavailable, figures from 2008.
[2]2010 data unavailable, figures from 2009.

Source: World Bank 2010, http://databank.worldbank.org.

ACRONYMS

AIDS	acquired immune deficiency syndrome
APEC	Asia-Pacific Economic Cooperation
APLN	Asia-Pacific Leadership Network
ASEAN	Association of Southeast Asian Nations
bcm	billion cubic meters
b/d	barrels a day
BRICS	Brazil, Russia, India, China, and South Africa
CAG	Centre on Asia and Globalization
CEO	chief executive officer
CFC	chlorofluorocarbon
CGD	Center for Global Development
CIA	Central Intelligence Agency
CII	Confederation of Indian Industry
CPC	Communist Party of China
CTO	chief technical officer
DCR	Development Co-operation Report
DPT	diphtheria, pertussis, and tetanus
EBF	Extrabudgetary Fund
EU	European Union
FDI	Foreign Direct Investment
FYP	five-year plan
GDP	gross domestic product
GHG	greenhouse gas
GNP	gross national product
GRE	gross enrollment ratio

IAEA	International Atomic Energy Agency
IAS	Indian Administration Services
ICC	International Cricket Council
ICC	International Criminal Court
ICG	International Crisis Group
ICJ	International Court of Justice
ICTR	International Criminal Tribunal for Rwanda
ICTY	International Criminal Tribunal for Yugoslavia
IIE	International Institute of Education
IGO	intergovernmental organization
IIT	Indian Institute(s) of Technology
IMF	International Monetary Fund
IT	information technology
KAUST	King Abdullah University of Science and Technology
KGB	Komitet Gosudarstvennoy Bezopasnosti (Committee for State Security)
LRA	Lord's Resistance Army
MAD	mutual assured destruction
MCC	Marylebone Cricket Club
MDG	Millennium Development Goal
MIT	Massachusetts Institute of Technology
NATO	North Atlantic Treaty Organization
NGO	nongovernmental organization
NSC	National Security Council
NSG	Nuclear Suppliers Group
NUS	National University of Singapore
OECD	Organization for Economic Cooperation and Development
OEEC	Organisation for European Economic Cooperation
OLA	Office of Legal Affairs (UN Secretariat)
PLA	People's Liberation Army
PPP	purchasing power parity
PPWSA	Phnom Penh Water Supply Authority
PRIO	Peace Research Institute Oslo
QE	quantitative easing
RBF	Regular Budget Fund
SDR	special drawing rights

SOE	state-owned enterprise
UDHR	Universal Declaration of Human Rights
UNAMA	UN Assistance Mission in Afghanistan
UNAMI	UN Assistance Mission in Iraq
UNCLOS	UN Convention on the Law of the Sea (Law of the Sea Treaty)
UNDP	UN Development Programme
UNDR	Universal Declaration of Human Rights
UNEP	UN Environment Program
UNESCO	United Nations Educational, Scientific, and Cultural Organization
UNFPA	UN Population Fund
UNGA	UN General Assembly
UNHCR	UN High Commissioner for Refugees
UNICEF	UN Children's Fund
UNSC	UN Security Council
UNWTO	UN World Tourism Organization
USAID	US Agency for International Development
USTR	US Trade Representative
WEF	World Economic Forum
WFP	World Food Programme
WHO	World Health Organization
WMD	weapon of mass destruction
WTO	World Trade Organization

ACKNOWLEDGMENTS

One important life lesson I have learned with the writing of this book—my fourth—is that it is probably mad to work full-time as a dean of a school of public policy and write books at the same time. Since my very fulfilling day job keeps me busy during the week, I can write only on weekends. It has been stressful. In the end, I succeeded in completing this book because I have been helped by a wonderful community of people. I wish to acknowledge these people, who have, in effect, created an outstandingly supportive "ecosystem."

All my three bosses have been very supportive. The president of NUS, Professor Tan Chorh Chuan; the provost of NUS, Professor Tan Eng Chye; and the chairman of the board of governors of the Lee Kuan Yew School of Public Policy (LKY School), Professor Wang Gungwu, have always given me a lot of leeway to develop my ideas. They have encouraged me to write more. Similarly, my colleagues in the LKY School have been equally supportive. I hope it is not self-delusion that makes me believe that my writing has also helped to raise the profile of the LKY School.

The Dean's Office team has also been very supportive. I must thank Amirah Binte Mohamed Fadali, Karen Kor, Ann Verbeek, and, especially, Carol Chan, my secretary, for their tremendous support. Over the last eight years as dean, I have also been blessed with good research assistants. Benjamin Shatil (in 2010) and Yvonne Guo (2011–mid-2012) did most of the research for this book. Rhoda Severino joined at the end to help complete the last lap.

I live in Singapore. My publisher, PublicAffairs, is in New York. As this is my third book with PublicAffairs, the close friendships I have built up working on the previous two books with its excellent team have helped a lot. This is the third time that my editor, Clive Priddle, has had to suffer my first drafts. He has always been frank and open with his criticisms. His support has meant a lot to me. I also wish to thank his subeditors Michelle Welsh-Horst, Jan Kristiansson, and Melissa Raymond. While thanking all these people, I must also thank the late singer Mohamed Rafi, whose songs keep me company through all my writing.

It's been critical to know I have the support and encouragement of my children even though they were away from Singapore for most of 2011 and 2012. All those who know me well know that I would not have accomplished anything without the support of my wife, Anne.

Finally, as I approach the age of sixty-five in 2013, I join many of my peers in thinking more often of mortality. The best thing I can do is to nurture the next generation. Over the past sixty years or so, my generation has had relatively good innings. I am convinced that the next sixty years could be even better. A Zeitgeist of pessimism is seeping into the discussion in some of the world's leading capitals, especially in the West. With this book, I want to inject some optimism. As a mark of my faith in the future, I am dedicating this book to the eight grandchildren of my parents, as I am confident that a great future lies ahead for them with the coming great convergence.

NOTES

Introduction

1. Martin Wolf, "In the Grip of a Great Convergence," January 4, 2011, http://www.ft.com/intl/cms/s/0/072c87e6–1841–11e0–88c9–00144feab49a.html#ixzz22YmCfrmm.

2. On a purchasing-power-parity basis.

3. Yuval Atsmon, Peter Child, Richard Dobbs, and Laxman Narasimhan, "Winning the $30 Trillion Decathlon: Going for Gold in Emerging Markets," *McKinsey Quarterly*, August 2012, https://www.mckinseyquarterly.com/Winning_the_30_trillion_decathlon_Going_for_gold_in_emerging_markets_3002.

4. Adam LeBor, "How We Dined with Mladic and Failed Our Duty," *Financial Times*, May 27, 2011, 9.

5. Bill Clinton, "Global Challenges," public address at Yale University, October 31, 2003.

6. Strobe Talbott, *The Great Experiment: The Story of Ancient Empires, Modern States, and the Quest for a Global Nation* (New York: Simon and Schuster, 2009), 330.

7. Ibid., 330–331.

8. "Written Testimony of Hillary Rodham Clinton, Secretary, U.S. Department of State, Before the Senate Foreign Relations Committee on May 23, 2012, Accession to the 1982 Law of the Sea Convention and Ratification of the 1994 Agreement Amending Part xi of the Law of the Sea Convention," http://www.foreignpolicy.com/files/fp_uploaded_documents/120523_0_Secretary_Clinton_Testimony.pdf.

9. Ibid.

10. Shultz said in a letter to Senator Dick Lugar in 2007, "The treaty has been changed in such a way with respect to the deep sea-beds that it is now acceptable, in my judgment. Under these circumstances, and given the many desirable aspects of the treaty on other grounds, I believe it is time to proceed with ratification." Quoted in "Written Testimony of Hillary Rodham Clinton."

11. Jeffrey Sachs, letter to the editor, *Financial Times*, February 9, 2012, http://www.ft.com/intl/cms/s/0/9160571e-5191–11e1-a99d-00144feabdc0.html#axzz1yrgRRBMF.

12. Gideon Rachman, *Zero-Sum World* (London: Atlantic Books, 2010), xix.

13. "The Redistribution of Hope," *The Economist*, December 16, 2010, http://www.economist.com/node/17732859.

14. Ibid.

15. James Politi, "US Budget: Pushed to the Brink," *Financial Times*, July 5, 2012, http://www.ft.com/intl/cms/s/0/9abd560e-c5c2–11e1-a5d5–00144feabdc0.html.

Chapter 1: A New Global Civilization

1. Albert Einstein, *Ideas and Opinions by Albert Einstein*, trans. Sonja Bargmann, ed. Carl Seelig (New York: Crown, 1954), 13.

2. Gunnar Myrdal, "Nobel Prize Lecture: The Equality Issue in World Development," September 26, 2012, http://www.nobelprize.org/nobel_prizes/economics/laureates/1974/myrdal-lecture.html.

3. Seth Borenstein, "Bombings, Beheadings? Stats Show a Peaceful World," *Guardian*, October 22, 2011, http://www.guardian.co.uk/world/feedarticle/9908513.

4. Andrew Mack, "2010 Human Security Report," Simon Fraser University, http://hsrgroup.org/press-room/latest-news/latest-news-view/10–12–02/Canadian_Study_Reports_New_Threats_to_Global_Security_but_Reveals_Encouraging_Long-Term_Trends.aspx.

5. Ibid.

6. Halvard Buhaug, Scott Gates, Håvard Hegre, and Håvard Strand, "Global Trends in Armed Conflict," Centre for the Study of Civil War, International Peace Research Institute, Oslo, 2007, http://www.regjeringen.no/nb/dep/ud/kampanjer/refleks/innspill/engasjement/prio.html?id=492941.

7. Ronald Bailey, "How Scared of Terrorism Should You Be?," *Reason*, September 6, 2011, http://reason.com/archives/2011/09/06/how-scared-of-terrorism-should.

8. "President Bush Discusses Terror Plot upon Arrival in Wisconsin," August 20, 2006, http://georgewbush-whitehouse.archives.gov/news/releases/2006/08/20060810-3.html.

9. John Lewis Gaddis, *The Long Peace: Inquiries into the History of the Cold War* (Oxford: Oxford University Press, 1987).

10. Charles A. Fisher, "Southeast Asia: The Balkans of the Orient? A Study in Continuity and Change," *Geography* 47(4), November 1962, http://www.jstor.org/pss/40565457.

11. *The Millennium Development Goals Report 2011*, http://mdgs.un.org/unsd/mdg/Resources/Static/Products/Progress2011/11–31339%20(E)%20MDG%20Report%202011_Book%20LR.pdf.

12. "US Intelligence Predicts Poverty Plummet by 2030," Fox News, July 28, 2012, http://www.foxnews.com/politics/2012/07/28/us-intelligence-predicts-poverty-plummet-by-2030/.

13. Jeffrey Kluger, "Millennium Success: The World Gets Healthier, Richer," *Time*, June 24, 2010, http://www.time.com/time/world/article/0,8599,1999516,00.html.

14. *Millennium Development Goals Report 2011*.

15. Charles Kenny, "Getting Better in Pictures," Center for Global Development, 2011, http://www.cgdev.org/files/1424862_file_Getting_Better_in_Pictures_FINAL .pdf.

16. "Africa Rising: Jeffrey Sachs Says Ghana's Future Looks Bright," *Christian Science Monitor*, January 11, 2012, http://www.csmonitor.com/World/Africa/2012/0111 /Africa-Rising-Jeffrey-Sachs-says-Ghana-s-future-looks-bright.

17. Ibid.

18. Kenny, "Getting Better in Pictures."

19. Ramon Magsaysay Award for Government Service, "Citation for Ek Sonn Chan," August 31, 2006, http://www.rmaf.org.ph/Awardees/Citation/Citation EkSon.htm.

20. Joel E. Cohen, David E. Bloom, Martin B. Malin, and Helen Anne Curry, "Introduction: Universal Basic and Secondary Education," in *Educating All Children: A Global Agenda*, ed. Joel E. Cohen, David E. Bloom, and Martin B. Malin (Cambridge, MA: American Academy of Arts and Sciences, 2006), 2–3.

21. Kenny, "Getting Better in Pictures," 25–26.

22. Ibid., 25.

23. Peter Singer, "Is Violence History?" review of *The Better Angels of Our Nature* by Steven Pinker, *New York Times*, October 9, 2011, http://www.nytimes.com /2011/10/09/books/review/the-better-angels-of-our-nature-by-steven-pinker-book -review.html?_r=1&bl=&gwh=199BA89E3201D6A56147CD35873E787C&page wanted=all.

24. Homi Kharas, "The Emerging Middle Class in Developing Countries," Working Paper No. 285 (Paris: OECD Development Centre, 2010), http://www.oecd.org /dataoecd/12/52/44457738.pdf.

25. Ibid.

26. Homi Kharas, "The Emerging Middle Class in Developing Countries," OECD Development Centre, Working Paper No. 285, January 2010, http://www.oecd.org /dataoecd/12/52/44457738.pdf.

27. Stiglitz, whose book on the subject is titled *The Three Trillion Dollar War: The True Cost of the Iraq Conflict*, notes that "this war is the first war ever that's been totally financed by borrowing, by deficits," http://www.bloomberg.com/apps/news ?pid=newsarchive&sid=acX.yk56Ko.

28. Geoffrey Blainey, *The Causes of War* (New York: Free Press, 1973), 3.

29. Institute of International Education, "Open Doors 2011: Report on International Education Exchange," November 14, 2011, http://www.iie.org/Research-and -Publications/~/media/Files/Corporate/Open-Doors/Open-Doors-2011-Briefing -Presentation.ashx.

30. Institute of International Education, "International Students: Leading Places of Origin," *IIE.Org*, 2012, http://www.iie.org/Research-and-Publications/Open-Doors /Data/International-Students/Leading-Places-of-Origin.

31. Amanda Wilson, "U.S.: 2010 Saw Record Number of International Students," Inter Press Service, November 15, 2011, http://ipsnews.net/news.asp?idnews =105842.

32. "A Work in Progress," *The Economist*, March 17, 2011.

33. Sean Coughlan, "End of Empire for Western Universities?," *BBC*, July 10, 2012, http://bbc.co.uk/news/business-18646423.

34. Zhao Litao and Sheng Sixin, "China's 'Great Leap' in Higher Education," East Asia Institute background brief no. 394, July 24, 2008, http://www.eai.nus.edu.sg /BB394.pdf.

35. Yao Li, John Whalley, Shunming Zhang, and Xiliang Zhao, "China's Higher Education Transformation and Its Global Implications," *VoxEU.org*, April 18, 2008, http://www.voxeu.org/index.php?q=node/1066.

36. "PM's Inaugural Address at the 'PAN IIT-2008—IIT Alumni Global Conference," Press Information Bureau, Government of India, December 19, 2008, http:// pib.nic.in/newsite/erelease.aspx?relid=45899.

37. John Cook, "Vinod Khosla on Failure, Thinking Big and Why the Best Entrepreneurs Are Under 25," *Geekwire.com*, September 30, 2011, http://www.geekwire. com/2011/vinod-khosla-failure-thinking-big-entrepreneurs-25.

38. "Betting on Green," *Economist*, March 10, 2011, http://www.economist.com /node/18304172.

39. "I'm One of the Hardest Working People I Know: Narayan Murthy," *Financial Express*, September 25, 2011, http://www.financialexpress.com/news/im-one-of-the -hardest-working-people-i-know-narayan-murthy/851242/0.

40. Arab Knowledge Report 2009: Towards Productive Intercommunication for Knowledge, http://www.mbrfoundation.ae/English/pages/AKR2009.aspx.

41. Roger Highfield, "The Renaissance of Arabic Science," *New Scientist*, October 29, 2010, http://www.newscientist.com/blogs/thesword/2010/10/the-renaissance-of -arabic-scie.html.

42. Adnan Badran and Moneef R. Zou'bi, "Arab States" in *UNESCO Science Report 2010*, http://www.unesco.org/new/fileadmin/MULTIMEDIA/HQ/SC/pdf/sc_usr10 _arab_states_EN.pdf.

43. Ibid.

44. Ibid.

45. Highfield, "The Renaissance of Arabic Science."

46. Badran and Zou'bi, *UNESCO Science Report 2010*.

47. Ali Dadpay, "Iran Parliament and Women in Higher Education," *Bazaar Dispatch*, February 12, 2008, http://bazardispatch.blogspot.com/2008/02/iran-parliament-and -women-in-higher.html.

48. UNESCO Institute for Statistics, http://www.uis.unesco.org/Pages/default .aspx.

49. Robert D. Kaplan, *The Ends of the Earth: From Togo to Turkmenistan, from Iran to Cambodia, a Journey to the Frontiers of Anarchy* (New York: Random House, 1996), 182.

50. Singer, "Is Violence History?"

51. President Eisenhower's News Conference, April 7, 1954, Public Papers of the Presidents, 1954, 382, http://www.saylor.org/site/wp-content/uploads/2011/02 /Eisenhower-News-Conference.pdf.

52. Donald E. Nuechterlein, "Southeast Asia in International Politics: A 1975 Perspective," *Asian Survey* 15, no. 7 (July 1975): 576.

53. Martin Loffelholz and Danilo A. Arao, "The ASEAN Guide: A Journalist's Handbook to Regional Integration in Southeast Asia," December 2010, http://www3.giz.de/imperia/md/content/a-internet2008/iij/20110407_asean_guide.pdf.

54. Adam Smith, *An Inquiry into the Nature and Causes of the Wealth of Nations* (Oxford: Clarendon Press, 1869), 2:28.

55. "Premier Wen urges officials to better use power, serve the people wholeheartedly," *Xinhua*, June 22, 2012, http://news.xinhuanet.com/english2010/china/2011-06/22/c_13944515.htm.

56. Ibid.

57. "HIGHLIGHTS—China Premier Wen Jiabao's Comments at NPC Press Conference," March 14, 2012, http://www.reuters.com/article/2012/03/14/china-npc-highlights-idUSL4E8EE11K20120314.

58. "Bangladesh to Clock 7 pct GDP Growth in 2011–12 Fiscal: Central Bank," January 30, 2011, http://news.xinhuanet.com/english2010/world/2011–01/30/c_13713995.htm.

59. "Africa Rising," *The Economist*, December 3, 2011, http://www.economist.com/node/21541015.

60. Ibid.

61. Shibani Mahtani, "Singapore Presses Its Advantage in Myanmar," *Wall Street Journal*, February 15, 2012, http://blogs.wsj.com/searealtime/2012/02/15/singapore-presses-its-advantage-in-myanmar/.

62. Najib Razak, "The Asean Way Won Burma Over," *Wall Street Journal*, April 3, 2012, http://online.wsj.com/article/SB10001424052702303816504577321242628750250.html.

63. Mahtani, "Singapore Presses Its Advantage in Myanmar."

64. "Profile: John Bolton," *BBC*, December 4, 2006, http://news.bbc.co.uk/2/hi/4327185.stm.

65. *Good News*, July 13, 2006, "Blair Calls for SA to Join G8," *South Africa Good News*, July 13, 2006, http://www.sagoodnews.co.za/south_africa_in_the_world/blair_calls_for_sa_to_join_g8.html.

66. Thomas Friedman, *The Lexus and the Olive Tree* (New York: Anchor Books, 2000). 101–111.

67. See John Williamson, "What Should the World Bank Think About the Washington Consensus?," *World Bank Research Observer* 15, no. 2 (August 2000): 251–264. Williamson first coined the term.

Chapter 2: A Theory of One World

1. Bill Clinton speech in Mukono, Uganda, March 23, 1998, http://clinton3.nara.gov/Africa/19980324–3374.html.

2. Bill Clinton speech at Zellerbach Hall, UC-Berkeley, January 29, 2002.

3. Ibid.

4. Bill Clinton speech at Harvard University, November 19, 2001.

5. http://en.wikiquote.org/wiki/Al_Gore.

6. Al Gore speech on Iraq, with MoveOn PAC at New York University, May 26, 2004.

7. "Tony Blair: As the World Becomes Smaller, the Need to Understand Each Other's Faith Grows," *The Independent*, June 14, 2008, http://www.independent.co.uk /opinion/commentators/tony-blair-as-the-world-becomes-smaller-the-need-to -understand-each-others-faith-grows-846964.html.

8. Tony Blair speech at Seton Hall University, February 3, 2009, http://blogs.shu .edu/diplomacy/files/archives/02%20Blair_Layout%201.pdf.

9. Gordon Brown, *Beyond the Crash: Overcoming Crisis Globalization* (New York, NY: Simon & Schuster, 2010).

10. Gordon Brown speech to the Young Global Leaders Forum, http://www .managementexchange.com/hack/juccce-%E2%80%9Cblueprint-impact%E2%80 %9D-crowdsourcing-solutions-societal-challenges.

11. Gordon Brown speech at Georgetown University, April 14, 2011, http://www .georgetown.edu/story/gordonbrown.html.

12. Ibid.

13. "Brown Calls for Overhaul of UN, World Bank, and IMF," *The Guardian*, January 18, 2007.

14. Jagdish Bhagwati, *In Defense of Globalization* (Oxford: Oxford University Press, 2004), 3; Martin Wolf, *Why Globalization Works* (New Haven, CT: Yale University Press, 2004), 14.

15. http://en.wikipedia.org/wiki/List_of_environmental_issues, accessed 3 April 2012.

16. Summary by Stewart Brand of a talk by Mark Lynas on green global perspectives, sent to me via e-mail on February 26, 2012.

17. Bess Levin, "Hank Paulson Has a New Job," *Dealbreaker*, June 27, 2011, http:// dealbreaker.com/2011/06/hank-paulson-has-a-new-job/.

18. Beth Daley, "Number of Small Environmental NGOs Are on the Rise—and They Want Your Money," *Boston Globe*, December 2, 2008, http://www.boston.com /lifestyle/green/greenblog/2008/12/number_of_smaller_environmenta_1.html.

19. Christine Xu, "China: Locals Turn to Environmental Activism," Climate Institute, April 2008, http://www.climate.org/topics/international-action/chinese -environmental-action.html; David Kirby, "Made in China: Our Toxic, Imported Air Pollution," Discover, April 2011, http://discovermagazine.com/2011/apr/18-made -in-china-our-toxic-imported-air-pollution/article_view?b_start:int=4&-C=.

20. Meng Jing, "NGO's Role Evolves in Changing China," *China Daily*, May 12, 2012, http://www.chinadaily.com.cn/cndy/2012–05/12/content_15275471.htm.

21. Larry Lee and Chen Weihua, "Young People Dream of a Sustainable World," *China Daily*, June 22, 2012, http://usa.chinadaily.com.cn/epaper/2012–06/22 /content_15518402.htm.

22. Ibid.

23. "China's Yellow River Conservancy Commission wins this year's Lee Kuan Yew Water Prize," *People's Daily*, 3 March 2012, http://english.people.com.cn/90001/90776 /90883/6908053.html.

24. "International Climate Change Negotiations: Key Lessons and Next Steps," Smith School of Enterprise and the Environment, University of Oxford, July 2011, http://edition2a.intellimag.com/?id=ssee-july2011&page=19.

25. Jing Cao, Mun Ho, and Dale Jorgenson, "Benefits of Carbon Control Policy," *China Daily*, September 2, 2011, http://www.chinadaily.com.cn/opinion/2011–09/02/content_13601127.htm.

26. Al Gore speech at the National Sierra Club Convention, San Francisco, September 9, 2005, http://www.commondreams.org/views05/0912–32.htm.

27. "Be Worried, Be Very Worried," *CNN*, March 26, 2006, http://articles.cnn.com/2006–03–26/us/coverstory_1_cubic-miles-greenland-ice-sheet-global-warming/2?_s=PM:US.

28. Tony Blair speech to the Labour conference, September 27, 2005, http://www.guardian.co.uk/uk/2005/sep/27/labourconference.speeches.

29. "Financial Support," Berkeley Earth Service Temperature, http://berkeley earth.org/donors/.

30. Richard A. Muller, "The Conversion of a Climate-Change Skeptic," *New York Times*, July 28, 2012, http://www.nytimes.com/2012/07/30/opinion/the-conversion-of-a-climate-change-skeptic.html?_r=4&pagewanted=all.

31. Yilmaz Argüden, "Rio+20 Was a Bust," *The Globalist*, July 11, 2012, http://www.theglobalist.com/printStoryId.aspx?StoryId=9683.

32. John Maynard Keynes, *The General Theory* (New York, Harcourt Brace and World, 1964), 383.

33. Paola Subacchi, personal e-mail, February 29, 2012.

34. Paola Subacchi, personal e-mail, March 24, 2012.

35. Eswar Prasad, personal e-mail, July 20, 2012.

36. T. N. Srinivasan, person e-mail, March 18, 2012.

37. Stella Dawson, "Scenarios: Impact of Euro Zone Crisis on U.S. Economy," *Reuters*, November 30, 2011, http://www.reuters.com/article/2011/11/30/us-usa-economy-scenarios-idUSTRE7AT1V720111130.

38. Otmar Issing, "Europe's Political Union Is an Idea Worthy of Satire," *Financial Times*, July 29, 2012, http://www.ft.com/intl/cms/s/0/d5efc38a-d64b-11e1-b547–00144feabdc0.html#axzz236vE5pCO.

39. Sanya Declaration, Third Summit, para. 16, http://www.contexto.org/pdfs/BRIChist.pdf.

40. "Delhi Declaration," March 29, 2012, http://www.brics.utoronto.ca/docs/120329-delhi-declaration.html.

41. Gregg Fields, "Is QE3 About to Set Sail?" *Bankrate.com*, July 13, 2011, http://www.bankrate.com/financing/federal-reserve/is-qe3-about-to-set-sail/.

42. "China Minister Says Dollar Printing 'Out of Control,'" Reuters, October 26, 2010, http://uk.reuters.com/article/2010/10/26/uk-china-dollar-minister-idUKTRE69P3S020101026.

43. Alan Beattie and Joe Leahy, "Brazil blames Fed move on fiscal inaction," *Financial Times*, September 22, 2011, http://www.ft.com/intl/cms/s/0/69f2c362-e538–11e0–852e-00144feabdc0.html.

44. Alan Wheatley, "Anger in Arab World Creates Risks in Asia," *New York Times*, January 31, 2011, http://www.nytimes.com/2011/02/01/business/global/01inside .html.

45. Robert J. Carbaugh and David W. Hedrick, "Will the Dollar Be Dethroned as the Main Reserve Currency?," *Global Economy Journal* vol.9, no. 3, 2009, http://www .eclac.org/noticias/paginas/3/35143/Will-the-dollar-be-dethroned.pdf.

46. "Statement of the Honorable Lawrence Summers, Under-Secretary of the Treasury for International Affairs, Before the Committee on Small Business, U.S. House of Representatives," May 26, 1993.

47. Charles Duhigg and Keith Bradsher, "How the U.S. Lost Out on iPhone Work," *New York Times*, January 21, 2012, http://www.nytimes.com/2012/01/22/business /apple-america-and-a-squeezed-middle-class.html?pagewanted=print.

48. Ibid.

49. "The Global Information Technology Report 2012: Living in a Hyperconnected World," World Economic Forum, 2012, http://reports.weforum.org/global -information-technology-2012/.

50. Donald Melanson, "UN: Worldwide Internet Users Hit Two Billion, Cellphone Subscriptions Top Five Billion," *Endgadget.com*, January 28, 2011, http://www .engadget.com/2011/01/28/un-worldwide-internet-users-hit-two-billion-cellphone -subscript/.

51. Mary Lennighan, "Number of phones exceeds population of world," *Total Telecom*, May 20, 2011, http://www.totaltele.com/view.aspx?ID=464922.

52. Christina Bonnington, "Global Smartphone Adoption Approaches 30 Percent," *Wired.com*, November 28, 2011, http://www.wired.com/gadgetlab/2011/11/smart phones-feature-phones.

53. Ibid.

54. "iPad 2 as Fast as Cray 2 Supercomputer, Fraction of the Size," *Electronista.com*, May 20. 2011, http://www.electronista.com/articles/11/05/10/ipad.2.benches.as.fast .as.cray.2.from.1985/.

55. http://en.wikipedia.org/wiki/Wikipedia.

56. Matt Craze and Nathan Crooks, "Chile Is Rescuing Trapped Miners Through Escape Tube," *Bloomberg*, October 31, 2010, http://www.bloomberg.com/news/2010 –10–13/chile-frees-first-of-33-miners-in-world-s-longest-underground-mine -rescue.html.

57. http://en.wikipedia.org/wiki/Wenzhou_train_collision.

58. James McKeigue, "Profit from the New Tourism Boom," *Moneyweek*, November 18, 2011, http://www.moneyweek.com/investment-advice/how-to-invest/strategies /pack-away-some-tourism-stocks-56434.

59. Quoted in ibid.

60. "UN Launches Major Push to Improve Global Sanitation by 2015," *UN News Centre*, June 21, 2011, http://www.un.org/apps/news/story.asp?NewsID=38783&Cr =sanitation&Cr1=.

61. "Energy for All: Financing Access for the Poor" in *World Energy Outlook 2011*, International Energy Agency, October 2011, http://www.iea.org/Papers/2011 /weo2011_energy_for_all.pdf.

62. "Monitoring the WSIS Targets: A Mid-term Review," World Telecommunication /ICT Development Report 2010, http://www.itu.int/ITU-D/ict/publications/wtdr _10/material/WTDR2010_Target8_e.pdf.

63. World Bank indicators. data.worldbank.org/data-catalog/world-development -indicators.

64. "Pakistanis, Indians Want Peace: Poll," *The News*, January 1, 2011, http:// www.thenews.com.pk/article-8446-Pakistanis,-Indians-want-peace:-poll.

65. Singer and Sen quoted in Dani Rodrik, "The Nation-State Reborn," http:// www.project-syndicate.org/commentary/the-nation-state-reborn.

66. "United Nations and the Rule of Law," http://www.un.org/en/ruleoflaw /index.shtml.

67. Lee Kuan Yew, cited in S. Jayakumar and Tommy Koh, *Pedra Branca: The Road to the World Court* (Singapore: NUS Press, 2009), xiii.

68. "ICJ Awards Pedra Branca's Sovereignty to Singapore," *Channel News Asia*, May 23, 2008, http://www.channelnewsasia.com/stories/singaporelocalnews/view /349592/1/.html.

69. Rodolfo C. Severino, "The Asean Way and the Rule of Law," address at the International Law Conference on ASEAN Legal Systems and Regional Integration, Asia-Europe Institute and the Faculty of Law, University of Malaya, Kuala Lumpur, September 3, 2001, http://www.aseansec.org/3132.htm.

70. Mahdev Mohan, "Rule of Law for Human Rights in the ASEAN Region: A Synthesis," in *Rule of Law for Human Rights in the Asean Region: A Base-Line Study*, ed. David Cohen, Kevin Tan Yew Lee, and Mahdev Mohan (Jakarta: Human Rights Resource Centre, University of Indonesia, 2011), 10, http://hrrca.org/system/files /Rule_of_Law_for_Human_Rights_in_the_ASEAN_Region.pdf.

71. Dani Rodrik, "The Nation-State Reborn," *Project Syndicate*, February 13, 2012, http://www.project-syndicate.org/commentary/rodrik67/English.

72. Dr. Manmohan Singh, speech at the India-China Economic, Trade, and Investment Summit, Beijing, January 14, 2008.

73. Premier Wen Jiabao, speech at the India-China Business Cooperation Summit, New Delhi, December 15, 2010.

Chapter 3: Global Irrationality

1. Robert Bolt, "A Man for All Seasons: A Play in Two Acts," in *Three Plays* (London: Heinemann, 1967), 147.

2. Jimmy Carter, "A Cruel and Unusual Record," *New York Times*, June 24, 2012, http://www.nytimes.com/2012/06/25/opinion/americas-shameful-human-rights -record.html.

3. In this book, the "West" refers to the US, Canada, the European Union member states, Australia, New Zealand, and Switzerland.

4. Madeleine K. Albright, "Who Broke the U.N.?," *Foreign Policy*, September/October 2012, http://www.foreignpolicy.com/articles/2012/08/13/who_broke_the_un.

5. "Statement by Ambassador Joseph M. Torsella, U.S. Representative to the United Nations for UN Management and Reform, on the Adoption by the General

Assembly of the UN 2012–2013 Regular Budget," US Mission to the United Nations, New York, December 24, 2011, http://usun.state.gov/briefing/statements /2011/179776.htm.

6. "The 62nd United Nations General Assembly: A Look Forward at the U.S.-United Nations Relationship," Better World Campaign, September 2007, http://www .globalproblems-globalsolutions-files.org/unf_website/PDF/bwc_congressional _briefing_book_092007.pdf.

7. (81.34 billion / 520.5 billion) × 100 = 15.6272815; (3.55200 trillion / 14.6 trillion) × 100 = 24.3287671; http://www.whitehouse.gov/sites/default/files/omb/budget /fy2013/assets/hist01z1.xls.

8. 65.7 million / 1.35 trillion × 100 = 0.00486666667; 2.7 billion / 63 trillion × 100 = 0.00428571429.

9. Martin Wolf, "The World's Hunger for Public Goods," *Financial Times*, January 24, 2012, http://www.ft.com/intl/cms/s/0/517e31c8–45bd-11e1–93f1–00144feabdc0 .html.

10. Ibid.

11. Peter J. Hotez, "Tropical Diseases: Poverty's New Plague," *International Herald Tribune*, August 21, 2012.

12. J. Patrick Vaughan, Sigrun Mogedal, Stein-Erik Kruse, Kelley Lee, Gill Walt, and Koen de Wilde, *Cooperation for Health Development: Extrabudgetary Funds in the World Health Organisation* (London: Governments of Australia, Norway, and the UK, 1995).

13. The Geneva Group represents fourteen member states that are major donors to UN agencies. The members are Australia, Belgium, Canada, France, Germany, Italy, Japan, the Netherlands, the Russian Federation, Spain, Sweden, Switzerland, the United Kingdom, and the United States.

14. Kelley Lee, *The World Health Organization (WHO)* (New York: Routledge, 2009), 9.

15. Ibid., 72.

16. Ibid., 73.

17. Ibid., 79.

18. Ibid., 65.

19. Ibid., 116.

20. Ibid., 117.

21. Ibid., 109.

22. Kishore Mahbubani, "The World Health Organization (WHO)," *Global Public Health: An International Journal for Research, Policy, and Practice* 7, no. 3 (2012), http://www.tandfonline.com/doi/abs/10.1080/17441692.2011.652972.

23. "Global Health Governance," Centre on Asia and Globalisation, http://www .caglkyschool.com/node/50.

24. All Kickbusch quotes are from http://www.globalhealtheurope.org/index .php?option=com_content&view=article&id=306:the-10-challenges-of-global -health-governance&catid=85:opinion-pieces&Itemid=139.

25. "Full Text: Tony Blair's Speech," *The Guardian*, March 18, 2003, http://www .guardian.co.uk/politics/2003/mar/18/foreignpolicy.iraq1.

26. Barack Obama speech at the Nuclear Security Summit, April 2010, http://www.cfr.org/proliferation/obamas-speech-nuclear-security-summit-april-2010/p21889.

27. Ibid.

28. Scott Ritter interview with *Buzzflash*, November 15, 2005, http://www.buzzflash.com/interviews/05/11/int05045.html.

29. Scott Peterson, "Iran Nuclear Talks: Why the Trust Gap Is So Great," *Christian Science Monitor*, April 12, 2012, http://www.csmonitor.com/World/Middle-East/2012/0412/Iran-nuclear-talks-Why-the-trust-gap-is-so-great.

30. Gary J. Bass, "How They Learned to Hate the Bomb," *New York Times*, December 30, 2011, http://www.nytimes.com/2012/01/01/books/review/the-partnership-five-cold-warriors-and-their-quest-to-ban-the-bomb-by-philip-taubman-book-review.html?pagewanted=all.

31. George P. Shultz, William J. Perry, Henry A. Kissinger, and Sam Nunn, "Deterrence in the Age of Nuclear Proliferation," *Wall Street Journal*, March 7, 2011, http://online.wsj.com/article/SB10001424052748703300904576178760530169414.html.

32. Thom Shanker, "Former Commander of U.S. Nuclear Forces Calls for Large Cut in Warheads," *New York Times*, May 15, 2012, http://www.nytimes.com/2012/05/16/world/cartwright-key-retired-general-backs-large-us-nuclear-reduction.html.

33. Ibid.

34. Heather Wokusch, "Women Activists Fighting Nuclear-Weapons Proliferation," *Activist*, April 2005, http://www.heatherwokusch.com/index.php?name=News&file=article&sid=68.

35. Ernest Corea, "New Network Seeks Nuke-Free World," *InDepthNews*, November 19, 2011, http://www.nuclearabolition.net/index.php?option=com_content&view=article&id=548:new-network&catid=16:nuclear-abolition-news-and-analysis&Itemid=17.

36. Kishore Mahbubani, "The Permanent and Elected Council Members," in *The UN Security Council: From the Cold War to the 21st Century*, ed. David Malone (Boulder, CO: Lynne Rienner, 2004), 253–266.

37. Costa Rica, Jordan, Liechtenstein, Singapore, and Switzerland, "Enhancing the Accountability, Transparency, and Effectiveness of the Security Council," revised draft resolution, May 3, 2012, http://www.un.org/ga/search/view_doc.asp?symbol=A/66/L.42/Rev.1.

38. "US 'Disgust' as Russia and China Veto UN Syria Resolution," *BBC*, February 4, 2012, http://www.bbc.co.uk/news/world-middle-east-16890434.

39. Joseph Logan and Patrick Worsnip, "Anger After Russia, China Block U.N. Action on Syria," Reuters, February 5, 2012, http://www.reuters.com/article/2012/02/05/us-syria-idUSTRE80S08620120205.

40. Colum Lynch, "Rise of the Lilliputians," *Foreign Policy*, May 10, 2012 http://turtlebay.foreignpolicy.com/posts/2012/05/10/rise_of_the_lilliputians.

41. Hans Corell, "Security Council Reform: Rule of Law More Important Than Additional Members," Letter to the Governments of the Members of the United Nations, Stockholm, December 10, 2008, http://www.havc.se/res/SelectedMaterial/20081210corelllettertounmembers.pdf.

42. Percy Bysshe Shelley, *Rosalind and Helen: A Modern Eclogue; with Other Poems* (London: C. and J. Ollier, 1819).

Chapter 4: Seven Global Contradictions

1. Joseph E. Stiglitz, *Freefall* (New York: Norton, 2010), 189.

2. "European Support for Lagarde as IMF Chief Grows," *Associated Press*, May 23, 2011, http://archive.hurriyetdailynews.com/n.php?n=european-support-for-lagarde-as-imf-chief-grows-2011–05–23.

3. Martin Wolf, "Europe Should Not Control the IMF," Financial Times, May 24, 2011, http://www.ft.com/intl/cms/s/0/28de825a-8640–11e0–9e2c-00144feabdc0.html.

4. Of the approximately 4 percent total, Australia has 1.31 percent, Canada has 2.56 percent, and New Zealand has 0.38 percent, http://www.imf.org/external/np/sec/memdir/members,aspx.

5. Charles Grant, "Is Europe Doomed to Fail as a Power?" (London: Centre for European Reform, July 2009), 10, http://www.cer.org.uk/pdf/essay_905.pdf.

6. Mihir Bose, "The ICC Becomes Democratic: How Cricket's Governing Body Grew from an Insular Club to a Commercial Entity," Lankanews.com, May 15, 2011, http://www.lankanewspapers.com/news/2011/5/66993_space.html.

7. Kishore Mahbubani, *Beyond the Age of Innocence* (New York: PublicAffairs, 2005), 97.

8. Kishore Mahbubani, "What Hillary Didn't Do in Asia," *Newsweek*, February 27, 2009, http://www.thedailybeast.com/newsweek/2009/02/27/what-hillary-didn-t-do-in-asia.html.

9. Kenneth Lieberthal and Wang Jisi, "Addressing U.S.-China Strategic Distrust," John L. Thornton China Centre at Brookings, March 2012, http://www.brookings.edu/~/media/research/files/papers/2012/3/30%20us%20china%20lieberthal/0330_china_lieberthal.pdf.

10. Hillary Clinton, "America's Pacific Century," *Foreign Policy*, November 2011, http://www.foreignpolicy.com/articles/2011/10/11/americas_pacific_century?hide comments=yes.

11. Simon Romero, "With Aid and Migrants, China Expands Its Presence in a South American Nation," *New York Times*, April 10, 2011, http://www.nytimes.com/2011/04/11/world/americas/11suriname.html?_r=1.

12. "Zambians Wary of 'Exploitative' Chinese Employers," Humanitarian News and Analysis, UN Office for the Coordination of Humanitarian Affairs, November 23, 2006, http://www.irinnews.org/Report.aspx?ReportId=61640.

13. Christian Fraser, "China's Chequebook Draws African Nations," *BBC*, November 9, 2009, http://news.bbc.co.uk/2/mobile/africa/8350228.stm.

14. Anissa Haddadi, "Is China Looking for a Profit by Dealing with the Libyan Rebels?," *International Business Times*, June 7, 2011, http://www.ibtimes.co.uk/articles/158605/20110607/is-china-looking-for-a-profit-by-dealing-with-the-libyan-rebels.htm.

15. Yitzhak Shichor, "Africa Warns China: Money Is Not enough," *Asia Times*, December 9, 2009, http://www.atimes.com/atimes/China_Business/KL09Cb01.html.

16. Ross E. Dunn, *The Adventures of Ibn Battuta, a Muslim Traveler of the Fourteenth Century* (Berkeley and Los Angeles: University of California Press, 1986), 3, 258.

17. "Dar al-Islam: the Muslim World," http://monkeytree.org/silkroad/battuta.html.

18. Thierry Ogier, "Brazil Vows to Deploy 'Arsenal' in Currency War," *Emerging Markets*, March 17, 2012, http://www.emergingmarkets.org/Article/2997035/Brazil-vows-to-deploy-arsenal-in-currency-war.html.

19. Arvind Subramanian, "China's Next Generation Should Look to Zhu," *Financial Times*, April 9, 2012, http://www.ft.com/intl/cms/s/0/de483c9e-7cb2-11e1-9d8f-00144feab49a.html#axzz1rnHRlOKm.

20. Please refer to discussion of this episode in Chapter 5.

21. Zhou Shengqi, "Sino–South Korean Trade Relations: From Boom to Recession," East Asia Institute Background Brief No. 508 (Seoul: East Asia Institute, March 2010).

22. Edward Wong, "Chinese Military Seeks to Extend Its Naval Power," *New York Times*, April 23, 2010, http://www.nytimes.com/2010/04/24/world/asia/24navy.html?pagewanted=all.

23. "American Shadow over South China Sea," *Global Times*, July 26, 2010, http://opinion.globaltimes.cn/editorial/2010–07/555723.html.

24. "China Says Its South China Sea Claims Are 'Indisputable'," *Bloomberg*, July 30, 2010, http://www.bloomberg.com/news/2010–07–30/china-has-indisputable-sovereignty-in-south-china-sea-defense-aide-says.html.

25. "The Framework for Strong, Sustainable, and Balanced Growth: Annex I," G-20 Seoul Summit Declaration, November 11–12, 2010, 10, http://www.g20.org/Documents2010/11/seoulsummit_declaration.pdf.

26. "Resolution Adopted by the General Assembly: 2005 World Summit Outcome," United Nations General Assembly Resolution A/RES/60/1, October 24, 2005, 12, http://daccess-dds-ny.un.org/doc/UNDOC/GEN/N05/487/60/PDF/N0548760.pdf?OpenElement.

27. Homi Kharas, "The Emerging Middle Class in Developing Countries," Working Paper No. 285 (Paris: OECD Development Centre, 2010), 28, http://www.oecd.org/dataoecd/12/52/44457738.pdf.

28. Jennifer Wheary, "The Global Middle Class Is Here: Now What?," *World Policy Journal* 26, no. 4 (December 2009): 75–83.

29. "US Intelligence Predicts Poverty Plummet by 2030," *Fox News*, July 28, 2012, http://www.foxnews.com/politics/2012/07/28/us-intelligence-predicts-poverty-plummet-by-2030/.

30. David Bornstein, "A Light in India," *New York Times*, January 10, 2011, http://opinionator.blogs.nytimes.com/2011/01/10/a-light-in-india/.

31. "India's Energy Woes Power New Business Opportunities," Knowledge@Wharton, July 28, 2011, http://knowledgetoday.wharton.upenn.edu/2011/07/india%E2%80%99s-energy-woes-power-new-business-opportunities/.

32. "Why India Might Save the Planet," *Newsweek*, March 13, 2011, http://www.newsweek.com/2011/03/13/why-india-might-save-the-planet.html.

33. Carbon dioxide emissions, total, per capita, UN Millennium Development Goals indicators, http://unstats.un.org/unsd/mdg/Default.aspx.

34. UN Charter, Art. 2, para.7.

35. John G. Ikenberry review of *A New World Order* by Anne-Marie Slaughter, *Foreign Affairs*, May/June 2004, http://www.foreignaffairs.com/articles/59730/g-john-ikenberry/a-new-world-order.

36. Colum Lynch, "Did Justice Scalia Really Call the ICC a Kangaroo Court?," *Turtle Bay*, August 2, 2012, http://turtlebay.foreignpolicy.com/posts/2012/08/02/did_justice_scalia_really_call_the_icc_a_kangaroo_court.

37. Moises Naim, "Five Myths About Davos," *Washington Post*, January 25, 2011, http://www.washingtonpost.com/wp-dyn/content/article/2011/01/25/AR2011012504781.html.

38. "Risk Management and Aung San Suu Kyi's Visit Define the World Economic Forum on East Asia 2012," *Asia Now*, June 11, 2012, http://asianowblog.com/2012/06/11/risk-management-and-aung-san-suu-kyi%E2%80%99s-visit-define-the-world-economic-forum-on-east-asia-2012/.

39. Gideon Rachman, "What's on the Mind of the Davos Man?," *Financial Times*, January 28, 2011, http://www.ft.com/intl/cms/s/2/3a6d0774-2977-11e0-bb9b-00144feab49a,dwp_uuid=c66ddce8-23dd-11e0-8bb1-00144feab49a.html#axzz1Z2nkg3RK.

40. Jim Yardley, "Industry in India Helps Open a Door to the World," *New York Times*, April 1, 2012, http://www.nytimes.com/2012/04/01/world/asia/private-sector-helps-propel-india-onto-world-stage.html?pagewanted=all.

41. "India Tries Business Diplomacy," *New York Times*, April 8, 2012, http://imcms images.mediacorp.sg/CMSFileserver/documents/006/PDF/20120408/0804NYP034.pdf.

Chapter 5: Will Geopolitics Derail Convergence?

1. "Geopolitics," *Oxford Dictionaries*, http://oxforddictionaries.com/definition/geopolitics?region=us&q=geopolitics.

2. Robert H. Jackson and Georg Sørensen, *Introduction to International Relations: Theories and Approaches* (New York: Oxford University Press, 2007), 97–99.

3. Ibid., 60–61.

4. "Chances of US-China War Remote, Says Gates," *Straits Times*, July 1, 2011.

5. All Kissinger quotes are from http://www.nytimes.com/2011/05/10/books/on-china-by-henry-kissinger-review.html?pagewanted=all.

6. See Kishore Mahbubani, *The New Asian Hemisphere: The Irresistible Shift of Global Power to the East* (New York: PublicAffairs, 2008), 225.

7. Frank Ching, "Why China Needed Bin Laden," *The Diplomat*, May 26, 2011, http://the-diplomat.com/2011/05/26/why-china-needed-bin-laden/?all=true.

8. Yoichi Funabashi, "Japan-China Relations Stand at Ground Zero," East Asia Forum, October 20, 2010, http://www.eastasiaforum.org/2010/10/20/japan-china-relations-stand-at-ground-zero/.

9. Christopher C. Joyner, "The Spratly Islands Dispute in the South China Sea: Problems, Policies, and Prospects for Diplomatic Accommodation," *Investigating Confidence-building Measures in the Asia-Pacific Region*, ed. Ranjeet K. Singh (Washington, DC: Henry L. Stimson Center, 1999), 57.

10. "Clinton's Comments on South China Sea Territorial Dispute Press China-U.S. Relations," *2point6billion.com*, July 27, 2010, http://www.2point6billion.com/news /2010/07/27/clinton%E2%80%99s-comments-on-south-china-sea-territorial-dispute -press-china-u-s-relations-6528.html.

11. Carlyle A. Thayer, "Recent Developments in the South China Sea: Grounds for Cautious Optimism?," December 14, 2010, http://www.rsis.edu.sg/publications /WorkingPapers/WP220.pdf.

12. Lee Kuan Yew quoted in Jeremy Au Yong, "The Way to Solve Border Disputes: MM," *Straits Times*, September 29, 2010.

13. Huy Duong, "The South China Sea Is Not China's Sea," *Asia Times*, October 5, 2011, http://www.atimes.com/atimes/Southeast_Asia/MJ05Ae03.html.

14. Fareed Zakaria, "Why Defense Spending Should Be Cut," *Washington Post*, August 4, 2011, http://www.washingtonpost.com/opinions/why-defense-spending -should-be-cut/2011/08/03/gIQAsRuqsI_story.html.

15. "Opinion Poll on Communist Party," *CNTV*, June 30, 2011, http://english .cntv.cn/program/newsupdate/20110630/106660.shtml.

16. Mitt Romney, "How I'll Respond to China's Rising Power," *Wall Street Journal*, February 16, 2012, http://online.wsj.com/article/SB10001424052970204880404577 225340763595570.html.

17. Ibid.

18. "If This Isn't a World-Altering Economic Shift, Then What Is?," *Financial Times*, February 9, 2012, http://www.ft.com/intl/cms/s/0/9160571e-5191–11e1-a99d-001 44feabdc0.html.

19. Ed Luce interview by David Rothkopf, "A Nation of Spoiled Brats," *Foreign Policy*, April 16, 2012, http://www.foreignpolicy.com/articles/2012/04/16/ed_luce _interview.

20. Saxby Chambliss, Bob Corker, Michael Froman. and Nita Lowey panel moderated by Kishore Mahbubani, World Economic Forum, January 27, 2012, http://www .weforum.org/videos/future-american-power-21st-century.

21. Charles A. Kupchan, "America's Place in the New World," *New York Times*, April 7, 2012, http://www.nytimes.com/2012/04/08/opinion/sunday/americas-place-in -the-new-world.html?hp=&pagewanted=all.

22. Romney, "How I'll Respond to China's Rising Power."

23. Bill Clinton, "State of the Union Address," February 17, 1993, http://www.wash ingtonpost.com/wp-srv/politics/special/states/docs/sou93.htm.

24. Bill Clinton speech at Warwick University, December 14, 2000, http://clinton6 .nara.gov/2000/12/2000–12–14-remarks-by-the-president-to-the-university-of-war wick.html

25. "WTO (World Trade Organization) Seattle Protest," December 8, 1999, http:// www.greatdreams.com/prep.htm.

26. "Strongman Zhu Rongji: I've Prepared 100 Coffins. 99 for Corrupt Officials and One for Myself" (Chinese language), *New Century News*, November 13, 2006, http://ncchinesenews.com/Article/china/200611/20061113232956.html.

27. WikiLeaks document release: "China-US Summitry: Premier Zhu Rongji's April 1999 Visit," http://stuff.mit.edu/afs/sipb/contrib/wikileaks-crs/wikileaks-crs-reports/RS20135.pdf.

28. Joseph Fewsmith, "China and the WTO: The Politics Behind the Agreement" in *NBR Analysis: South Korea, China, and the Global Economy*, National Bureau of Asian Research, December 1999, http://www.google.com/url?sa=t&rct=j&q=&esrc=s&frm=1&source=web&cd=8&ved=0CFQQFjAH&url=http%3A%2F%2Fkms1.isn.ethz.ch%2Fserviceengine%2FFiles%2FISN%2F106473%2Fichaptersection_singledocument%2Fd357fcc4-4f24-4a61-93f6-97b626259a24%2Fen%2F2.pdf&ei=_xoET9L4BcOHrAeT5tzrAQ&usg=AFQjCNG7Lxf3FlhxmZXQgn3puqQ3fb8Fmw&sig2=kssB7KQ2PgJ5bzhRMbFTFQ.

29. Steven Mufson and Robert G. Kaiser, "Missed U.S.-China Deal Looms Large," *Washington Post*, November 10, 1999.

30. Ibid.

31. http://professorannlee.com/; http://www.huffingtonpost.com/ann-lee.

32. Rong Xiaoqing, "Can the US Bring Itself to Learn from China?," *Global Times*, January 19, 2012, http://www.globaltimes.cn/NEWS/tabid/99/ID/692903/Can-the-US-bring-itself-to-learn-from-China.aspx.

33. Stephen Olson and Clyde Prestowitz, "The Evolving Role of China in International Institutions," report prepared for the U.S.-China Economic and Security Review Commission (Washington, DC: Economic Strategy Institute, January 2011).

34. "United States," *CIA World Factbook*, https://www.cia.gov/library/publications/the-world-factbook/geos/us.html.

35. Nina Easton, "America Sours on Free Trade," *CNN Money*, January 25, 2008, http://money.cnn.com/2008/01/18/news/economy/worldgoaway.fortune/.

36. Thomas L. Friedman, "Are We Going to Roll Up Our Sleeves or Limp On?," *New York Times*, September 20, 2011, http://www.nytimes.com/2011/09/21/opinion/friedman-are-we-going-to-roll-up-our-sleeves-or-limp-on.html?partner=rssnyt&emc=rss.

37. Brahma Chellaney quoted in "Belligerent on the Border," *India Today*, January 21, 2012, http://indiatoday.intoday.in/story/indo-china-talks-intelligence-bureau-report-exposes-intrusions-by-china/1/169823.html.

38. Brahma Chellaney, "Dragon's Familiar Dance," *India Today*, November 7, 2011, http://indiatoday.intoday.in/story/india-china-relations-current-and-pre-1962/1/157740.html.

39. Vikas Bajaj, "China's 'String of Pearls' Meant to Encircle India?" *New York Times*, February 15, 2010, http://www.nytimes.com/2010/02/16/business/global/16port.html.

40. "After 'Deep Love', PM Hails Bush as 'Great Friend of India'," *Rediff.com*, October 30, 2009, http://news.rediff.com/report/2009/oct/30/pm-hails-bush-as-great-friend-of-india.htm.

41. Mahbubani, *The New Asian Hemisphere*, 188–189.

42. "India China Take Common Stand on WTO Doha Round Issues India China Issue Joint Ministerial Statement in Beijing Kamal Nath Also Discusses Bilateral Trade with Chinese Minister," Alibaba.com, August 9, 2010, http://news.alibaba.com/article /detail/international-trade-special/100375728–1-india-china-take-common-stand .html.

43. "Government's Stance," Lead International, http://www.climate-leaders.org /climate-change-resources/india-and-climate-change/governments-stance.

44. Rob Elsworth, "China May Steal a March on Europe in Fight Against Climate Change," *Guardian*, April 24, 2012, http://www.guardian.co.uk/environment/2012 /apr/24/china-climate-change-carbon-emissions.

45. "The Rise of China and Its Energy Implications," James A. Baker III Institute for Public Policy Energy Forum, Rice University, http://www.rice.edu/energy/research /RiseOfChina/Rise%20of%20China.html.

46. "India's Power-Plant Coal Imports May Rise by 16% to Fuel Economic Growth," Bloomberg, October 20, 2010, http://www.bloomberg.com/news/2010–10–20/india-s -power-plant-coal-imports-may-rise-by-16-to-fuel-economic-growth.html; "China and India: A Rage for Oil," Bloomberg Businessweek, August 25, 2005, http://www.busi nessweek.com/bwdaily/dnflash/aug2005/nf20050825_4692_db016.htm?chan=gb.

47. "China, India to Cooperate in Oil Hunt," *China Daily*, January 13, 2006, http://www.chinadaily.com.cn/english/doc/2006–01/13/content_512118.htm.

48. Yejoo Kim, "Chinese and Indian Cooperation in Africa: The Case of Sudan," Consultancy Africa Intelligence, October 17, 2011, http://www.consultancyafrica .com/index.php?option=com_content&view=article&id=869:chinese-and-indian -cooperation-in-africa-the-case-of-sudan&catid=58:asia-dimension-discussion-papers &Itemid=264.

49. Raghuram Rajan, *Fault Lines: How Hidden Fractures Still Threaten the World Economy* (Princeton, NJ: Princeton University Press, 2010), 216.

50. Ibid., 217.

51. "Media Briefing by Official Spokesperson on Visit of Minister of Foreign Affairs of China," Ministry of External Affairs, Government of India, March 1, 2012, http:// www.mea.gov.in/media-briefings.htm?dtl/18853/Media+Briefing+by+Official +Spokesperson+on+visit+of+Minister+of+Foreign+Affairs+of+China.

52. Callum Roberts, "'The Ocean of Life'—And the Sorrow Beneath the Sea," *Newsweek*, May 14, 2012, http://www.thedailybeast.com/newsweek/2012/05/13/the -ocean-of-life-and-the-sorrow-beneath-the-sea.html.

53. "The Sunken Billions: The Economic Justification for Fisheries Reform," The International Bank for Reconstruction and Development/The World Bank, 2009, http://siteresources.worldbank.org/EXTARD/Resources/336681–1224775570533 /SunkenBillionsFinal.pdf.

54. Nicholas Stern, *The Economics of Climate Change: The Stern Review* (New York: Cambridge University Press, 2007), http://webarchive.nationalarchives.gov.uk /+/http://www.hm-treasury.gov.uk/d/Executive_Summary.pdf.

55. Kishore Mahbubani, "Letter to Netanyahu: Time Is No Longer on Israel's Side," *Financial Times*, November 10, 2011, http://www.ft.com/intl/cms/s/0/15537caa-0bc8–11e1–9310–00144feabdc0.html#axzz1oV3ttN9u.

56. Stephen Robert, "A Reset in Jewish Thinking," *New York Times*, April 24, 2012, http://www.nytimes.com/2012/04/25/opinion/a-reset-in-jewish-thinking.html?pagewanted=all.

57. Ibid.

58. Ami Ayalon, Orni Petruschka and Gilead Sher, "Peace Without Partners," *New York Times*, April 23, 2012, http://www.nytimes.com/2012/04/24/opinion/peace-without-partners.html?ref=opinion&gwh=A56CA627B5DE8E8BA7B59652A74BDF28&pagewanted=print.

59. Michael Barbaro, "A Friendship Dating to 1976 Resonates in 2012," *New York Times*, April 7, 2012, http://www.nytimes.com/2012/04/08/us/politics/mitt-romney-and-benjamin-netanyahu-are-old-friends.html?pagewanted=all.

60. Peter Cohan, "Will Saudi Arabia Support on Israeli Attack on Iran in June?," *Forbes.com*, February 26, 2012, http://www.forbes.com/sites/petercohan/2012/02/26/will-saudi-arabia-support-an-israeli-attack-on-iran-in-june/.

61. Murtaza Haider, "United Against Iran," *Dawn.com*, March 7, 2012, http://dawn.com/2012/03/07/united-against-iran/print/.

62. "Turkey's AKP: a Skillful Leader and a Tightening Grip," *France 24*, June 12, 2011, http://mobile.france24.com/en/20110612-turkey-erdogan-behind-akps-rise-skillful-leader-tightening-grip.

63. Gideon Rachman, *Zero-Sum World: Politics, Power, and Prosperity After the Crash* (London: Atlantic Books, 2010), 244.

64. Shashi Tharoor, "Peace in Kashmir?," *Project Syndicate*, February 20, 2012, http://beta.project-syndicate.org/commentary/peace-in-kashmir-.

65. Ibid.

66. Pankaj Mishra, "India and Pakistan Should Favor Cash Over Kashmir," *Bloomberg*, April 8, 2012, http://mobile.bloomberg.com/news/2012–04–08/india-and-pakistan-should-favor-cash-over-kashmir?category=%2F.

67. "Boeing Bullish on Southeast Asian Aircraft Demand," *The Nation*, March 16, 2011, http://www.nationmultimedia.com/2011/03/16/business/Boeing-bullish-on-Southeast-Asian-aircraft-demand-30150953.html.

68. Kazuhiko Togo, *Japan's Foreign Policy, 1945–2009: The Quest for a Proactive Policy* (Leiden, the Netherlands: E. J. Brill, 2010), 215.

69. "About the ASEAN Scholarships," Ministry of Education, Singapore, http://www.moe.gov.sg/education/scholarships/asean/.

70. "ASEAN Youth Movement," https://www.facebook.com/pages/ASEAN-Youth-Movement/141076287863.

71. Mong Palatino, "Disappointing ASEAN," *The Diplomat*, March 20, 2012, http://the-diplomat.com/asean-beat/2012/03/20/disappointing-asean/.

Chapter 6: A Barrier to Convergence

1. "Eastern Approaches," The Economist, February 7, 2008, http://www.economist.com/node/10640560.

2. John Lloyd, "US and Them," *Financial Times*, July 7, 2006, http://www.ft.com/intl/cms/s/2/de01f64e-0cba-11db-84fd-0000779e2340.html#axzz1YSlBRNQz.

3. Kishore Mahbubani, *Can Asians Think?* (Singapore: Marshall Cavendish International, 2004), 24.

4. "Official Development Assistance by Country as a Percentage of Gross National Income in 2009" (Paris: OECD, April 2010), http://www.oecd.org/document/11/0,3343,en_21571361_44315115_44981579_1_1_1_1,00.html.

5. "American Public Opinion on Foreign Aid," WorldPublicOpinion.org questionnaire, November 30, 2010, http://www.worldpublicopinion.org/pipa/pdf/nov10/ForeignAid_Nov10_quaire.pdf.

6. William Easterly, *The White Man's Burden: Why the West's Efforts to Aid the Rest Have Done So Much Ill and So Little Good* (New York: Penguin, 2006), 4.

7. Clare Lockhart, personal e-mail, June 12, 2012.

8. Ashraf Ghani and Clare Lockhart, *Fixing Failed States: A Framework for Rebuilding a Fractured World* (New York: Oxford University Press, 2008), 99.

9. Chinua Achebe, "Africa is People," November 6, 2005, http://www.africaresource.com/index.php?option=com_content&view=article&id=44:africa-is-people&catid=36:essays-a-discussions&Itemid=346.

10. Ghani and Lockhart, *Fixing Failed States*, 87.

11. Kishore Mahbubani, "The OECD: A Classic Sunset Organisation," *Global Policy* 3, no. 1 (February 2012).

12. Judith Clifton and Daniel Díaz-Fuentes, "From 'Club of the Rich' to 'Globalisation à la Carte'? Evaluating Reform at the OECD," *Global Policy*, 2011, http://www.globalpolicyjournal.com/articles/global-governance/%E2%80%98club-rich%E2%80%99-%E2%80%98globalisation-%C3%A0-la-carte%E2%80%99-evaluating-reform-oecd.

13. Mahbubani, "The OECD."

14. Ibid.

15. Clifton and Díaz-Fuentes, "From 'Club of the Rich.'"

16. Ibid.

17. Ibid.

18. Mahbubani, "The OECD."

19. Clifton and Díaz-Fuentes, "From 'Club of the Rich.'"

20. Mahbubani, "The OECD."

21. Harlan Cleveland, *Birth of a New World: An Open Moment for International Leadership* (San Francisco: Jossey-Bass, 1993), 178–179.

22. Clare Lockhart, "The Failed State We're In," *Prospect*, June 2008.

23. Ibid., 40.

24. Ghani and Lockhart, *Fixing Failed States*.

25. Ibid., 86.

26. Ibid., 88.

27. Axel Dreher, Jan-Egbert Sturm, and James Raymond Vreeland, "Does Membership on the UN Security Council Influence IMF Decisions?," Leitner Program Working Papers 2006–11 (New Haven, CT: Leitner Program in International and Comparative Political Economy, Yale University, 2006), http://www.polisci.umn.edu/pdf/unsc_imf.pdf.

28. Ilyana Kuziemko and Eric Werker, "How Much Is a Seat on the Security Council Worth?: Foreign Aid and Bribery in the United Nations," *Journal of Political Economy* 114, no. 5 (2006).

29. Ibid.

30. Ibid.

31. James D. Wolfensohn, *A Global Life: My Journey Among Rich and Poor, from Sydney to Wall Street to the World Bank* (New York: PublicAffairs, 2010), 320–321.

32. Joseph Stiglitz, "Thanks for Nothing," *The Atlantic*, October 2001, http://www.theatlantic.com/magazine/archive/2001/10/thanks-for-nothing/2315/.

33. "The IMF Ignored Crisis Warnings, Says Watchdog," *Straits Times*, February 12, 2011.

34. Letter from Peter Doyle to Shakour Shalaan, Dean of the IMF Executive Board, published by CNN, June 18, 2012, http://cnnibusiness.files.wordpress.com/2012/07/doyle.pdf.

35. Joseph Stiglitz, "What I Learned at the World Economic Crisis," *New Republic*, April 17, 2000, http://www.tnr.com/article/politics/the-insider.

36. Ian Goldin, The World Bank Is Flirting with Irrelevance," *Financial Times*, March 5, 2012, http://www.ft.com/intl/cms/s/0/56555e28–6468–11e1-b50e-00144fe-abdc0.html#axzz1pdWYoE3m.

37. Danny Leipziger, "Next World Bank Chief Must Restore Its Vision," *Financial Times*, March 9, 2012, http://www.ft.com/intl/cms/s/0/36a7542a-67bd-11e1-b4a1–00144feabdc0.html#axzz1pdWYoE3m.

38. Ghani and Lockhart, *Fixing Failed States*, 97.

39. Frederic Mousseau, "Food Aid or Food Sovereignty? Ending World Hunger in Our Time" (Oakland, CA: Oakland Institute, 2005).

40. "Critics Call for Changes to U.S. Food Aid Policy," Iowa Public Television, July 8, 2005, http://www.iptv.org/mtom/story.cfm/feature/6379/mtom_20050708_3044_feature.

41. "Band Aids and Beyond: Tackling Disasters in Ethiopia 25 Years After the Famine," Oxfam, October 22, 2009, http://www.oxfam.org/sites/www.oxfam.org/files/bp133-band-aids-beyond.pdf.

42. "Paris Declaration and Accra Agenda for Action" (Paris: OECD, 2005), http://www.oecd.org/document/18/0,3343,en_2649_3236398_35401554_1_1_1_1,00.html.

43. Ghani and Lockhart, *Fixing Failed States*, 100.

44. Julio Godoy, "Aid Fragmentation Worse Despite Paris Declaration," Inter Press Service, March 10, 2009, http://ipsnews.net/africa/nota.asp?idnews=46043.

45. Barbara Unmuessig quoted in ibid.

46. Stephen Walt, "The Myth of American Exceptionalism," *Foreign Policy*, November 2011, http://www.foreignpolicy.com/articles/2011/10/11/the_myth_of_american_exceptionalism?page=full.

Chapter 7: Converging on Global Governance

1. "What Is the G20?," http://g20.org/index.php/en/g20.

2. Gordon Brown, "Decisive Euro Action Is Needed at the G20 Summit," June 15, 2012, http://blogs.reuters.com/great-debate/2012/06/15/decisive-euro-action-is-needed-at-the-g20-summit/.

3. Daniel D. Bradlow, "Europeans Must Pay to Head IMF," *Foreign Policy in Focus*, 9 June 2011, http://www.fpif.org/articles/europeans_must_pay_to_head_imf.

4. "London Summit—Leaders' Statement," April 2, 2009, http://www.wcoomd .org/files/1.%20Public%20files/PDFandDocuments/Highlights/G20_Final_London _Communique.pdf.

5. Valentina Pop, "Europeans Wary of Losing IMF Chair After Sex Scandal," *EU-Observer.com*, May 17, 2011, http://euobserver.com/19/32342. "We know that in the mid-term developing countries have a right to the post of IMF chief and the post of World Bank chief. I think that in the current situation, when we have a lot of discussions about the euro, that Europe has good candidates to offer," German chancellor Angela Merkel told reporters, http://www.reuters.com/article/2012/02/15/us-world bank-zoellick-idUSTRE81E1A120120215.

6. Lesley Wroughton, "World Bank's Zoellick to Step Down, U.S.

Eyes Spot," *Reuters*, February 15, 2012, http://mobile.reuters.com/article/id USTRE81E1A120120215?irpc=932.

7. Jan-Aart Scholte, "Global Governance, Accountability and Civil Society," in *Building Global Democracy?: Civil Society and Accountable Global Governance*, ed. Jan-Aart Scholte (Cambridge: Cambridge University Press, 2011), 8.

8. Hans Morgenthau, *Politics Among Nations* (New York: Knopf, 1948), 13.

9. Inis L. Claude, *Swords into Plowshares: The Problems and Process of International Organization* (New York: Random House, 1971), 154.

10. David Bosco, *Five to Rule Them All: The UN Security Council and the Making of the Modern World* (New York: Oxford University Press, 2009), 97.

11. Ibid., 239.

12. Ibid., 200.

13. "In 2005, Security Council Addresses Broad Range of Concerns, Including Terrorism, Situations in Africa, Middle East, Iraq, Afghanistan," Department of Public Information, United Nations Secretariat, January 20, 2006, http://www.un.org /News/Press/docs/2006/sc8614.doc.htm.

14. Kishore Mahbubani, "The Permanent and Elected Council Members," in *The UN Security Council: From the Cold War to the 21st Century*, ed. David Malone (Boulder, CO: Lynne Rienner, 2004), 259.

15. Raghuram G. Rajan, *Fault Lines: How Hidden Fractures Still Threaten the World Economy* (Princeton, NJ: Princeton University Press, 2010), 211.

16. Ibid., 214.

17. "Integrated and Coordinated Implementation of and Follow-up to the Outcomes of the Major United Nations Conferences and Summits in the Economic, Social and Related Fields," United Nations General Assembly, September 15, 2005, http://www.who.int/hiv/universalaccess2010/worldsummit.pdf.

18. E. P. Thomson, *Whigs and Hunters: The Origin of the Black Act* (Harmondsworth, UK: Penguin, 1977), 266.

19. Simon Chesterman, "An International Rule of Law?," Public Law and Legal Theory Research Paper Series, Working Paper No. 08–11 (New York: New York University School of Law, April 2008), http://ssrn.com/abstract=1081738.

20. Leo Gross, "The Double Veto and the Four-Power Statement on Voting in the Security Council," *Harvard Law Review* 67, no. 2 (December 1953): 251–281.

21. Sean D. Murphy, "The United States and the International Court of Justice: Coping with Antinomies," in *The Sword and the Scales: The United States and International Courts and Tribunals* ed. Cesare Romano (Cambridge: Cambridge University Press, 2009), 46–111.

22. Chesterman, "An International Rule of Law?"

23. "Strengthening Targeted Sanctions Through Fair and Clear Procedures," Watson Institute Targeted Sanctions Project, Brown University, March 30, 2006, http://watsoninstitute.org/pub/Strengthening_Targeted_Sanctions.pdf.

24. Franklin Delano Roosevelt quoted in "F.D.R. and the Stuff of His War," *New York Times*, February 3, 2006, http://www.nytimes.com/2006/02/03/arts/design/03fdr.html.

25. Diplomatic cable from Ambassador Zalmay Khalilzad to Secretary of State Condoleezza Rice, December 29, 2007, http://wikileaks.org/cable/2007/12/07USUN NEWYORK1225.html.

26. Ibid.

27. France, Germany, United Kingdom, Italy, the European Union, Turkey, and Russia.

Conclusion: Because Everything That Rises Must Converge

1. Alfred Lord Tennyson, "Locksley Hall," http://en.wikisource.org/wiki/Locksley_Hall.

2. Kishore Mahbubani, *The New Asian Hemisphere: The Irresistible Shift of Global Power to the East* (New York: PublicAffairs, 2008).

3. Tony Blair's foreign policy address at Georgetown University, May 26, 2006, http://blogs.georgetown.edu/?id=15721.

4. 2010 figures, according to the World Bank.

5. "Recent trends in military expenditure," Stockholm International Peace Research Institute, http://www.sipri.org/research/armaments/milex/resultoutput/trends.

6. "United Nations' 2010–2011 Budget Pushes Past $5 Billion," *Reuters*, December 25, 2009, http://www.dnaindia.com/world/report_united-nations-2010–2011-budget-pushes-past-5-billion_1327278. The UN budget for 2010 and 2011 was $5.16 billion (therefore $2.58 billion per year). World total military expenditures in 2010, according to SIPRI, were $1,630 billion.

7. John Bolton, *Surrender Is Not an Option: Defending America at the United Nations and Abroad* (New York, NY: Threshold Editions, 2007), 279.

8. Ewen MacAskill, Ed Pilkington, and Jon Watts, "Despair at UN over Selection of 'Faceless' Ban Ki-moon as General Secretary," *Guardian*, October 7, 2006, http://www.guardian.co.uk/world/2006/oct/07/northkorea/print.

9. "London Summit—Leaders' Statement," April 2, 2009, http://www.wcoomd.org/files/1.%20Public%20files/PDFandDocuments/Highlights/G20_Final_London_Communique.pdf.

10. Dani Rodrik, "The Nation-State Reborn," *Project Syndicate*, February 13, 2012, http://www.project-syndicate.org/commentary/rodrik67/English.

11. David Rodin, "Towards a Global Ethic," *Ethics and International Affairs* 26, no. 1 (Spring 2012).

12. *Kony 2012*, Invisible Children, March 5, 2012, http://youtu.be/Y4MnpzG5Sqc.

13. Scott Wong, "Joseph Kony Captures Congress' Attention," Politico, March 22, 2012, http://www.politico.com/news/stories/0312/74355.html.

14. Rodney Muhumuza, "Troops Join Hunt for Kony," *Chronicle Herald*, March 24, 2012, http://thechronicleherald.ca/world/76927-troops-join-hunt-kony.

15. "Uganda Displays Captive Kony Lieutenant," CNN, May 14, 2012, http://www.cnn.com/2012/05/14/world/africa/uganda-lra-capture/index.html.

16. 2005 World Summit Outcome Document, para. 139, http://www.who.int/hiv/universalaccess2010/worldsummit.pdf.

17. Rodin, *Towards a Global Ethic*.

18. Martin Luther King, Jr. sermon on "conquering self-centeredness" delivered at Dexter Avenue Baptist Church, Montgomery, Alabama, August 11, 1957, http://mlk-kpp01.stanford.edu/index.php/encyclopedia/documentsentry/conquering_self_centeredness.

INDEX

Kishore Mahbubani is a writer, professor, and former Singaporean diplomat who served twice as ambassador to the UN. Currently, he is the dean of the Lee Kuan Yew School of Public Policy at the National University of Singapore. A prolific writer, he has published three books and numerous articles in leading global journals and newspapers like *Foreign Affairs*, *Foreign Policy*, and the *Financial Times*. *Foreign Policy* listed him as one of the top 100 global thinkers in 2005, 2010, and 2011.

PublicAffairs is a publishing house founded in 1997. It is a tribute to the standards, values, and flair of three persons who have served as mentors to countless reporters, writers, editors, and book people of all kinds, including me.

I. F. STONE, proprietor of *I. F. Stone's Weekly*, combined a commitment to the First Amendment with entrepreneurial zeal and reporting skill and became one of the great independent journalists in American history. At the age of eighty, Izzy published *The Trial of Socrates*, which was a national bestseller. He wrote the book after he taught himself ancient Greek.

BENJAMIN C. BRADLEE was for nearly thirty years the charismatic editorial leader of *The Washington Post*. It was Ben who gave the *Post* the range and courage to pursue such historic issues as Watergate. He supported his reporters with a tenacity that made them fearless and it is no accident that so many became authors of influential, best-selling books.

ROBERT L. BERNSTEIN, the chief executive of Random House for more than a quarter century, guided one of the nation's premier publishing houses. Bob was personally responsible for many books of political dissent and argument that challenged tyranny around the globe. He is also the founder and longtime chair of Human Rights Watch, one of the most respected human rights organizations in the world.

·   ·   ·

For fifty years, the banner of Public Affairs Press was carried by its owner Morris B. Schnapper, who published Gandhi, Nasser, Toynbee, Truman, and about 1,500 other authors. In 1983, Schnapper was described by *The Washington Post* as "a redoubtable gadfly." His legacy will endure in the books to come.

Peter Osnos, *Founder and Editor-at-Large*